GENDERING MUSICAL MODERNISM

The music of Ruth Crawford, Marion Bauer, and Miriam Gideon

This book explores the work of three significant American women composers of the twentieth century: Ruth Crawford, Marion Bauer, and Miriam Gideon. It offers a unique approach to a rich body of music that deserves theoretical scrutiny and provides information on both the lives and music of these fascinating women, skillfully interweaving history and musical analysis in ways that both the specialist and the more general reader will find compelling. In this important new study, Ellie Hisama has employed a form of analysis by which she links musical characteristics with aspects of the composers' identities. This is revealing both for questions of music and gender and for the continuing search for meaning in music. The book thus draws attention to the value of the music of these three composers and contributes to the body of analytical work concerned with the explanation of musical language.

ELLIE M. HISAMA is Associate Professor of Music at Brooklyn College and the Graduate Center, City University of New York and is Director of the Institute for Studies in American Music at Brooklyn College.

CAMBRIDGE STUDIES IN MUSIC THEORY AND ANALYSIS

GENERAL EDITOR: IAN BENT

Published titles

GENDERING
MUSICAL MODERNISM

The music of
Ruth Crawford, Marion Bauer,
and Miriam Gideon

ELLIE M. HISAMA

CAMBRIDGE
UNIVERSITY PRESS

PUBLISHED BY THE PRESS SYNDICATE OF THE UNIVERSITY OF CAMBRIDGE
The Pitt Building, Trumpington Street, Cambridge, United Kingdom

CAMBRIDGE UNIVERSITY PRESS
The Edinburgh Building, Cambridge CB2 2RU, UK
40 West 20th Street, New York, NY 10011-4211, USA
10 Stamford Road, Oakleigh, VIC 3166, Australia
Ruiz de Alarcón 13, 28014 Madrid, Spain
Dock House, The Waterfront, Cape Town 8001, South Africa

http://www.cambridge.org

First published 2001

Printed in the United Kingdom at the University Press, Cambridge

Typeface Monotype Bembo 11/13 pt.   *System* QuarkXPress™ [SE]

A catalogue record for this book is available from the British Library

Library of Congress Cataloguing in Publication data

ISBN 0 521 64030 X hardback

To my parents,
Toshiaki and Kay K. Hisama

CONTENTS

FIGURES

TABLES

EXAMPLES

FOREWORD BY IAN BENT

Theory and analysis are in one sense reciprocals: if analysis opens up a musical structure or style to inspection, inventorying its components, identifying its connective forces, providing a description adequate to some live experience, then theory generalizes from such data, predicting what the analyst will find in other cases within a given structural or stylistic orbit, devising systems by which other works – as yet unwritten – might be generated. Conversely, if theory intuits how musical systems operate, then analysis furnishes feedback to such imaginative intuitions, rendering them more insightful. In this sense, they are like two hemispheres that fit together to form a globe (or cerebrum!), functioning deductively as investigation and abstraction, inductively as hypothesis and verification, and in practice forming a chain of alternating activities.

Professionally, on the other hand, "theory" now denotes a whole subdiscipline of the general field of musicology. Analysis often appears to be a subordinate category within the larger activity of theory. After all, there is theory that does not require analysis. Theorists may engage in building systems or formulating strategies for use by composers; and these almost by definition have no use for analysis. Others may conduct experimental research into the sound-materials of music or the cognitive processes of the human mind, to which analysis may be wholly inappropriate. And on the other hand, historians habitually use analysis as a tool for understanding the classes of compositions – repertories, "outputs," "periods," works, versions, sketches, and so forth – that they study. Professionally, then, our ideal image of twin hemispheres is replaced by an intersection: an area that exists in common between two subdisciplines. Seen from this viewpoint, analysis reciprocates in two directions: with certain kinds of theoretical enquiry, and with certain kinds of historical enquiry. In the former case, analysis has tended to be used in rather orthodox modes, in the latter in a more eclectic fashion; but that does not mean that analysis in the service of theory is necessarily more exact, more "scientific," than analysis in the service of history.

The above epistemological excursion is by no means irrelevant to the present series. Cambridge Studies in Music Theory and Analysis is intended to present the work of theorists and of analysts. It has been designed to include "pure" theory – that is, theoretical formulation with a minimum of analytical exemplification; "pure" analysis – that is, practical analysis with a minimum of theoretical underpinning; and writings that fall at points along the spectrum between the two extremes. In these capacities, it aims to illuminate music, as work and as process.

However, theory and analysis are not the exclusive preserves of the present day. As subjects in their own right, they are diachronic. The former is coeval with the very study of music itself, and extends far beyond the confines of Western culture; the latter, defined broadly, has several centuries of past practice. Moreover, they have been dynamic, not static fields throughout their histories. Consequently, studying earlier music through the eyes of its own contemporary theory helps us to escape (when we need to, not that we should make a dogma out of it) from the preconceptions of our own age. Studying earlier analyses does this too, and in a particularly sharply focused way; at the same time it gives us the opportunity to re-evaluate past analytical methods for present purposes, such as is happening currently, for example, with the long-despised methods of hermeneutic analysis of the late nineteenth century. The series thus includes editions and translations of major works of past theory, and also studies in the history of theory.

In this volume, Ellie Hisama offers a fascinating critique of the place of women in the movement that historians nowadays call musical modernism – a movement pervasively associated with male composers such as Schoenberg, Stravinsky, Webern, and Bartók. Her critique invokes three women composers who occupied significant roles in American musical life during the twentieth century, and who have attracted growing attention in recent times: Ruth Crawford, Marion Bauer, and Miriam Gideon, all of whom composed a substantial amount of music in a post-tonal idiom, either free-atonal, or serial.

Hisama's critique is purposefully focused on a small number of works: a string quartet (Crawford), two songs (Crawford, Gideon), two solo piano pieces (Bauer), and a violin and piano work (Gideon). She examines the musical fabric of each piece or movement in detail, using ingenious methods of analysis designed specially for the music concerned. She contends persuasively that when such a "close reading" recognizes and takes into account the impact of the composer's gender and political views on a work, then it can offer us valuable ways to hear and apprehend that work.

Her readings, carried out with the utmost skill, suggest ways in which the three composers severally coped with a male-dominated world – challenging it, accepting while undercutting it, even getting the upper hand (literally!) over it temporarily, and so forth – and at the same time dealing with a social and political world in which their views were sometimes far from orthodox. Indeed, it shows them working against the background of the Great Depression and later the fanatical oppression of the McCarthyist era. Hisama gives us enough historical and biographical information to see also how the musical processes that she uncovers reflect aspects of their family, social, and professional lives.

Her book brings together the general fields of feminist theory and social critique, and the specific field of formalist music theory, and intertwines them so successfully, with such depth of insight, and with such cleverly invented analytical tools, that it will surely set a new standard not only for gender discourse about music, but also for discourse concerning race, sexuality, and class.

ACKNOWLEDGMENTS

Portions of this study were delivered at the University of Minnesota, the Graduate Center of the City University of New York, Wesleyan University, Ithaca College, Mount Holyoke College, University of California at Riverside, Ohio State University, Princeton University, Connecticut College, and Pennsylvania State University. For their helpful responses I would like to thank Elizabeth West Marvin, Richard Hermann, Marianne Kielian-Gilbert, Leo Treitler, Joel Lester, Catherine Torpey, John Rahn, Taylor Greer, Jeff Stadelman, Marion Guck, Suzanne Cusick, Fred Maus, Nicholas Cook, Rachel Joffe Falmagne, Arlene Dallalfar, Jyl Lynn Felman, Margaret Hunt, Miriam Whaples, Barbara Whitten, Ruth Busch, Monica Jakuc, Roger Graybill, Lori Burns, Lyn Ellen Burkett, Naomi André, David Brackett, Michele Edwards, Cathy Shuman, and Amy Dooling. I am indebted to Alexander Vishio, David Sanjek, Shaugn O'Donnell, Tim Campbell, and Joanne Burkholder for their generous assistance with various questions, and to the late Martin Bernstein, Maurice Peress, the late Irene Heskes, Barbara Petersen, Şahan Arzruni, Leo Kraft, George Perle, and Lucille Field Goodman for graciously allowing me to interview them. I am grateful to Milton Babbitt, from whom I first heard of Marion Bauer, for sharing his memories about American music's recent past. I thank my colleagues at Brooklyn College, City University of New York for their support, especially Ray Allen, Nancy Hager, Bruce MacIntyre, Philip Rupprecht, and Jeff Taylor. Warmest thanks to Kathleen Mason Krotman, Lorraine Reilly, and Peg Rivers for their kind assistance, and to my students at Brooklyn College, Connecticut College, Ohio State University, and the University of Virginia for sharing their enthusiasm and ideas.

I am deeply grateful to Alexander Ewen, Herbert Kurz, and Mike Seeger for allowing me access to materials pertaining to this study. I thank Vanessa Chow for contributing her artwork and David Smey for preparing several musical examples. I would also like to recognize the members of the faculty seminar in Gender and Women's Studies at Connecticut College for their intellectual companionship and friendship during 1998–99. I am especially grateful to Jacqui Alexander, from whom I learned a great deal about feminism and politics in a brief time, and to Lisa Wilson for her generosity and support.

I deeply appreciate the research assistance of George Boziwick of the Research Division of the New York Public Library for the Performing Arts; Nancy Cricco of the Bobst Library Archives, New York University; Wayne Shirley and Kevin Layne at the Library of Congress; and Honora Raphael and the staff at the Walter W. Gerboth Music Library, Brooklyn College. I would also like to thank the staffs at the Mina Rees Library of the City University of New York, Graduate Center; the American Music Center; Houghton Library, Harvard University; and Library Archives, Mount Holyoke College. Support from the Five College Women's Studies Research Center at Mount Holyoke College, the Elizabeth D. Gee Award for Research on Women, and a research leave and university seed grant from Ohio State University gave me the time and resources necessary to complete the book. I acknowledge gratefully a grant from the Society of Music Theory's 1999 Publication Subvention Fund.

I owe my greatest intellectual debt to Joseph Straus, who has enabled and sustained my work over the years through his astute suggestions, keen criticisms, and general enthusiasm. A turning point for me was a course he taught in which I first encountered Crawford's music; our subsequent conversations about possible linkages between feminism and music theory became the foundation for this study. Carol Oja's unfailingly perceptive readings enriched and strengthened several chapters. David Lewin offered valuable suggestions that stimulated my thinking and strengthened my work. Carl Schachter first ignited my enthusiasm for analyzing music. His teaching immeasurably shaped the ways I hear and write about music. I am indebted to Philip Lambert for shepherding the initial study to completion; to Maurice Peress for his insights and for sharing memories about Marion Bauer; and to Allan Atlas for facilitating my professional development over the years. I owe a special thanks to Susan McClary for her rigorous and sympathetic critiques, and to Adrienne Fried Block and Judith Tick, whose kind encouragement and inspiring scholarship made it possible for this study to come into existence.

One could not have a finer research assistant than Kate Bohonos – these pages bear the mark of her scrupulous work and many thoughtful suggestions. My ideas have benefited immensely from Ian Bent's meticulous readings and exemplary editing. I am indebted to Penny Souster for her interest in the project. It has been a distinct pleasure to work with them.

From our first week of graduate school together, Anton Vishio has articulated countless useful critiques of my work. I value his insights, humor, and companionship. Heartfelt thanks go to my parents-in-law, Anton and Patricia Vishio, for their continual love and support. My parents, Kay and Toshiaki Hisama, have encouraged and sustained me in all my endeavors. I am happy to dedicate this work to them.

A version of Chapter 2 appears in *Concert Music, Rock, and Jazz Since 1945: Essays and Analytical Studies*, ed. Elizabeth West Marvin and Richard Hermann (Rochester: University of Rochester Press, 1995). Portions of Chapters 7 and 8 were published in different form in "(Re)discovering Miriam Gideon," *Institute for Studies in American Music Newsletter* XXVII/2 (Spring 1998), 4–5.

Copyrighted material is here by kind permission of the following:

Marion Bauer, "Chromaticon" and Toccata from *Four Piano Pieces* © 1930 by Boosey & Hawkes, Inc. Copyright Renewed. Reprinted by permission.

Ruth Crawford, "Chinaman, Laundryman" © 1973 by Merion Music, Inc. Used by permission of the publisher.

Ruth Crawford Seeger, String Quartet 1931, third and fourth movements © 1941 by Merion Music, Inc. Used by permission of the publisher.

Miriam Gideon, "Night is my Sister," from *Sonnets from Fatal Interview* for voice and string trio, published by American Composers Alliance © 1961 by Miriam Gideon. Used by permission of Herbert Kurz.

Miriam Gideon, "Esther," from *Three Biblical Masks* for violin and piano, published by American Composers Alliance © 1979 by Miriam Gideon. Used by permission of Herbert Kurz.

"Contour Reduction Algorithm" from Robert D. Morris, "New Directions in the Theory and Analysis of Musical Contour," *Music Theory Spectrum* 15/2 (Fall 1993), 212, © 1993 by the Society for Music Theory, Inc. Used by permission of Robert D. Morris and the University of California Press.

ABBREVIATIONS

Complete publishing information for the following can be found in the Bibliography.

JNS-MRCS   Joseph N. Straus, *The Music of Ruth Crawford Seeger*

JT-RCS   Judith Tick, *Ruth Crawford Seeger: A Composer's Search for American Music*

MB-TCM   Marion Bauer, *Twentieth Century Music: How It Developed, How to Listen to It* (1947 edn unless otherwise noted)

MBp-NYU   Marion Bauer papers, 1936–51, New York University, Bobst Library Archives

MG-RCS   Matilda Gaume, *Ruth Crawford Seeger: Memoirs, Memories, Music*

MGf-BMI   Miriam Gideon files, Broadcast Music, Inc.

MGj-NYPL   Journals of Miriam Gideon, Miriam Gideon papers, New York Public Library, Music Research Division

MGp-NYPL   Miriam Gideon papers, New York Public Library, Music Research Division

NLS-SPM   Nancy Louise Stewart, "The Solo Piano Music of Marion Bauer"

NYPL   New York Public Library for the Performing Arts, Music Research Division

RCd-LC   Ruth Crawford diary, Seeger Collection, Library of Congress

RCl-LC   Ruth Crawford letters, Seeger Collection, Library of Congress

SC-LC   Seeger Collection, Library of Congress

NOTE ABOUT TECHNICAL TERMS

For readers unfamiliar with post-tonal theory, I provide a definition of technical terms the first time they are used and give the page reference for these definitions in the index. These definitions are not meant to be exhaustive, and readers may wish to consult texts by Joseph N. Straus and John Rahn that introduce the fundamentals of post-tonal theory.[1] Some of the terms used are of my own devising.

Pitches will be identified according to the Acoustical Society of America's system of notation, where C4 equals middle C.

Contours will be identified by cseg names according to the conventions established by Elizabeth West Marvin and Paul Laprade.[2]

Pitch–class sets will be identified by their Forte name followed by their prime form given in brackets, or in abbreviated form by their prime form.[3]

---

[1] Joseph N. Straus, *Introduction to Post-Tonal Theory*, 2nd edn (Upper Saddle River, NJ: Prentice Hall, 2000); John Rahn, *Basic Atonal Theory* (New York: Longman, 1980).

[2] Elizabeth West Marvin and Paul A. Laprade, "Relating Musical Contours: Extensions of a Theory for Contour," *Journal of Music Theory* 31/2 (1987), 257-62.

[3] Allen Forte, *The Structure of Atonal Music* (New Haven: Yale University Press, 1973), 179-81.

CULTURAL ANALYSIS AND POST-TONAL MUSIC

Given the vast, marvelous repertoire of feminist approaches to literary analysis introduced over the past two decades, a music theorist interested in bringing feminist thought to a project of analyzing music by women might do well to look first to literary theory. One potentially useful study is Sandra Gilbert and Susan Gubar's landmark work *The Madwoman in the Attic*, which asserts that nineteenth-century writing by women constitutes a literary tradition separate and distinct from the writing of men and argues more specifically that writings of women, including Austen, Shelley, and Dickinson, share common themes of alienation and enclosure.[1] Some feminist theorists have claimed that a distinctive female tradition exists also in modernist literature; Jan Montefiore, for example, asserts that in autobiographical writings of the 1930s, male modernists tended to portray their experiences as universal in contrast to female modernists who tended to represent their experiences as marginal.[2]

But because of the singular nature of the modernist, post-tonal musical idiom, an analytical project intended to explore whether a distinctive female tradition indeed exists in music immediately runs aground. Unlike tonal compositions, which draw their structural principles from a more or less unified compositional language, post-tonal works are constructed according to highly individualized schemes whose meaning and coherence derive from their internal structure rather than from their relation to a body of works. Milton Babbitt has characterized these contrasting qualities of post-tonal and tonal music as "contextual" and "communal," respectively, a distinction that will be useful in establishing the approach, boundaries, and intentions of this study.[3]

Babbitt defines "contextual" compositions as largely self-enclosed works that

[1] Sandra M. Gilbert and Susan Gubar, *The Madwoman in the Attic: The Woman Writer and the Nineteenth-Century Literary Imagination* (New Haven: Yale University Press, 1979; 2nd edn, 1984).

[2] Jan Montefiore, "Case-histories versus the 'Undeliberate Dream': Men and Women Writing the Self in the 1930s," in *Difference in View: Women and Modernism*, ed. Gabriele Griffin (London: Taylor & Frances, 1994), 56–74. Other explorations of the relationship between women and literary modernism are Sandra M. Gilbert and Susan Gubar, *No Man's Land: The Place of the Woman Writer in the Twentieth Century,* vol. 1: *The War of the Words* (New Haven: Yale University Press, 1988), and Sandra M. Gilbert and Susan Gubar, eds., *The Female Imagination and the Modernist Aesthetic* (New York: Gordon and Breach, 1986).

[3] Milton Babbitt, *Words about Music*, ed. Stephen Dembski and Joseph N. Straus (Madison: University of Wisconsin Press, 1987), 9, 167–68.

establish their premises and materials within themselves – he gives as examples compositions by Schoenberg, Webern, and himself – and argues that these pieces can be understood on their own terms without reference to other works. In contrast, the coherence of music that he calls "communal," like common-practice tonal compositions, depends on its relation to external principles which are shared with other works.

If we accept Babbitt's premise that post-tonal compositions are by nature contextual and self-enclosed, then the task of drawing them into broader analytic categories like "music by women" for the purpose of comparative study proves to be extremely difficult, if not impossible; it follows that the enterprise of integrating gender into a set of close readings of post-tonal compositions might not best be served by a comparative method with the intent to generalize about the distinctiveness or "difference" of modernist music by women but by an alternative strategy.

Thus, I shall not seek to argue that specific compositions share some sort of commonality because they were written by women who were working within a specific idiom and historical moment. Instead, I propose to relate the music and identities of three twentieth-century American women: Ruth Crawford (1901–53), Marion Bauer (1887–1955), and Miriam Gideon (1906–96).[4] I offer analyses of their music that are informed by the conditions of gender and politics within which they exist. By the term "gender" I mean, following historian Joan Scott's definition, the social organization of sexual difference; under this definition, gender is regarded as distinct from biological sex.[5] By "politics" I am referring to the network of relations between people in a society. This book explores the impact of gender on the structure of the compositions discussed, and addresses the impact of the composers' political views on their music. As a work rooted in musical analysis, this study contributes to a growing body of scholarly literature that brings feminist insights to bear upon music theory.[6]

---

[4] Ruth Crawford is also known by her married name, Ruth Crawford Seeger. Because she composed the three works analyzed in this study under the name Ruth Crawford, I shall refer to her as such.

In her article "Why Can't We Listen to Marion Bauer's Music?", *Providence Journal-Bulletin* (Rhode Island), 23 August 1994, Susan Pickett asserts that Marion Bauer lied about the year of her birth and maintains that Bauer was born on 15 August 1882 rather than on 15 August 1887. Pickett supports this assertion in an unpublished typescript ("Marion Bauer Lecture") by referring to a local newspaper's announcement in 1882: "On August 15, born to the wife of J. Bauer, a daughter." Since this evidence does not clearly state that "a daughter *Marion*" was born on this day, the possibility remains that another daughter – not Marion – was born on 15 August 1882. The question of Bauer's birth year is not answered by consulting the birth records of her hometown. The Walla Walla, WA, health department does not have a birth certificate for Marion Bauer on file – before 1907, it was not required to register births or deaths there. The year of Bauer's birth thus remains unverified, and requires further research. I thank Professor Pickett for providing me with a copy of her typescript.

[5] Joan Wallach Scott, *Gender and the Politics of History* (New York: Columbia University Press, 1988), 2.

[6] Examples of feminist music-theoretical writing include Lori Burns, "Analytic Methodologies for Rock Music: Harmonic and Voice-Leading Strategies in Tori Amos's 'Crucify'," in *Expression in Pop-Rock Music: A Collection of Critical and Analytical Essays*, ed. Walter Everett (New York: Garland, 2000), 213–46; Marcia J. Citron, "Music as a Gendered Discourse," Chap. 4 of *Gender and the Musical Canon* (Cambridge: Cambridge University Press, 1993), 120–64; Marion A. Guck, "A Woman's (Theoretical) Work," *Perspectives of New Music* 32/1 (1994),

The seven compositions that I analyze are Crawford's String Quartet, movements three and four, composed in 1931; her song "Chinaman, Laundryman" from *Two Ricercari* for voice and piano, composed in 1932; two of Bauer's *Four Piano Pieces*, "Chromaticon" and Toccata, premiered and published in 1930;[7] and Gideon's "Night is my Sister" from *Sonnets from Fatal Interview* for voice and string trio, composed in 1952; and "Esther" from *Three Biblical Masks* for violin and piano, composed in 1960.[8] Each analytical chapter first offers information about the composer relevant to the piece, and then presents an analysis informed by the biographical material. This approach thus employs another sense of the term "contextual" – in addition to Babbitt's meaning of "self-referential," these analyses are also contextual because they relate the techniques and strategies used in each piece to its social contexts. What I aim to demonstrate is that formalist readings acknowledging the impact of a composer's gender and political views on the work itself impart valuable ways of hearing and apprehending these compositions.

The following biographical survey provides a portrait of these three composers. Ruth Crawford was born in 1901 in East Liverpool, Ohio. Her father was a Methodist minister, and her mother a pianist who gave Crawford piano lessons.[9] She continued studying piano with Djane Lavoie Herz and composition with Adolf Weidig at the American Conservatory of Music in Chicago. Crawford spent the summer of 1929 at the MacDowell Colony in Peterborough, New Hampshire, where she met Marion Bauer, who was also in residence there. That fall Crawford moved to New York and began studying composition with Charles Seeger. In August of 1930 she went to Europe to continue her musical education in Berlin, supported by a Guggenheim fellowship – the first in composition awarded to a woman. Crawford was active in New York's modern music community during the late 1920s and early 1930s, and earned some measure of recognition from her colleagues for her musical accomplishments.

After Crawford married Seeger in 1932, their son Michael was the first of four children they would have together. Raising four children, giving piano lessons, teaching music at her daughter Barbara's school, and acting as a music consultant to several schools took up enormous amounts of her time, and for the next two decades she stopped composing modernist works, devoting her creative energies

28–43; Marianne Kielian-Gilbert, "On Rebecca Clarke's Sonata for Viola and Piano: Feminine Spaces and Metaphors of Reading," in *Audible Traces: Gender, Identity, and Music* (Zurich: Carciofoli Press, 1999), 71–114; Judy Lochhead, "Joan Tower's 'Wings' and 'Breakfast Rhythms I and II': Some Thoughts on Form and Repetition," *Perspectives of New Music* 30/1 (1992), 132–57; and Joseph N. Straus, *The Music of Ruth Crawford Seeger* (JNS-MRCS).

[7] A date of composition has not yet been firmly established for Bauer's *Four Piano Pieces*. In a Works Progress Administration Composers' Forum-Laboratory of 22 January 1936 in which Bauer was the featured composer, the program gives the date 1930 for her *Four Piano Pieces*, and I am provisionally using this as the date of its composition (program in Harrison Potter file, Library Archives, Mount Holyoke College).

[8] Gideon originally composed *Three Biblical Masks* for organ in 1958 as a commission from Herman Berlinski.

[9] The first extended study of Crawford's life and music was Matilda Gaume's *Ruth Crawford Seeger* (MG-RCS). Judith Tick's biography, *Ruth Crawford Seeger: A Composer's Search for American Music* (JT-RCS), is a rich resource about Crawford.

instead to transcribing and arranging numerous American folk tunes, many of which were published.[10] Crawford returned to modernist composition in the 1950s, just before she died of cancer in Chevy Chase, Maryland, at the age of 52. Her compositions have enjoyed a renaissance during the past decade: scores, recordings, and information about her life and work are fortunately being made available, and her String Quartet 1931 is now rightfully regarded as one of the finest modernist works of the genre.

The compositional style that Crawford forged in Chicago bears the influence of Skryabin in its harmonic language, a quality about which Seeger was highly critical. Early pieces include her *Nine Preludes for Piano*, the first five composed in 1924–25 and the last four in 1927–28; the Violin Sonata of 1925–26; and her *Five Sandburg Songs*, composed at the MacDowell Colony in the summer of 1929. After beginning to study composition with Seeger in 1929, Crawford became much more concerned with contrapuntal procedures in her music, as is evident in some works composed during this period, including her second, third, and fourth *Diaphonic Suites* of 1930, her String Quartet 1931, and her 1930–32 song cycle *Rat Riddles*, with texts by Carl Sandburg.[11]

Born in 1887 as the youngest child of French Jewish immigrants, Marion Bauer first studied piano with her sister Emilie in her hometown of Walla Walla, Washington, and later with Henry Holden Huss and Eugene Heffley in New York.[12] In 1906 she

---

[10] Collections of Crawford's transcriptions and arrangements include *Our Singing Country*, ed. John A. and Alan A. Lomax (New York: Macmillan, 1941) and *American Folk Songs for Children* (Garden City, NY: Doubleday, 1950; repr., Hamden, CT: Shoe String Press, 1993). A complete list of Crawford's published transcriptions and arrangements appears in JT-RCS, 364–71.

[11] In JNS-MRCS, Joseph N. Straus discusses the relationship between Crawford's music and Charles Seeger's theories of dissonant counterpoint and new music composition, as outlined in Seeger's article "On Dissonant Counterpoint," *Modern Music* 7/4 (1930), 25–31 and in his treatise "Tradition and Experiment in (the New) Music," in Charles Seeger, *Studies in Musicology II, 1929–1979*, ed. Ann M. Pescatello (Berkeley: University of California Press, 1994), 39–273. Judith Tick explores the impact of Seeger's theories on Crawford's String Quartet in her essay "Dissonant Counterpoint Revisited: The First Movement of Ruth Crawford's String Quartet 1931," in *A Celebration of American Music: Words and Music in Honor of H. Wiley Hitchcock*, ed. Richard Crawford, R. Allen Lott, and Carol J. Oja (Ann Arbor: University of Michigan Press, 1990), 405–22, as does Taylor A. Greer in his essay "The Dynamics of Dissonance in Seeger's Treatise and Crawford's Quartet," in *Understanding Charles Seeger, Pioneer in American Musicology*, ed. Bell Yung and Helen Rees (Urbana: University of Illinois Press, 1999), 13–28.

[12] The most thorough biographical study of Bauer currently available is Nancy Louise Stewart's "The Solo Piano Music of Marion Bauer" (NLS-SPM). Information on Bauer also appears in Christine Ammer, *Unsung: A History of Women in American Music* (Westport, CT: Greenwood Press, 1980), 123–27 (rev. edn, Portland, OR: Amadeus Press, forthcoming); David Ewen, *American Composers Today: A Biographical and Critical Guide* (New York: H. W. Wilson, 1949), 20–22; Madeline Goss, *Modern Music-Makers: Contemporary American Composers* (New York: Dutton, 1952; repr., Westport, CT: Greenwood Press, 1970), 129–40; Carol J. Oja, *Making Music Modern: New York in the 1920s* (New York: Oxford University Press, in press); and Claire R. Reis, *Composers in America: Biographical Sketches of Contemporary Composers With a Record of Their Works* (New York: Macmillan, 1938; rev. and enl., 1947), 19–20. Three interviews with the following people yielded additional information about Bauer: Martin Bernstein, who was Bauer's colleague at New York University for twenty-five years (interview with the author, 22 March 1994); Maurice Peress, who studied with Bauer at New York University (interview with the author, 11 April 1994); and Irene Heskes, who also studied with Bauer at New York University (interview with the author, 8 July 1997).

traveled to Paris for the first time; there she studied with Nadia Boulanger, exchanging English lessons for instruction in harmony and analysis, and studied piano as well, with Raoul Pugno. Bauer studied counterpoint and form in Berlin with Paul Ertel in 1910–11, and composition in New York City during World War I with Walter Henry Rothwell.

During the 1930s, Bauer continued her career as a composer, writer, and university professor while living with her sister Flora in New York. In 1926 she became the first woman faculty member to join New York University's music department, where she taught generations of students during her twenty-five-year career, among them composers Milton Babbitt, J. Vincent Higginson, and Julia Frances Smith.[13] In 1933 she published *Twentieth Century Music*, an introductory guide which was then particularly valuable for its reproductions of extracts from hard-to-find music by composers of atonal music, including Schoenberg and Webern.[14] She was a correspondent for the Chicago-based periodical *The Musical Leader*, and her orchestral work *Sun Splendor*, noteworthy as the second piece by a woman to be performed by the New York Philharmonic, was premiered by the Philharmonic in 1947 under the direction of Leopold Stokowski.[15]

Bauer's music is more conservative than Crawford's. Many of her compositions from the 1910s and 1920s rely upon a pitch center; she turned to serialism relatively late, in the 1940s, in her piano works *Patterns*, op. 41 (1946), and *Moods*, op. 46 (1950/54). Although her writings and lectures of the early 1930s embraced modernism and atonality, her own music remained less experimental than the music she advocated by Schoenberg, Webern, Cowell, and others.[16] This seeming inconsistency may be partly explained by the reluctance of her publisher, Arthur P. Schmidt, to support her early leanings toward modernist composition.[17] Two piano works illustrating Bauer's tonal style are *Three Impressions* (1918) and *From the New Hampshire Woods* (1922).

Bauer's study at the Paris Conservatory from 1923 to 1926 with André Gédalge, who taught Ravel, Milhaud, and Honegger, marked a turning point in her compositional style from a tonal to a post-tonal idiom.[18] Her interest in innovative

---

13 Ammer, *Unsung*, 267.

14 Marion Bauer, *Twentieth Century Music: How It Developed, How to Listen to It* (MB-TCM). Babbitt states that reading Bauer's book was for him "one of the great turning points," convincing him to transfer from the University of North Carolina at Chapel Hill to New York University, from which he graduated in 1935. Babbitt is quoted in William Duckworth, *Talking Music: Conversations with John Cage, Philip Glass, Laurie Anderson, and Five Generations of American Experimental Composers* (New York: Schirmer Books, 1995), 61–62. Babbitt provides an introduction to the 1978 reissue of Bauer's *Twentieth Century Music* (New York: Da Capo Press, 1978).

15 Ammer, *Unsung*, 98.   16 Bauer's *Twentieth Century Music* is an example of her pro-modernist writing.

17 Letters to Bauer's publisher Arthur P. Schmidt dated 29 September 1916 and 6 October 1916 attest to Schmidt's preference for a more conservative musical style than Bauer wished to maintain; cited in NLS-SPM, 17. In addition, Bauer describes her unfortunate experience of having her violin sonata marked down from first to second place in the 1928 Society for the Publication of American Music competition expressly for its "modern tendencies" (letter by Bauer dated 18 June 1927 to Henry R. Austin of the Arthur P. Schmidt Publishing Company; cited in NLS-SPM, 39–40).

18 Two works that Bauer composed in Paris in 1924, *Quietude* and *Turbulence*, demonstrate her departure from tonality.

compositional procedures is apparent also in one of her tonal works, her 1922 Prelude in D minor for piano, op. 15/3, in which a melodic line is presented by the right hand in a continuous rhythm of short note values and is doubled at the octave by the left hand.[19] Bauer continued composing in a post-tonal style from the 1930s through the mid-1950s; these works include her *Dance Sonata*, op. 24 (1932); *Two Aquarelles*, op. 39 (1944/50); and *Anagrams*, op. 48 (1950).

Miriam Gideon was born in Greeley, Colorado, in 1906.[20] Her father, Abram, taught philosophy and modern languages at Colorado State Teachers College, and her mother, Henrietta, taught at a local elementary school. Both were of German-Jewish extraction and spoke German at home. In 1916, the Gideon family moved to Yonkers, New York. Gideon studied piano with Hans Barth in New York City and took music courses at Yonkers High School, but because her parents did not own a piano or phonograph, her contact with music at home was limited. To provide their daughter with a proper musical education, Gideon's parents sent her to Boston at the age of fifteen to study music with her uncle Henry, who was an organist and conductor, as well as the music director of Temple Israel. In Boston, Gideon immersed herself in the study of piano, organ, and music theory, and she continued to live with her uncle while attending Boston University. There she majored in French and minored in math while taking music courses and studying piano with Felix Fox. After graduating at the age of nineteen, she returned to New York and took courses in music at New York University with Martin Bernstein, Marion Bauer, Charles Haubiel, and Jacques Pillois, planning to earn a certificate to teach in the public schools. Bernstein encouraged Gideon to compose, and after a year at New York University, she aspired to teach at the university level.

From 1931 to 1934 Gideon studied harmony, counterpoint, and composition with Lazare Saminsky, a Russian émigré composer and conductor who had been a student of Rimsky-Korsakov. At Saminsky's suggestion, Gideon began to study composition with Roger Sessions, joining a number of other young musicians including Milton Babbitt, Edward Cone, David Diamond, and Vivian Fine. During the eight years that she studied with Sessions, her compositional style changed

---

[19] As Stewart notes, the rhythm and doubling of the melody in Bauer's third Prelude is strikingly similar to Ruth Crawford's 1930 *Piano Study in Mixed Accents* (NLS-SPM, 136).

[20] Biographical information on Miriam Gideon appears in Jane Weiner LePage, "Miriam Gideon," in *Women Composers, Conductors, and Musicians of the Twentieth Century: Selected Biographies*, vol. 2 (Metuchen, NJ: Scarecrow Press 1983), 118–41; Barbara A. Petersen, "The Vocal Chamber Music of Miriam Gideon," in *The Musical Woman*, vol. 2, ed. Judith Laing Zaimont, Catherine Overhauser, and Jane Gottlieb (New York: Greenwood Press, 1987), 223–55; Deena Rosenberg and Bernard Rosenberg, "Miriam Gideon," in *The Music Makers* (New York: Columbia University Press, 1979), 62–69; and in numerous biographical statements and descriptions of professional activities written by Gideon that are housed in the archives of Broadcast Music, Inc. (MGf-BMI). Interviews I conducted with the following people yielded additional information about Gideon: Irene Heskes, 8 July 1997; Barbara A. Petersen, 8 July 1997; Şahan Arzruni, 8 July 1997; Leo Kraft, 10 July 1999; George Perle, 8 September 1997; Milton Babbitt, 4 October 1997; Alexander Ewen, 17 December 1999; and Lucille Field Goodman, 21 December 1999.

markedly, abandoning its tonal foundations and moving to the free atonal style that she would maintain for the rest of her career.[21]

Gideon entered Columbia University's graduate musicology program in 1942, earning an M.A. in 1946 with a thesis focusing on Mozart's string quintets.[22] She began teaching at Brooklyn College, City University of New York (CUNY) in 1944 and at City College, CUNY in 1947. In 1949 she married Frederic Ewen, a member of Brooklyn College's English department.[23] During the 1950s, many leftist faculty in the City University of New York system were fired or their contracts not renewed because of McCarthyism. In 1952, at the age of 53, Ewen took early retirement from a tenured position in preference to going before a committee to discuss his and others' political views. Gideon noted in a 1991 interview that in 1954, because of her views and her relationship to Ewen, "at Brooklyn College, I was told my services were no longer required";[24] she resigned from City College the following year, so as not to be asked to identify other leftist faculty. At the invitation of Hugo Weisgall, Gideon began to teach in 1955 at the Jewish Theological Seminary of America, which awarded her a Doctor of Sacred Music degree in composition in 1970. She also taught at the Manhattan School of Music from 1967 until 1991. In 1971, Gideon was rehired at City College, where she was appointed as a full professor, and from which she retired in 1976. In 1983 Brooklyn College awarded her a Doctor of Humane Letters, *honoris causa*.[25]

Gideon was particularly interested in vocal music and set texts by Francis Thompson, Christian Morgenstern, Anne Bradstreet, Norman Rosten, and others for voice and chamber ensemble or piano. She also composed choral works, synagogue services, a cantata, and an opera, *Fortunato* which is based on the Spanish play by Serafin and Joaquín Quintero. Her instrumental compositions are primarily for chamber ensembles, and include a string quartet and a number of piano works. Gideon received awards and commissions from the Ford and Rockefeller Foundations, the National Endowment for the Arts, and the Elizabeth Sprague Coolidge Foundation, among others. In 1975 she was inducted into the American Academy and Institute of Arts and Letters, the second female composer to receive this honor (the first was Louise Talma, who was inducted in 1974).

My analytical approach varies according to the work under discussion. I relate Crawford's compositions to information about her life specifically during the time she composed each work. The chapters analyzing her music describe, in turn,

---

[21] Gideon contributed "Hommage à Roger" for solo piano to a festschrift in honor of her former teacher. In *Perspectives of New Music* 16/1 (Spring–Summer 1978), 118–19.

[22] Miriam Gideon, "The Secular Chamber Music of Mozart with Particular Reference to the Quintets" (M.A. thesis, Columbia University, 1946).

[23] Ewen's books include *Bertolt Brecht: His Life, Art, his Times* (New York: Citadel Press, 1967; repr., New York: Carol, 1992); and *Heroic Imagination: The Creative Genius of Europe from Waterloo (1815) to the Revolution of 1848* (Secaucus, NJ: Citadel Press, 1984).

[24] Linda Ardito, "Miriam Gideon: A Memorial Tribute," *Perspectives of New Music* 34/2 (Summer 1996), 208.

[25] In 1988, the annual Frederic Ewen Colloquium in Civil Liberties was established at Brooklyn College.

incidents of professional bias against women and her reactions to them, her self-image, and her leftist political beliefs, in order to suggest that these aspects of her experience, as recorded in her letters, diary entries, and other writings, shape her compositions. Because biographical information currently available on Bauer is scant, my readings of her compositions are not grounded in specific lived experiences to the extent of my analyses of Crawford's music. Rather, they speculate about possible relationships between the narratives in two of Bauer's piano works and her identity as constructed in her writings about music and in reflections by her contemporaries. Similarly, I link Gideon's music to her identity as it was shaped by her experiences and beliefs, some of which are just now coming to light in papers and interviews. Her setting of Millay's sonnet "Night is my Sister" and her musical interpretation of the story in the Book of Esther suggest a feminist sensibility sympathetic to the female characters. In the music of all three composers, their identity is expressed in the fabric of their music.

Though my approach to each composition differs, a unifying thread throughout the book is attention to various aspects of contour, working from the foundations of contour theory established by Robert Morris, Elizabeth West Marvin and Paul Laprade, and Michael Friedmann.[26] Morris defines contour space as "a pitch-space consisting of elements arranged from low to high disregarding the exact intervals between the elements."[27]

I apply Morris's conception of musical contour to a variety of musical spaces. Chapter 2 presents an analysis of the third movement of Crawford's String Quartet 1931. By using an original analytical tool that measures the "degree of twist" of the four instrumental voices as compared to their normative arrangement with the first violin as the highest voice, second violin as the second highest voice and so forth, I suggest that this work speaks in a "double-voiced discourse" (a phrase coined by literary theorist Elaine Showalter) by presenting both a dominant narrative and a "muted" narrative that is recoverable only when applying the twist tool to its dimension of voice leading.[28] Chapter 3 offers a narrative hearing of the fourth movement of Crawford's quartet. As in Chapter 2, I argue that Crawford's personal experience of bias against women composers informs the structure of a movement from her string quartet, and suggest that a female persona is given voice in the first violin, its music actively opposing the other three instruments which represent male authority. Chapter 4 presents an analysis of a composition with text, Crawford's song "Chinaman, Laundryman." Introducing the notion of "contour deviance," an

---

[26] Robert D. Morris, *Composition with Pitch-Classes: A Theory of Compositional Design* (New Haven: Yale University Press, 1987); Morris, "New Directions in the Theory and Analysis of Musical Contour," *Music Theory Spectrum* 15/2 (1993), 205–28; Michael L. Friedmann, "A Methodology for the Discussion of Contour: Its Application to Schoenberg's Music," *Journal of Music Theory* 29/2 (1985), 223–48; Elizabeth West Marvin and Paul Laprade, "Relating Musical Contours: Extensions of a Theory for Contour," *Journal of Music Theory* 31/2 (1987), 225–67; and Friedmann, "My Contour, Their Contour," *Journal of Music Theory* 31/2 (1987), 268–71.

[27] Morris, *Composition with Pitch-Classes*, 341.

[28] Elaine Showalter, "Feminist Criticism in the Wilderness," in *The New Feminist Criticism: Essays on Women, Literature, and Theory*, ed. Elaine Showalter (New York: Pantheon Books, 1985), 263.

analytical measure analogous to the "twist tool" which I employed in Chapter 2, I assert that measuring the contour deviance of the piano's music underscores a particular reading of the text, one that can be linked to Crawford's political sympathies with the ethnic immigrant worker.

In Chapter 5, I argue that Bauer's beliefs about the organization of society are suggested in her prose writings about music; her piano piece "Chromaticon" can be heard as musically representing such views. Through an analysis of the piece that maps out a narrative of conflict between specific melodic contours, I propose that Bauer's belief in the necessity of challenging the status quo is reflected in the structure of the piece. Chapter 6 examines Bauer's Toccata through an aspect of its performance – the relationship of the pianist's hands – and traces a narrative in terms of one hand's dominance over the other. Its particular approach to contour space is one that has not yet been examined in the contour literature: I discuss the relationship of the pianist's hands in performing the predominant four-note simultaneities of the piece, whose precise pitches remain secondary in my analysis to the physical arrangement of the performer's hands. I argue that within this performative dimension, a narrative based on a playful reversal of hand dominance is present in the work; my analysis also contemplates whether this reading of the piece might be understood to resonate with Suzanne Cusick's recent speculations about the relationships between musical experience and sexuality.[29]

Chapter 7 examines Gideon's song "Night is my Sister" for voice and string trio. The text of "Night is my Sister," a sonnet by Edna St. Vincent Millay, offers a tale of a drowned woman "weedily washed ashore," one for whom there is "Small chance . . . in a storm so black / A man will leave his friendly fire and snug / For a drowned woman's sake"; it thus provides an opportunity to consider Gideon's music in relation to an overtly gendered narrative. Gideon's setting presents an intensely sympathetic portrait of the unfortunate female protagonist while it criticizes the male character's refusal to help her. Chapter 8 explores Gideon's "Esther" from *Three Biblical Masks* for violin and piano, which portrays the Biblical figure in the Purim story after which the piece is named in relation to the two other primary characters, Mordecai and Haman. My analysis traces the transformation of the title character from passive and dutiful to assertive and authoritative, a shift enacted by Gideon's treatment of pitch and rhythm.

This project of presenting analyses that are inflected by historical and social context does not argue that these strategies exist *uniquely* in compositions by women. There is, obviously, no biological imperative for women to compose one way and men another, and it is certainly possible that structures similar to those I describe here are present in music by male composers. If one indeed discovered similar strategies in compositions by men, their existence would not alter my argument about the relationship between gender and structure in these pieces by

---

[29] Suzanne G. Cusick, "On a Lesbian Relationship with Music: A Serious Effort Not to Think Straight," in *Queering the Pitch: The New Gay and Lesbian Musicology*, ed. Philip Brett, Gary C. Thomas, and Elizabeth Wood (New York: Routledge, 1994), 67–83.

Crawford, Bauer, and Gideon. I would not identify their presence as being related to gender and female identity in the ways that I claim here.

Four additional points will further clarify the goals and limits of this study. First, the compositions analyzed are not meant to be representative of the *œuvre* of Crawford, Bauer, or Gideon, or of post-tonal music by American women composers of the twentieth century more generally. Rather, I argue that these pieces may be related to their composers' subjectivities in specific ways; other compositions by Crawford, Bauer, or Gideon may not exemplify the specific relationships I claim here.

Second, I believe the task of identifying common structural elements or strategies in such a diverse group of compositions by three women is futile and, accordingly, this study does not have such a goal; rather, it presents close readings of individual works by three women. Exploring the question of whether music that belongs to a particular category (e.g., "twentieth-century music by American women") is somehow structurally distinctive would necessitate detailed readings of a number of compositions, and of music by both male and female composers.

Third, my argument is not based on compositional intention, i.e., that Crawford, Bauer, and Gideon consciously constructed these musical narratives and strategies in order to express their personal situation or views. There is no documentary evidence that they intended to present the particular narratives I offer, though it remains a possibility. Rather, this study demonstrates that making connections between biography and musical structure enables a listener to experience new and compelling ways of understanding music. Indeed, composers do not always provide the most convincing interpretations of their music, nor are they necessarily cognizant of the analytical implications of their music: Crawford once remarked that sounds in the third movement of her String Quartet 1931 were inspired by foghorns she heard at New Year's, while Bauer dismissed the last two chords of her Toccata as "arbitrary chords at the point of movement and repose."[30] My analyses of both of these pieces offer different readings than their composers articulated.

Fourth, I aim to present feminist accounts of post-tonal music that are pro-modernist. I thus respond to Catherine Parsons Smith's influential article which considers the historical phenomenon of musical modernism through the lens of gender.[31] She argues that because American male composers such as Ives described musical modernism by using language fraught with masculine imagery, modernism itself is marked as male: "It appears that modernism in music, as in literature, may indeed be understood as a reaction to the first wave of feminism. One must painfully conclude that while this reaction was productive for many males, it was profoundly destructive for female composers."[32] She suggests that this rhetoric of masculinity may even have ultimately driven women from fully pursuing their

---

[30] Quoted in JT-RCS, 156–57, and Marion Bauer, *Twentieth Century Music* (MB-TCM), 119.

[31] Catherine Parsons Smith, "'A Distinguishing Virility': Feminism and Modernism in American Art Music," in *Cecilia Reclaimed: Feminist Perspectives on Gender and Music*, ed. Susan C. Cook and Judy S. Tsou (Urbana: University of Illinois Press, 1994), 90–106.   [32] *Ibid.*, 99.

modernist art. As one example, Smith cites Ruth Crawford, who, she asserts, "abandoned the development of her own modernist compositional language in the early 1930s, just as she seemed to have gained creative maturity."[33]

Smith's conclusions are problematic on two grounds: first, in the case of Crawford, there is no historical evidence that modernism's alleged misogyny dissuaded her from continuing to compose. Rather, Crawford's desire to embrace folk music combined with her duties raising a family of four and of teaching music were, as Tick has amply demonstrated in her recent biography, the reasons she chose to sidestep the world of art music until the 1950s. Second, that male composers like Ives wished to ascribe to modernism stereotypically masculine characteristics is not sufficient reason to claim that modernist music actually *is* a male preserve. Unlike Gilbert and Gubar, or Marianne DeKoven, who have convincingly claimed that misogyny is part and parcel of specific modernist literary texts, Smith does not demonstrate the inherent misogyny of musical matter itself – that is, pitch, rhythm, and other elements of structure.[34]

The difference in the medium marks an important distinction between feminist literary studies and feminist music studies. Because musicology has lagged behind other disciplines in drawing upon feminism, it may be tempting to transfer insights gleaned from feminist literary studies or other disciplines to musical texts. But because music is distinct from literature or art, made up of sound but not necessarily of image or representation, it deserves new theoretical models that acknowledge its unique features.

These analyses of compositions by Crawford, Bauer, and Gideon illustrate my belief that the aesthetic and techniques of musical modernism are not inherently misogynist, but that modernism indeed provides a space for forms of expression by women. Because it released these composers from the strictures of a common musical style by giving them the technical means to forge new musical procedures and narratives, modernism did not prove harmful to them, but rather stimulated their work in inventive and liberating ways. If twentieth-century composers including Crawford, Bauer, and Gideon embraced modernism, I believe that feminists of the twenty-first century have the responsibility to include them and their music in our accounts of modernism, rather than leaving its legacy to men.

---

[33] *Ibid.*, 93.

[34] Gilbert and Gubar, *No Man's Land*; Marianne DeKoven, "Modernism and Gender," *The Cambridge Companion to Modernism*, ed. Michael Levenson (Cambridge: Cambridge University Press, 1999), 174–93. DeKoven complicates the argument that misogyny and masculinism mark modernist literary works by men by claiming that the "masculinist misogyny [of male modernists] . . . was almost universally accompanied by its dialectical twin: a fascination and strong identification with the empowered feminine" (174).

2

THE QUESTION OF CLIMAX IN RUTH CRAWFORD'S STRING QUARTET, THIRD MOVEMENT

The opening bars of the third movement of Ruth Crawford's String Quartet 1931 present a strikingly original musical conception. They draw the listener into an unfamiliar sound world, one in which the voices twist over, then under, one another, come together and veer apart, creeping up all the while. As Example 2.1 shows, about three-quarters of the way through the work, the voices crescendo to *fff*, attack triple-stops, and snap apart – that is, the piece reaches a climax. The voices then swiftly descend and return to the soft and slow quality of the opening to conclude the movement.

The presence of a climax suggests a significant critical issue for the piece: as a remnant of nineteenth-century musical procedures, it seems at odds with the work's particular innovative structure and aesthetic.[1] I know of no string quartet movement composed within a decade of Crawford's that draws upon her techniques of placing the viola and cello in high registers so that they produce unusual timbres, of presenting the four instrumental voices as more or less equal in importance, and of writing the piece as a counterpoint of dynamics. Two pieces composed much later – the seventh of Elliott Carter's 1950 *Eight Etudes and a Fantasy* for Woodwind Quintet and the ninth of György Ligeti's 1968 *Zehn Stücke für Bläserquintett* – evoke comparison with Crawford's composition through their emphasis on timbre and the communal labor of the instruments. By remarking on the oddness of the climax's inclusion in Crawford's quartet movement, I am not making an *a priori* claim that climaxes are incongruous with modernist music, but rather am suggesting that this particular climax does not match the rest of its musical fabric.

While musing over the various possibilities with which I could explore the question of climax in the work, it struck me that feminist theory might prove

---

[1] Judith Tick has discovered that the third movement's climax over mm. 68–75 was not present in the 1931 version but was added seven years later. The original version of 1931 presents a single harmony, A3–G♯4–D♯6–E5, beginning on m. 68, beat 3, which is sustained through m. 72; it does not include double-stops or the culminating triple-stop chord at m. 75. The version included in Example 2.1 was written in 1938 and published in 1941. Tick's findings appear in JT-RCS (215–16, 218), which includes a partial transcription of the original version.

useful to such a study, for over the past two decades feminism has transformed entire disciplines; I believed it could bring crucial insights to music theory as well.[2]

Ruth Crawford's string quartet seemed a promising piece to begin forging an example of feminist music theory.[3] The work has always struck me as an inappropriate specimen to slide under the microscope of set theory (one of the most frequently used modes of music analysis for post-tonal music), for it is not composed of a few set classes which a set theorist would locate and trace through their various manifestations. Consequently, I have developed another method to analyze the quartet's third movement. What I hope to demonstrate by applying this model to the composition is that close readings of musical structure and formalist music theory may indeed address, and in fact grow out of, a feminist consciousness.

In attempting to reconcile feminism with music theory, I want to commit myself to close readings of musical structure for two reasons. The first is personal: I enjoy it. The second is more global. If we are to build a feminist community of music scholars, we need to leave open as many ways of reading as possible. Although some feminists reject rational and formalist approaches as masculinist, I do not find it necessary or desirable to stop analyzing music from codified principles – in short, to designate formalism as the Other in feminist music analysis.[4] I want to claim instead that hearing pieces of music *as feminists* may lead us to reject our traditional analytical tools and encourage us to develop new ones, which may be formalist as a particular piece warrants. Because some works might exceed our received ways of hearing, theorizing, and criticizing, I believe they deserve consideration through alternative theoretical models.

In the fall of 1929, Ruth Crawford moved to New York in order to continue her musical education. Only 28, she had already rightfully earned the admiration and support of colleagues who could wield a good deal of influence. With the aid of

---

[2] Many feminist theorists have argued against the standard academic writing style that takes on a disembodied voice of authority. Instead, as in my discussion here, the first-person narrative and an explicit subjective position is often crucial to a feminist stance. I hope it will become apparent that I hear the piece in the way I am suggesting because of the construction of my own identity. Examples of this style of writing include bell hooks, *Yearning: Race, Gender, and Cultural Politics* (Boston: South End Press, 1990); Trinh T. Minh-ha, *Woman, Native, Other: Writing Postcoloniality and Feminism* (Bloomington: Indiana University Press, 1989); Michele Wallace, *Invisibility Blues: From Pop to Theory* (London: Verso, 1990); and Patricia J. Williams, *The Alchemy of Race and Rights* (Cambridge, MA: Harvard University Press, 1991).

[3] Joseph N. Straus analyzes the third movement of Crawford's quartet (JNS-MRCS, 158–72). His examination differs from mine by focusing on a composite melody formed by all the instruments, pitch and duration contours, and harmonic and motivic organization, rather than on the aesthetic issue of the climax's inclusion, relative register of the instruments, and gender; Straus also discusses some of the issues encountered in viewing Crawford's music through a feminist lens (220–26). Suzanne G. Cusick, Marion A. Guck, Marianne Kielian-Gilbert, and Susan McClary offer dazzling insights into this fledgling area of research in a quartet of papers published in *Perspectives of New Music* 32/1 (1994), 8–85.

[4] One such writer who has questioned the compatibility of rationalism and formalism with feminism is Mary Daly, *Beyond God the Father: Toward a Philosophy of Women's Liberation* (Boston: Beacon Press, 1973).

Example 2.1 Crawford, String Quartet 1931, third movement

Example 2.1 (*cont.*)

Example 2.1 (*cont.*)

Example 2.1 (*cont.*)

Henry Cowell, she moved into the home of music patron Blanche Walton and began to study composition with Charles Seeger, who had been Cowell's own mentor. Walton provided Crawford both financial and emotional support, and the composer Marion Bauer, whom she had met at the MacDowell Colony, became her mentor.[5] In 1930, the Guggenheim Foundation awarded her a year-long fellowship in composition, its first to a woman.[6]

Yet Ruth Crawford was no stranger to the many barriers that resulted from sexist opinions about women composers. Charles Seeger was initially reluctant to accept her as a student because he believed women to be incapable of composing; the director of the Guggenheim Foundation, Henry Allen Moe, did not want even to consider her application on the simple grounds of her sex.[7] Crawford's diary entry from 22 February 1930 records a memory of being shut out:

The musicologists meet. It is decided that I may sit in the next room and hear [Joseph] Yasser [a visiting Russian musicologist] about his new supra scale. Then when I come out for this purpose, I find someone has closed the doors. Blanche is irate, so am I. Men are selfish, says Blanche. You just have to accept the fact. Perhaps, I wonder, their selfishness is one reason why they accomplish more than women. . . . I walk past the closed door to my room, and when I pass I turn my head toward the closed door and quietly but forcibly say, "Damn you," then go on in my room and read Yasser's article. Later, my chair close to the door, I hear some of the discussion.[8]

I have chosen to lead into my analysis with this image because it powerfully illustrates Crawford's status as a composer. Living in the Walton home, she could gain access to important musical resources, but as a woman she was still kept from entering the drawing room on the occasion of Yasser's visit and was reduced to

---

[5] Carol J. Oja provides further information about Walton and other female patrons in "Women Patrons and Crusaders for Modernist Music: New York in the 1920s," in *Cultivating Music in America: Women Patrons and Activists since 1860*, ed. Ralph P. Locke and Cyrilla Barr (Berkeley: University of California Press, 1997), 237–61.

[6] Biographical information on Crawford is provided in JT-RCS and MG-RCS.

[7] Seeger recalls how Henry Cowell convinced him to give Crawford composition lessons despite his negative view of women composers in Ray Wilding-White, "Remembering Ruth Crawford Seeger: An Interview with Charles and Peggy Seeger," *American Music* 6/4 (1988), 446. Dane Rudhyar successfully persuaded Moe to review Crawford's application (MG-RCS, 41).

[8] RCd-LC, 22 February 1930; quoted in MG-RCS, 196. A supra scale is a scale based on the twelve-tone scale in which the half steps are divided further into microtones. Some of Yasser's ideas about music are developed in his book *A Theory of Evolving Tonality* (New York: American Library of Musicology, 1932; repr. New York: Da Capo Press, 1975).

Contrary to what Crawford had apparently been told, Yasser's supra scale was not the only topic discussed that day. In a 1972 interview, Charles Seeger mentioned that at the meeting the men had founded the New York Musicological Society, an organization which eventually developed into the American Musicological Society, and stated that he had purposefully excluded Crawford from this important event because he wanted to avoid the incipient criticism that musicology was "women's work": ". . . only women's clubs talked about music in the United States at that time, and we wanted to make it perfectly clear that we were men, and that we had to talk about music and women weren't in on it." (She was permitted to attend subsequent meetings to organize the Society.) Seeger's remarks appear in "Reminiscences of an American Musicologist," interviewers Adelaide Tusler and Ann Briegleb, Oral History Program, University of California at Los Angeles, 1972, 191. I would like to thank Taylor Greer for passing on this information.

pressing her ear to the door in order to pick up whatever scraps of information she could.[9]

While much of Crawford's music is obviously a product of her rigorous training in musical modernism, I will argue that her compositions also reflect her gender, or the social organization of sexual difference. I do not mean this in a biological or essentialist sense. Rather, I mean that as a woman, Ruth Crawford often found herself pushed to the outside of professional circles and that the structure of this string quartet movement mirrors her social, gender-based exclusion. As a result of this exclusion, her compositions became a site of resistance, speaking in what the literary theorist Elaine Showalter calls a "double-voiced discourse" that embodies both the muted and the dominant voices.[10] Because I am grounding my argument in the social exclusion and double participation that some women experience, rather than in their biology, I am not arguing that *all* women composers create such artistic spaces, nor that music by women is necessarily distinct from music by men. Such generalizations assume that women and men are monolithic groups, which I do not believe, and disregard historical context and individual experience, factors which are crucial to my reading of Crawford's work.[11]

The groundwork for my argument that links Crawford's string quartet movement to her gender is a theory offered by the anthropologist Edwin Ardener, who has suggested that women in a society operate both within a dominant group and in a space outside it. From his studies in Cameroon, he argues that Bakweri women, who are "muted" both socially and linguistically, express their views of the world not through direct expository speech but through the encoded realms of art, myth, or ritual.[12] Although some feminist theorists romantically urge us to celebrate such spaces as pure realms of female culture, unsullied by the dominant male culture, it is important to acknowledge that many of these models are not autonomous. As Showalter observes, because of the widespread influence and authority of the dominant male-generated model, and the necessity that women present their concerns in a form acceptable to men in order simply to be heard, a muted group's perceptions of the world and forms of self-expression are often transmitted through the dominant order.[13]

---

[9] Using this incident as a starting point, Suzanne G. Cusick explores the ways in which conceptions of gender have thoroughly infused the practice of American musicology from its founding to the present, in her essay "Gender, Musicology, and Feminism," in *Rethinking Music*, ed. Nicholas Cook and Mark Everist (Oxford: Oxford University Press, 1999), 471–98   [10] Showalter, "Feminist Criticism in the Wilderness," 263.

[11] Some of Rose Rosengard Subotnik's work may illuminate my argument about the relationship between this quartet movement and Crawford's subject position. She reflects upon what she understands to be structural parallelisms between a person's life and work in *Developing Variations: Style and Ideology in Western Music* (Minneapolis: University of Minnesota Press, 1991).

[12] Edwin Ardener, "Belief and the Problem of Women," in *Perceiving Women*, ed. Shirley Ardener (New York: John Wiley & Sons, 1975), 1–18, and his "The 'Problem' Revisited" in the same volume, 19–28. The term "muted group" was suggested by Charlotte Hardman.

[13] Showalter, "Feminist Criticism in the Wilderness," 261–63. Sandra M. Gilbert and Susan Gubar suggest that nineteenth-century writing by European and American women, including Jane Austen, Mary Shelley, Emily Brontë, and Emily Dickinson, generally displayed a normal surface design but often concealed other less accessible and acceptable levels of meaning. They present this argument in *The Madwoman in the Attic*.

Using Ardener's theoretical framework, I want to claim that while Crawford's quartet movement works its way up to a traditional climax, it also creates a musical space within which another procedure subverts the climax.[14] Because this undercurrent is much less obvious than the loudly trumpeted moment of climax, I will introduce an analytical model to account for its presence. Consequently, rather than having to conclude that the movement's promise of a new musical vision is spoiled by an unimaginative narrative strategy, we may alternatively understand it as challenging or even parodying a nineteenth-century climax and might contemplate the possibility that the foiling of the climax is in some way related to Crawford's experience as a woman.[15] Her composition, then, would be not just revolutionary but also distinctly feminist in undercutting a dominant, masculinist musical narrative by including a second narrative wholly independent of the first.

I do not know whether Crawford intended the movement to enact the specific feminist strategy I am suggesting here, or even whether she considered traditional musical climaxes to be a male domain. Although what she set out to do certainly interests me, the analysis I offer here does not depend upon compositional intent. Rather, my reading emerges from my knowledge of Crawford's strong feelings about the inequity of women compared to men, and my own identity as an Asian American woman who occupies social spaces analogous to the two musical spaces I perceive in this piece.

The quartet's third movement opens by establishing its unusual musical processes: instead of the instruments' keeping their distance, marking off their registral territory, they snuggle together a semitone apart and often pack themselves within the space of a minor third as they creep up toward the downbeat of m. 75, the point at which they break apart. The viola and cello are tossed up into registers alien to their usual tessituras, yielding unusual tone qualities; voices rub against each other at the

Footnote 13 (cont.)

> More explicit expressions of women's feelings of exclusion and invisibility in male-dominated social spaces have appeared in collections intended to provide a forum for such writings. Three such books are *This Bridge Called My Back: Writings by Radical Women of Color*, ed. Cherríe Moraga and Gloria Anzaldúa (Watertown, MA: Persephone Press, 1981; 2nd edn, Latham, NY: Kitchen Table, Women of Color Press, 1983); *All the Women Are White, All the Blacks are Men, But Some of Us Are Brave: Black Women's Studies*, ed. Gloria T. Hull, Patricia Bell Scott, and Barbara Smith (Old Westbury, NY: The Feminist Press, 1982); and *The Forbidden Stitch: An Asian American Women's Anthology*, ed. Shirley Geok-lin Lim and Mayumi Tsutakawa (Corvallis, OR: Calyx Books, 1989). Mitsuye Yamada describes her double invisibility as a Japanese American woman in "Invisibility is an Unnatural Disaster: Reflections of an Asian American Woman," in *This Bridge*, 35–40; Barbara Smith writes of her exclusion as a black lesbian in "Toward a Black Feminist Criticism," in *All the Women are White*, 157–75.

[14] Susan McClary has suggested reading musical climaxes in sexual terms in "Getting Down Off the Beanstalk: The Presence of a Woman's Voice in Janika Vandervelde's Genesis II," in *Feminine Endings: Music, Gender, and Sexuality* (Minneapolis: University of Minnesota Press, 1991), 112–31. Although I intend the traditional musical sense of "climax" here, another reading of the movement might usefully link it to sexuality.

[15] I mean "parody" in the sense proposed by Linda Hutcheon in her *A Theory of Parody: The Teaching of Twentieth-Century Art Forms* (New York: Methuen, 1985). In her examination of parody in twentieth-century painting, music, literature, and architecture, she suggests that modern parody does not necessarily ridicule, but possesses a range of intentions, including playfulness and irony as well as scorn.

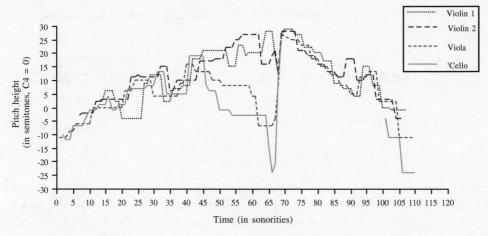

Figure 2.1 Graph of Crawford, String Quartet, third movement

space of a semitone; instruments shift pitch in turn. The movement rejects the predominant Classical string quartet model in which the first violin takes on the role of
leader over harmonic support provided by the second violin, viola, and cello.
Instead, the instruments work cooperatively, sharing in the same musical tasks.[16]

Yet in contrast to these innovative musical strategies, the movement takes on a
traditional narrative shape. As Figure 2.1 graphically demonstrates, the voices col-
lectively inch upward. They also gradually get louder. The four horizontally
directed lines in this figure represent each instrument's path through the piece.[17]

In m. 65 (sonority change 53 in Figure 2.1) the violins begin a game of one-
upmanship which brings all instruments to the pinnacle of the piece and to its subsequent collapse. Ten measures later, the movement becomes very loud, shifts from
legato bowing to attacks via triple-stops in all instruments, and sprawls across four
octaves. In a traditional musical narrative, this moment would serve as the climax.

[16] In her own analysis of this movement, which she sent to Edgard Varèse in 1948, Crawford describes a melodic
line extending through the piece whose tones are distributed among the four instruments. As shown in a version
of the published score that she annotated, the melodic line in mm. 13–15, for example, is made up of the viola's
F♯, violin 2's A and B♭, and cello's G♯ and B. Crawford's analysis of the quartet's third and fourth movements is
available in SC-LC, and is published in JT-RCS, 357–60.
    Marion A. Guck has suggested that instead of conceiving of musical elements as competing with each other,
we might alternatively read them as working cooperatively. In my reading, I use both models in describing
different stretches of the music. Guck described these possibilities for perceiving music in "The Model of
Domination and Competition in Musical Analysis," a paper presented at the conference Feminist Theory and
Music, University of Minnesota, Minneapolis, in June 1991. The relationship of competition to gender is also
discussed in *Competition: A Feminist Taboo?*, ed. Valerie Miner and Helen E. Longino (New York: The Feminist
Press, 1987).
[17] I have assigned middle C the value of 0 on the y axis and have measured pitches in semitones. For the double-
and triple-stops, the graph displays the highest voice for the violins and the lowest voice for the viola and cello.
My thanks to Tim Campbell for his suggestions on the graph. Margaret E. Thomas offers other types of graphic
analyses in "The String Quartet of Ruth Crawford: Analysis With a View Toward Charles Seeger's Theory of
Dissonant Counterpoint" (M.A. thesis, University of Washington, 1991).

Example 2.2 Permutational notation for registral exchange between viola and cello

(viola, cello)

My analytical model, however, reveals a second narrative, which depends on the following paradigm. Think of the instruments as four strands of sound that are woven together throughout the piece. Each strand occupies a characteristic register, one not located in absolute pitch space but defined relative to the other strands' registral position. The reference state is that in which the sound-strands do not cross; that is, when the first violin occupies the highest register, the second violin the second highest register, the viola the third highest register, and the cello the lowest register. As the instrumental voices begin to twist and weave together, the pattern becomes more intricate. We can think of the piece as moving through varying patterns whose intricacy we can measure. The lowest possible measurement will indicate the state in which no strands cross; the highest possible measurement will indicate the greatest degree of "twist" possible for the four sound-strands.[18]

A closer look at the first three notes of the movement will introduce the mechanics of the analysis. The viola enters on a barely audible C♯3, quickly crescendos and dies away. As it swells a second time to *p*, the cello enters a semitone above it, *ppp*, and similarly pulsates between *p* and *ppp* in turn, alternating with the viola in dynamic prominence. The cello then moves underneath the viola in m. 5 to sound the pitch a semitone below the viola's sustained C♯3. With the cello's move to C♮3 in m. 5, the two instruments swap registral places. The cello becomes the lower voice, the viola the higher.[19]

Using the conventions introduced in Example 2.2, we can explore this registral exchange in greater detail. At the beginning of m. 5, the cello is higher than the

[18] In Seeger's treatise "Tradition and Experiment in (the New) Music," which he drafted with Crawford's assistance during the summer of 1930, Seeger uses the term "twist" to indicate a single musical line consisting of at least three pitches whose contour goes up and then down, or down and then up. In contrast, I use "twist" to describe the pattern of all four voices at any given moment. Taylor Aitken Greer discusses Crawford's quartet movement in relation to Seeger's treatise in *A Question of Balance: Charles Seeger's Philosophy of Music* (Berkeley: University of California Press, 1998), 137–44.

[19] The following section of theory is derived from Daniel Harrison's work on permutations in "Some Group Properties of Triple Counterpoint and Their Influence on Compositions by J. S. Bach," *Journal of Music Theory* 32/1 (1988), 23–49. Permutations are an example of transformational theory, an area which David Lewin has explored in *Generalized Musical Intervals and Transformations* (New Haven: Yale University Press, 1989). Henry Klumpenhouwer lucidly engages Harrison's and Lewin's work in "A Generalized Model of Voice-Leading for Atonal Music" (Ph.D. diss., Harvard University, 1991).

Example 2.3 Numerical notation for registral exchange in a two-voice sonority

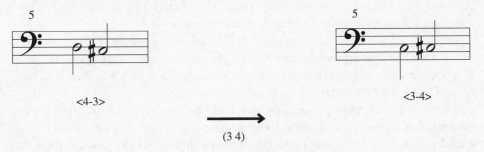

<4-3>   <3-4>

(3 4)

Example 2.4 Numerical notation for registral exchange in a four-voice sonority

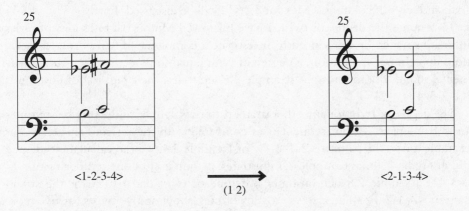

<1-2-3-4>   <2-1-3-4>

(1 2)

viola; at the end of m. 5, the viola is higher than the cello. (Throughout the examples that follow, the notes of violin 2 and cello have downward stems; the notes of violin 1 and viola have upward stems.)

The change from Example 2.2a to Example 2.2b is labeled with the permutation symbol (viola, cello) that denotes an interchange between the viola and cello. This interchange transforms Example 2.2a, <cello-higher-than-viola>, into Example 2.2b, <viola-higher-than-cello>. Example 2.3 illustrates an abbreviation of this terminology; by calling the viola "instrument 3" and the cello "instrument 4," the two situations may be notated as <4-3> and <3-4>. The first situation, <4-3>, is thus transformed into the second, <3-4>, by the permutation (34), which simply means that instruments 3 and 4 exchange registral roles. Regarding the movement of the voices as an exchange helps us to chart the crossing of each sound-strand.

Example 2.4 applies this permutational notation to the sonorities of m. 25, two examples of the four-voice sonority patterns that predominate in the piece. The only instrument to change pitch in m. 25 is violin 1, which moves from F♯4 to D4. The registral disposition of the first sonority of Example 2.4 is represented as <1-2-3-4>. That is, instrument 1 is in the highest register, instrument 2 in the second highest register, and so forth. The second sonority is represented as <2-1-3-4>;

instrument 2 is now in the highest register and instrument 1 is in the second highest register. The permutational notation (12) shows that instruments 1 and 2 have switched places, and the others remain in relative position.

Example 2.5 is a score reduction that displays all the sonorities of the piece using two staves. The first row below each system gives the measure numbers; when more than one sonority appears in a measure, the measure number is followed by a letter (e.g., 8a, 8b). The second row numbers the sonorities.

Table 2.1 lists all strand patterns greater than two strands from Example 2.5 using numerical notation. Its first three columns list the measure number, sonority, and strand pattern(s) for that measure. The fourth column lists the permutations that connect successive strand patterns. The number in the fifth column measures the "degree of twist" of the sound-strands at any given moment. The numbers in the sixth and seventh columns, "Max" and "N", will be discussed shortly.

To measure the degree of twist, I have borrowed Milton Babbitt's idea of order inversions which he introduced to investigate a completely different musical relationship.[20] In my application, a degree of twist equal to 0 occurs when the instrumental strands do not cross; as Example 2.6 illustrates, their registral disposition is <1-2-3-4>.

The degree of twist for any other strand pattern is defined as the number of times an instrument is "out of sequence" as compared with the reference pattern. For example, given the pattern <2-1-3-4> of Example 2.4, we can calculate its degree of twist to be 1, for as Example 2.7 illustrates, it contains just one reordering of <1-2-3-4>. Example 2.8 demonstrates a degree of twist equal to 5 for the strand pattern <3-4-2-1>. The arrows cross five times, showing five twists (or five reorderings) of the basic no-twist pattern.

Measuring the degree of twist for each sound-strand pattern throughout the piece enables us to describe the progression of these patterns. Although perceiving the exact degree at any one moment would require the musical ability to recognize each instrument's placement in relation to all the others – not an easy task, to be sure – many listeners do have the ability to hear that these strands are being continually woven and unwoven into configurations of varying intricacy, and to discern an increase or decrease in the degree of twist which the numbers reflect.[21]

In order to characterize the twining activity throughout the piece, Example 2.1 is annotated with the degree of twist for each sonority of three or more voices. The first three-instrument grouping occurs with the second violin's entrance in m. 13. Here, the degree of twist registers 0. It gradually reaches 2 in m. 18 through a progression of 0–0–1–2–2.

[20] Babbitt employs order inversions to investigate properties of twelve-tone row forms in "Twelve-Tone Invariants as Compositional Determinants," *Musical Quarterly* 46 (1960), 246–59.

[21] A performance can certainly bring out this reading. To consider one example, the recording by the Composers Quartet (Nonesuch H-71280, 1973) strives to keep each instrument's timbre indistinguishable from the others', making it more difficult to hear the twisting of voices from this performance than from one that preserves a separate identity for each instrument. The Composers Quartet's performance is based on a paradigm that Robert P. Morgan characterizes in the liner notes as a "sound mass" from which each voice emerges and recedes in turn.

Example 2.5 List of sonorities in String Quartet 1931, third movement

Example 2.5 (*cont.*)

At m. 19, the first violin enters, bringing the total of voices to four, and the degree of twist collapses back to 0. (Table 2.1 lists this moment as a *three*-voice strand pattern, <2-3-4>, in order to suggest that instrument 1 is doubling instru-

(1)

ment 2, having not yet asserted its first-violin identity.) On beat 3 of m. 19, the cello's change to C♯4 increases the degree to 1; in m. 20, the second violin's move to E♭4 effects an increase to 2; and in m. 24, the cello's subsequent drop to B3 brings the degree back down to 0. To summarize, the opening gesture of the three instruments (mm. 13–19) begins with no degree of twist, increases to 1, then 2, then drops back down to 0; it immediately repeats this sequence in mm. 19–24. (The drop from degree 2 to 1 in m. 21 is relatively brief, and does not affect the overall profile.)

This twisting activity of the voices is quite different from the overall upward registral climb toward the moment of climax and release. Within the dimension of voice-weaving, an increase is followed immediately by a decrease. The musical movement, then, is not simply a vector pointed toward m. 75; rather, it rocks back and forth.

In using the terms "increase" and "decrease" to describe progessions of twist values, I am not drawing a parallel between an increase in the degree of twist and an increase of "tension" in the weaving of sound strands. First, equating a greater degree of twist with a higher level of tension is incompatible with my metaphor: a high twist number for any particular sound-strand pattern would not be considered

Table 2.1 *Data Summary, Crawford String Quartet, third movement*

Meas.	Sonority	Strand Pattern [hi–mid–lo]	Permutation	Degree of Twist	Max	N=Degree/ Max
13b	7	<2-3-4>	( )	0	3	0
14a	8	<2-3-4>	(34)	0	3	0
14b	9	<2-4-3>	(24)	1	3	.33
15	10	<4-2-3>	(243)	2	3	.67
18	11	<3-4-2>	(243)	2	3	.67
19a	12	<2-3-4> (1)	(34)	0	3	0
19b	13	<2-4-3> (1)	—	1	3	.33
20	14	<2-1-4-3>	(12)	2	6	.33
21	15	<1-2-4-3>	(24)	1	6	.17
22	16	<1-4-2-3>	(234)	2	6	.33
24	17	<1-2-3-4>	(12)	0	6	0
25	18	<2-1-3-4>	(34)	1	6	.17
26	19	<2-1-4-3>	(13)	2	6	.33
29	20	<2-3-4-1>	(23)	3	6	.5
30	21	<3-2-4-1>	(234)	4	6	.67
32	22	<4-3-2-1>	(234)	6	6	1.0
33	23	<2-4-3-1>	(34)	4	6	.67
34[1]	24	<2-3-4-1>	(14)	3	6	.5
37a	25	<2-3-1-4>	( )	2	6	.33
37b	26	<2-3-1-4>	(132)	2	6	.33
39a	27	<1-2-3-4>	(34)	0	6	0
39b	28	<1-2-4-3>	(142)	1	6	.17
40	29	<4-1-2-3>	(142)	3	6	.5
43	30	<2-4-1-3>	(13)	3	6	.5
45	31	<2-4-3-1>	( )	4	6	.67
46	32	<2-4-3-1>	( )	4	6	.67
47	33	<2-4-3-1>	(1342)	4	6	.67
49	34	<1-2-4-3>	(12)	1	6	.17
50a	35	<2-1-4-3>	(134)	2	6	.33
50b	36	<2-3-1-4>	( )	2	6	.33
51	37	<2-3-1-4>	(23)	2	6	.33
53	38	<3-2-1-4>	(1234)	4	6	.67
56a	39	<4-3-2-1>	(123)	6	6	1.0
56b	40	<4-1-3-2>	( )	4	6	.67
57	41	<4-1-3-2>	(23)	4	6	.67
58a	42	<4-1-2-3>	(14)	3	6	.5
58b	43	<1-4-2-3>	(234)	2	6	.33
59	44	<1-2-3-4>	( )	0	6	0
60	45	<1-2-3-4>	( )	0	6	0
61a	46	<1-2-3-4>	( )	0	6	0
61b	47	<1-2-3-4>	( )	0	6	0
62a	48	<1-2-3-4>	( )	0	6	0
62b	49	<1-2-3-4>	(12)	0	6	0
63a	50	<2-1-3-4>	( )	1	6	.17

Table 2.1 (*cont.*)

Meas.	Sonority	Strand Pattern [hi–mid–lo]	Permutation	Degree of Twist	Max	N=Degree/ Max
63b	51	<2-1-3-4>	( )	1	6	.17
64	52	<2-1-3-4>	( )	1	6	.17
65a	53	<2-1-3-4>	( )	1	6	.17
65b	54	<2-1-3-4>	( )	1	6	.17
66	55	<2-1-3-4>	( )	1	6	.17
67	56	<2-1-3-4>	( )	1	6	.17
68	57	<3-1-2-4-5>	—	2	9	.22
69	58	<3-1-2-4-5-6>	—	2	13	.15
70a	59	<3-1-4-2-5-6-7>	—	3	18	.17
70b	60	<3-1-4-2-7-5-6-8>	(68)	5	24	.21
71a	61	<3-1-4-2-7-5-8-6>	(13)(274)	6	24	.25
71b	62	<1-3-2-7-4-5-8-6>	( )	5	24	.21
72	63	<1-3-2-7-4-5-8-6>	(457)(68)	5	24	.21
73	64	<1-3-2-4-5-7-6-8>	—	2	24	.08
75a	65	<1-4-5-2-7-6-8-3-10-9-11-12>	—	9	46	.20
75b	66	<2-1-3-4>	(14)(23)	1	6	.17
75c	67	<3-4-2-1>	—	5	6	.83
75d	68	<5-6-7-3-1-8-4-2>	—	17	24	.71
76	69	<2-3-1-4>	—	2	6	.33
77a	70	—	—	—	—	—
77b	71	—	—	—	—	—
77c	72	<1-2-3>	(12)	0	3	0
77d	73	<2-1-3>	(132)	1	3	.33
78a	74	<1-3-2>	( )	1	3	.33
78b	75	<1-3-2>	(13)	1	3	.33
78c	76	<3-1-2>	( )	2	3	.67
78d	77	<3-1-2>	(123)	2	3	.67
79a	78	<1-2-3>	( )	0	3	0
79b	79	<1-2-3>	(23)	0	3	0
79c	80	<1-3-2>	(23)	1	3	.33
79d	81	<1-2-3>	( )	0	3	0
80a	82	<1-2-3>	(23)	0	3	0
80b	83	<1-3-2>	(23)	1	3	.33
80c	84	<1-2-3>	(123)	0	3	0
81a	85	<2-3-1>	(23)	2	3	.67
81b	86	<3-2-1>	(132)	3	3	1.0
81c	87	<2-1-3>	(13)	1	3	.33
82a	88	<2-3-1>	( )	2	3	.67
82b	89	<2-3-1>	(13)	2	3	.67
82c	90	<2-1-3>	(13)	1	3	.33
83a	91	<2-3-1>	( )	2	3	.67
83b	92	<2-3-1>	(23)	2	3	.67
84a[2]	93	<3-2-1>	(123)	3	3	1.0
84b	94	<1-3-2>	(23)	1	3	.33
85a	95	<1-2-3>	(23)	0	3	0
85b	96	<1-3-2>	(132)	1	3	.33

Table 2.1 (*cont.*)

Meas.	Sonority	Strand Pattern [hi-mid-lo]	Permutation	Degree of Twist	Max	N= Degree/ Max
86a	97	<3-2-1>	(12)	3	3	1.0
86b	98	<3-1-2>	(123)	2	3	.67
87a	99	<1-2-3>	(123)	0	3	0
87b	100	<2-3-1>	—	2	3	.67
88a	101	<2-3-1-4>	( )	2	6	.33
88b	102	<2-3-1-4>	( )	2	6	.33
90a	103	<2-3-1-4>	(123)	2	6	.33
90b	104	<3-1-2-4>	—	2	6	.33
90c	105	<1-2-3> (4)	—	0	3	0
91	106	<1-2-3-4>	—	0	3	0
94a	107	<1-3-4>	—	0	3	0

Notes:
[1] There appears to be a misprint in the published version of the score in m. 35: in the composer's personal copy (SC-LC), C5 in Violin 2 is crossed out and a B4 is written in, and is tied to the B4 in m. 34.
[2] In the composer's score (SC-LC), a slur connects violin 2's pitch in m. 84 to its last note in m. 83, making the pitch a B♭ rather than B♮.

a more "tense" moment in the weave. Second, regarding the degree of twist as a measurement of tension or stress that is alleviated would be inconsistent with my argument that this hidden dimension subverts the dominant, traditional narrative. Doing so would greatly diminish the feminist content of my argument, one aspect of which is the refusal of this second musical space merely to reflect the first, to borrow Virginia Woolf's metaphor of a looking-glass to describe women's expected roles in relation to men.[22] Rather, in my analysis the primary significance of the twisting activity is its cyclic organization.

Measure 24 initiates a steady increase in twist, from 0 to the maximum degree of 6 in m. 32, where the cello reaches G4. The degree of twist then immediately decreases, 6–4–3–2–2, returning to degree 0 at m. 39.

The permutations, listed in Table 2.1, help to articulate the increasing and decreasing degrees of twist. In mm. 13b–15, the rising degree–numbers correspond either to no change, symbolized by (), or to change in which two elements swap places, to which I shall refer as two-element permutations, or "2-cycles." I shall refer to three-element permutations in which three elements swap places as 3-cycles, and so forth.

The return to degree 0 at m. 19a takes place over a 3-cycle, (243). In mm. 19a–22, the numbers correspond to 2-cycles, while the approach to degree 0 at m. 24 corresponds to a 3-cycle. Furthermore, a 3-cycle over mm. 30–32 accompanies

[22] Virginia Woolf, *A Room of One's Own* (San Diego: Harcourt Brace Jovanovich, 1989 [1929]), 35.

Example 2.6 Degree of twist = 0 in a four-voice sonority

<1-2-3-4>

Example 2.7 Degree of twist = 1 in a four-voice sonority

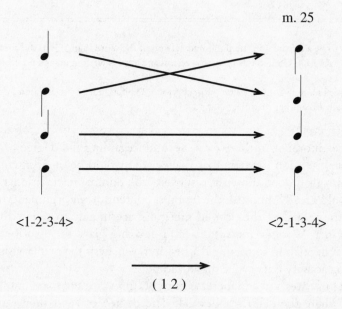

m. 25

<1-2-3-4>   <2-1-3-4>

(1 2)

the move from degree 4 to 6, and a 3-cycle also marks the return at m. 39a to degree 0. To summarize this section of the piece, 3-cycles accompany movement to degrees 0 or 6; 2-cycles and ()-cycles are used to move between other degrees of twist.

Attending to the permutations thus makes it easier to hear the continual transformation of strand patterns. I would like to suggest two additional listening strategies. The first is to listen for prominent melodic leaps. For example, at m. 24 the cello drops a fourth from E4 to B3, bringing the degree-of-twist progression back to 0. At mm. 31–32, the cello also signals the move to degree 6, the greatest degree of twist, with its distinct tritone ascent from C♯4 to G4. The second listening strategy is to trace the path of a single strand. For instance, over mm. 24–32 the cello moves

Example 2.8 Degree of twist = 5 in a four-voice sonority

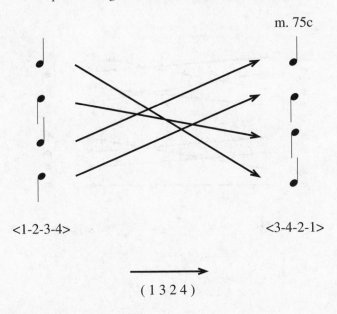

m. 75c

<1-2-3-4>   <3-4-2-1>

(1 3 2 4)

up from the lowest registral position to the highest while the degree of twist increases from 0 to 6.[23]

Returning in m. 39 to the musical narrative, we hear the degree of twist drop to 0, then increase to 1, 3, and then to 4, yielding the value of 4 three times over mm. 45–47. While the twisting activity pauses in these three measures, each instrument abandons its climb upward: the viola sustains its E4 throughout; in m. 45 the first violin dives 10 semitones, from C5 to D4; in m. 46 the cello drops 8 semitones from C♯5 to F4; and in m. 47, the second violin falls 9 semitones from D♯5 to F♯4. (Figure 2.1 shows the similar downward motion of the three instruments over sonorities 31–33.) This stretch of music thus exemplifies a local correspondence between the upward ascent and the steady twining activity of the sound-strands; both are temporarily abandoned. This moment does not, to me, indicate mutual recognition or reinforcement of the two musical spaces; indeed, points of coincidence might be expected of two forces operating independently of one another.

To move out of degree 4, the first violin ascends a fourth at m. 49 from D4 to G4, and the degree drops to 1.[24] This drop is accompanied by permutation (1342), the first 4-cycle to occur in the piece. The degree of twist then increases to 2 and swiftly reaches the maximum degree 6 at m. 56a with another 4-cycle. Degree 6 is displaced on the next beat by 4, which in turn decreases to 2 at m. 58b. With the assistance of the 3-cycle (234), the degree of twist returns to 0 at m. 59. Figure 2.1

---

[23] In mm. 13–15, the cello similarly moves from the lowest register to the highest register while the degree of twist increases from 0 to its local maximum of 2.

[24] The first violin's ascent by a fourth in m. 49, bringing the degree down from 4 to a local low of 1, mirrors the cello's earlier drop of a fourth in m. 24, which brought the degree down from 2 to 0.

Example 2.9 Degree of twist = 5 in an eight-voice sonority

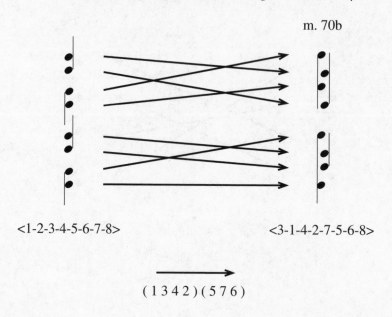

m. 70b

<1-2-3-4-5-6-7-8>   <3-1-4-2-7-5-6-8>

(1 3 4 2) (5 7 6)

shows this passage, in which the violins begin to split off registrally from the viola and cello over sonorities 44 to 65 (mm. 59–75).

After the strand pattern reaches degree 0 at m. 59, it returns this value for four measures until the second violin ascends in mm. 62–63 by a major third, F♯5 to A♯5, a move that shifts the degree to 1. The value of 1 is returned seven times before violin 1 plays its first double-stop in m. 68. In other words, the sound-strands cease their continual to-and-fro motion and grind to a halt. What I want to emphasize in mm. 59–67 is the slowing and stopping of the twisting activity, not the relatively low degree of twist. The moment of relative repose occurs because the weaving stops, not because it has reached degrees 0 and 1. In striking contrast, it is at this moment of relative repose, when the continual shifting of patterns pauses for quite a long time, that the tension of the piece starts to build more quickly, soon to become unbearable.

When the double- and triple-stops commence in m. 68, we cannot continue to calculate their degree-of-twist values as we did for the three- and four-strand patterns. The model can be generalized in the following way to accommodate this increase in the number of registral voices in a sound-strand pattern from four to five, six, seven, eight, or twelve as needed.

Example 2.9 represents the sonority at m. 70b as <3-1-4-2-7-5-6-8>. The strand patterns are ordered, as before, from high to low, but the first violin's double-stop notes are designated 1 and 2, the second violin's notes 3 and 4, etc. Since the sonority contains five reorderings of <1-2-3-4-5-6-7-8>, it would be assigned a degree of twist of 5.

The overall increase in degree of twist in Table 2.1, for mm. 68–75a from 2 to 9 is a bit misleading because with an increase in the number of registral voices, the maximum possible degree of twist increases proportionally. The sixth column in Table 2.1 contains the maximum possible degree of twist for each expanded strand pattern. A three-voice sonority has maximum degree of 3 (e.g., <4-3-2>); a four-voice sonority has a maximum degree of 6 (e.g., <4-3-2-1>). A five-voice sonority has a maximum degree of 9; a six-voice sonority has a maximum degree of 13, and so forth.[25]

A sonority's degree of twist divided by its maximum possible degree of twist gives a more accurate figure for comparing the degrees of twist among sonorities of different sizes. The seventh column in Table 2.1, labeled N, lists these relative values. For mm. 68–74, the values range from .08 to .25. In contrast to the heightening intensity of this passage as it progresses toward the climax, the degree of twist stays within a relatively small range. The climax sonority of m. 75 registers degree 9, which appears on first glance to be a local high, but with a maximum degree of 46 for a twelve-note sonority, its N-value is merely .20, remaining well within the small range already established. The highest N-value for mm. 68–75 is .83 at m. 75c, which is less than the N-value of 1 obtained at m. 32 and m. 56a. The events on the surface of the music are therefore not reinforced at the level of voice-twisting activity; the weaving of the sound-strands has slowed considerably, in contrast to the bells and whistles going off that signal a climax. This disjunction between the two dimensions continues after the moment of climax. During the release of surface tension, the twisting again commences – the sonority on the last beat of m. 75 registers 17 out of a maximum 24, or .71, a prominent increase from .20 of m. 75's downbeat sonority.

Calculating the degree of twist for the slurred eighth- and sixteenth-note figures that connect the climax sonority to the octachord in m. 75 beautifully illustrates the twisting activity. If we count the four beginning pitches and four end pitches of the slurred figures in m. 75 as each constituting a strand pattern, we can measure the degree of twist for these figures before and after their two-and-a-half octave sweep. Table 2.1 lists the beginning pitches in m. 75b as pattern <2-1-3-4> with degree of twist 1, and lists the end pitches in m. 75c as pattern <3-4-2-1> with a degree of twist 5. The increase from 1 to 5 suggests that over the second and third beats of m. 75 the strands plait rapidly from a nearly untwisted state into a highly twisted pattern.[26]

As Example 2.1 shows for m. 77 to the end of the piece, the steady increase and

---

[25] Although the maximum degree of twist for a five-voice strand (e.g., <5-4-3-2-1>) would be 10, the maximum number for the sonority in m. 68 is 9. Since a double-stop played by violin 1 would always be notated numerically as <1-2> and never as <2-1>, to count <2-1> as a twist would inflate the Max number. The ten twists that would be possible for five distinct instrumental voices is thus decreased by one when two of the voices are played by a single instrument, thus bringing the maximum number down to 9. The same reasoning applies when calculating the Max numbers for all the other double- and triple-stops in the passage. I am indebted to Jeff Stadelman for alerting me to this feature of Max numbers.

[26] My thanks to Anton Vishio for his suggestions on how to apply my model to the inner pitches of m. 75.

decrease of the degree of twist is mostly absent. Now the patterns shift much more rapidly, beat to beat, in what seems an almost random fashion in contrast to the instruments' steady collective descent after their triple-stop attacks: they sink downward, moving as relentlessly to the piece's nadir as they did to its peak.

In a 1976 interview, Charles Seeger acknowledged his former prejudice against women composers:

I was very snooty in those days about women composers and had come more or less to the conclusion that the great tradition of European music, say from 1200 to about 1930, had been created mostly by men and that it was a bit absurd to expect women to fit themselves into a groove which was so definitely flavored with machismo (and, of course, the early music of the twentieth century and the late music of the nineteenth century was machismo with a capital M).[27]

My reading of his wife's string quartet movement suggests how a woman composer did manage to situate herself simultaneously "within the groove" and outside it, to flow with the mainstream and to run a countercurrent underneath it. Rather than refusing to answer the compositional call to machismo, Crawford's quartet movement replies in part within the dominant discourse – but answers deviously, to borrow a phrase from Teresa de Lauretis.[28] Thus it manages to speak the language of the "great tradition" while also maintaining a space of resistance.

By tracing these twists systematically through the quartet movement, we are able to perceive a musical space through which an alternative narrative is written, one that proceeds alongside the more prominent narrative of the music's surface that drives toward the climax. My analysis thus draws a parallel between the structure of Crawford's quartet movement and her existence as a woman composer whose music seemingly accepts the conventions of the dominant group while it in actuality resists them. As I have argued, Crawford's gender animates this work in a way not readily evident, but which can be made audible, in this case, through formalist analysis.

---

[27] Wilding-White, "Remembering Ruth Crawford Seeger," 445. Seeger's designation of 1930 as the year that concluded men's dominance in European music composition may have had something to do with the fact that Crawford composed most of her mature works in the early 1930s: she wrote the String Quartet and *Diaphonic Suite No. 4* in 1931; the first three *Diaphonic Suites*, *Piano Study in Mixed Accents*, and *Three Chants for Women's Chorus* in 1930; *Three Songs to Poems by Carl Sandburg* over 1930–32; and her songs "Chinaman, Laundryman" and "Sacco, Vanzetti" – which he described as "extraordinary" and "magnificent" (quoted in JT-RCS, 194) – in 1932. Tick gives a chronological list of Crawford's works in JT-RCS, 361–71. Seeger further discusses the question of difference between the music of men composers and women composers in his essay "Ruth Crawford," in *American Composers on American Music: A Symposium*, ed. Henry Cowell (Stanford: Stanford University Press, 1933), 116–17.

[28] Teresa de Lauretis, *Alice Doesn't: Feminism, Semiotics, Cinema* (Bloomington: Indiana University Press, 1984), 7.

3

INSCRIBING IDENTITIES IN
CRAWFORD'S STRING QUARTET,
FOURTH MOVEMENT

In the late spring of 1930, Ruth Crawford travelled with Charles Seeger to Patterson, New York, where Seeger usually spent the summer with his three sons. Crawford was to continue her composition lessons with him, which she had begun in the fall of 1929 in New York City. In Patterson, these lessons took a different form – they consisted of Seeger dictating a treatise on modernist music to her every morning and afternoon, which she transcribed and typed. The projected two-part work, eventually called "Tradition and Experiment in (the New) Music," was based upon her tutorials during the previous nine months and on the composition lessons of Seeger's other students, including Henry Cowell. In addition to these secretarial responsibilities, she commented extensively on a complete draft of the manuscript before leaving in August to begin a year as a Guggenheim fellow in Berlin.[1]

Crawford's willingness to give up the opportunity to spend a second summer composing at the MacDowell Colony for this arrangement in Patterson, which concentrated on drafting Seeger's book rather than on developing her compositional skills, underscores her commitment to working with him. Her correspondence documents the extent to which her relatively brief period of study with Seeger had influenced her. In a letter to Seeger written in November 1930, she recounts how in Germany she had begun describing him to others as "a man whose ideas have the disciplinary advantages of Schoenberg's but with a vision and a vista that reaches *far* beyond. . . ."[2] In a letter to Nicholas Slonimsky, she writes that

[He] shared with me his conception of the aspects and as yet untried possibilities, both in form and content, of a new music, and his views as to various means of bringing some organic coordination out of the too often superabundance of materials in use at present. As a result of this study, my work began at last to take a "handleable" shape, to present itself in some sort of intelligible continuity.[3]

---

[1] Because of Crawford's extensive work on "Tradition and Experiment," Seeger dedicated the treatise to her (41). Background information on the writing of "Tradition and Experiment" is provided in Ann M. Pescatello, Introduction to Seeger, *Studies in Musicology II*, 9; JNS-MRCS, 2–4; JT-RCS, 131–32; and Greer, *A Question of Balance*, 8–9.

[2] Letter to Seeger, 11 November 1930, quoted in Tick, "Dissonant Counterpoint Revisited," 419. In this essay, Tick describes the circumstances of the quartet's composition, discusses the autograph draft of its first movement, and analyzes this movement in the context of Seeger's work in two versions of "Tradition and Experiment" and in his article "On Dissonant Counterpoint," 25–31.

[3] Letter to Nicholas Slonimsky, 29 January 1933; quoted in MG-RCS, 64–65.

35

"Tradition and Experiment in (the New) Music" gives both a speculative account of modern music and practical guidelines for composing it. One theme that emerges is Seeger's emphasis on the importance of a composer's musical feeling or intuition which he believed must accompany technical proficiency. In a section devoted to the idea of "mood," which concerns the composer's artistic conception of a piece and which is distinct from its systematic organization, he writes the following:

So far we have dealt with the technique of music as if it were entirely a matter of intrinsic organization. Perhaps it is necessary again to point out that this is only half the story. Probably at least half the time the composer does what he does not on the grounds of technical procedure at all, but at the behest of mood, literary program, a conception of the lyric, declamative, dramatic, or antiphonal, or a grand conception of a work as a whole . . . [I]n even the strictest exercises in organic composition, mood and external suggestion of every kind must be expected to play its indispensable role. For if it does not, the result will not be musical.[4]

Seeger's view was one with which Crawford was familiar, and it may well have influenced the conception of her own music. In a letter she wrote to Seeger in February 1931, she described the inception of the quartet's first movement by giving human agency to specific musical entities:[5] "[I] took the little monody which is lyric and gave it a leggiero pal with a bass voice and it insisted on becoming a string quartet."[6]

One of Crawford's markings in her personal copy of the score alludes to her conception of the piece as an instrumental vocalization. Scratching out "Allegro possibile" as the tempo indication in the published score, she adds "half note = circa 100" and writes "Allegro quasi recitative," invoking a style of text setting in order to suggest that speech should be simulated in a piece that has no text.[7] Her own brief analysis of the movement makes no mention of the program I shall present in which the instruments carry out a conflict between opposing parties, but the circumstances of her analysis warrant consideration: she prepared it in 1948 at Edgard Varèse's request for a course he was teaching at Columbia University. Although the audience for the analysis would surely have been interested in aspects of the quartet's form, pitch organization, and so forth, Crawford may have thought that inclusion of an extra-musical program would have been inappropriate. In a letter accompanying the analysis she sent to Varèse, Crawford writes that the enclosed

---

[4] Seeger, "Tradition and Experiment," 161.

[5] Crawford began the quartet in February 1931 and completed it during the spring of 1931 (JT-RCS, 155). By April, one movement was finished, while the third and fourth movements were still incomplete (*ibid.*, 156); she completed the quartet in the first week of June 1931, and sent the score to the Guggenheim Foundation on 13 June 1931 (*ibid.*, 170). During the question-answer period of the Works Progress Administration Composers' Forum-Laboratory held on 6 April 1938, she stated that she composed it in several months and that one of the movements had taken a week (MG-RCS, 204).

[6] Crawford, Letter to Seeger, 22 February 1931; quoted in Tick, "Dissonant Counterpoint Revisited," 407.

[7] SC-LC.

score is "analysed as to tone, rhythm, form, and dynamics," which leaves open the possibility that she chose *not* to analyze other aspects of the piece.[8]

In Chapter 2, I proposed that Crawford's music might be read as the record of a life, and argued that the compositional strategies in the third movement of her quartet can be heard as conveying her experiences of professional marginalization. In contrast, my analysis of the fourth movement presents a reading of its drama as representing a gender-based narrative that Crawford may have not been able or willing to articulate in speech or prose.

One such experience occurred in 1929, when Henry Cowell initially suggested to Seeger that he give composition lessons to Crawford, whose music had impressed him. Seeger initially refused, recalling his reasons fifty years later:

I had other women students at the time, and none of them was particularly interesting, so I made the arrangement that, all right, I would take her as a composer at my regular fee. Mrs. Walton, whom she was going to stay with, would pay for it and Ruth would promise to take six lessons. At the end of the six lessons we would have a discussion of the situation.[9]

Despite Seeger's reluctance to teach her, Crawford was able to produce compositional assignments that pleased even his prejudiced eye, and she was permitted to continue studying with him.

It is doubtful that Crawford could have so easily shrugged off the impact of Seeger's negative opinion of women composers. That she respected his opinion is evident: he was able to persuade her to leave behind her beloved Skryabin models; he introduced her to the new, "ultra-modern" style for which she had a real affinity; and he impressed her with his musical imagination and discipline. When she learned of his belief that female composition students were inherently dull, Crawford's dismay must have been acute.

After struggling against Seeger's preconceptions about women composers, Crawford encountered other professional barriers because of her sex. While in Vienna in May 1931, she visited the director of Universal Edition, Emil Hertzka, who suggested that, as a woman, she would find it difficult to get her music published, and that she could send her music "without hope."[10] Describing the visit in a letter to Seeger, Crawford seethed:

One thing he said made me rather boil, tho all I did outwardly was to ask him what he meant. The thing he said was that of course it would be particularly hard for a woman to get anything published. What is this for reasoning? He didn't see my music. He had lost money in publishing the music of Ethel [sic] Smyth.[11]

---

[8] Ruth Crawford Seeger, Letter to Edgard Varèse, 22 May 1948; repr. in MG-RCS, 212–15. Crawford's analyses and annotated scores of the quartet's third and fourth movements are housed in SC-LC.

[9] Seeger speculated about how Crawford reacted to his proposed contract for her studies: ". . . I was not present but I could see her eyes flashing: 'Well, I'm going to show that son of a bitch something.'" Quoted in Wilding-White, "Remembering Ruth Crawford Seeger: An Interview with Charles and Peggy Seeger," 446.

[10] Letter to Seeger, 6 May 1931; quoted in JT-RCS, 161–62.   [11] *Ibid.*, 162.

In her diary, that most private form of prose expression, Crawford described her feelings about women's status in society, which ranged from rueful to indignant, as in the following entry from August 1927:

I also vent my spleen today on the fact of being a woman, or rather on the fact that beastly men, not satisfied with their own freedom, encroach on that of women and produce in them a kind of necessitous fear which binds them about. For instance, what is more mysterious and delightful than to walk at night, especially on deserted and ill-lighted streets, when the few windows peek at one delightfully but do not intrude on one's aloneness – when shadows are deep and silent and the occasional whirrings of cars make swift crescendos and diminuendos on the night's symphony? Or to work one's way around the world, a poet-tramp, stoker, bell-boy, deck-hand, finding, probing into the essence of the roots of living; or a recluse for a few years, like Thoreau, building a hut off in the deep woods, feeling in his pulse a great freedom. Women have gained great independence, but men have that which women will never have.[12]

If Crawford felt the need to express in prose her anger about the limits placed upon women (anger that was often held in check in social situations such as in the meeting with Hertzka), she may well have done the same in her music. That anger can be heard in the narrative I shall propose for the last movement of her String Quartet 1931.[13] The basis for this claim is that Crawford's experiences of professional discrimination began to accrue during the late 1920s and early 1930s, a period just before she would compose the quartet.

Elie Siegmeister, a member of the Composers' Collective which Seeger helped to found in 1932–33, recalled Crawford's reserved demeanor during the few meetings of the Collective that she attended:

Ruth was always a little reticent and a little withdrawn. We'd sit around talking and she didn't say that much. It wasn't male chauvinism or anything, I mean, you know, we were I hope beyond that stage. But Ruth was just a little quieter than Charlie – we were big talkers anyway. She deferred a great deal to Charlie . . . I don't think that Charlie was in any way as I said, chauvinistic or the dominant male or anything like that. But you see, he had a gift of gab and she was very lovely and sweet and a little withdrawn. My impression was that Ruth was not essentially an intellectual. That's a hell of a thing to say about a composer, but I always felt that she was a lovely person who wasn't particularly interested in all these intellectual discussions and arguments.[14]

---

[12] RCd-LC, [26] August 1927; quoted in MG-RCS, 54.

[13] Interpreting instrumental compositions as narrative is a significant area in musicology. Among the central writings are Fred Everett Maus, "Music as Narrative," Indiana Theory Review 12/1–2 (1991), 1–24; Susan McClary, "Narrative Agendas in 'Absolute' Music: Identity and Difference in Brahms' Third Symphony," in Musicology and Difference: Gender and Sexuality in Music Scholarship, ed. Ruth A. Solie (Berkeley: University of California Press, 1993), 326–44; Jean-Jacques Nattiez, "Can One Speak of Narrativity in Music?," Journal of the Royal Musical Association (1989–90), 240–57; Anthony Newcomb, "Schumann and Late 18th-Century Narrative Strategies," 19th-Century Music 11/2 (Fall 1987), 164–74; Jann Pasler, "Narrative and Narrativity in Music," in Time and Mind: Interdisciplinary Issues, ed. J. T. Fraser (Madison, CT: International Universities Press, 1989), 233–57; and Eero Tarasti, "Pour une narratologie de Chopin," International Review of the Aesthetics and Sociology of Music 15/1 (1984), 53–75.

[14] Interview with Elie Siegmeister by Judith Tick, 18 December 1985; quoted in JT-RCS, 196.

In a diary entry from May 1930, Crawford gives a reason for her hesitancy in social situations, a trait that can partly be attributed to contemporary expectations of women.

Fear, I fear. I am afraid to tell others often my opinion. Not because I am afraid of hurting *them*, but because I am afraid of hurting their opinion of me. I am afraid to hold an opinion opposite to that of someone I respect. I am afraid, afraid.[15]

She alludes again to this fear a year later in a letter written to Seeger during the time she was completing the quartet, and describes how she is attempting to alter this behavior: "I am trying to develop a (polite) frankness and make myself lose my fear of expressing an opinion."[16]

In the quartet's last movement, the first violin is anything but reluctant to express an opinion. Example 3.1 gives the score. The first violin's *sforzando* marking, accents, and rising register immediately establish its assertive character, manifesting that personal quality with which Crawford was so concerned.[17]

By initially casting the first violin as a self-confident and assertive subject, Crawford is able to situate a quality that she wished to acquire herself within the fabric of her music. The movement can be understood as a site in which she was able to bring to life a persona that she herself found difficult to project in everyday discourse.[18] Moreover, it may be heard to play out a narrative that was familiar to Crawford, one in which her musical efforts were not readily acknowledged or accepted by men who were in positions of power. These compositional "moods" can, I believe, be linked to gender issues.

It cannot be convincingly claimed that an individual's struggle against a larger group in power is an exclusive concern of women and not of men; nor should one make the essentialist assertion that women are diffident while men are self-assured. However, in Crawford's case, her writings document her frustrations stemming from her encounters with fixed, traditional beliefs about appropriate roles for women and her inhibitions about expressing contrary opinions, a psychological state effected by her female subjectivity.

---

[15] Quoted in MG-RCS, 198.

[16] Letter to Seeger, 14 May 1931; quoted in JT-RCS, 163. Crawford's diffidence marked her later years, as well: Tick notes that "others sensed Ruth's lack of confidence" and that Crawford "projected a sense of personal unworth" as a result of comparing herself to Seeger, whom she believed to possess much more musical talent than she (JT-RCS, 308).

[17] The fourth movement of Crawford's quartet may be fruitfully compared to the second movement of Charles Ives's Second String Quartet (1901–13). According to Ives, the instruments personified "4 men" whose vigorous "Arguments" in the second movement take place between the second violin and the other three instruments. See John Kirkpatrick, *A Temporary Mimeographed Catalogue of the Music Manuscripts and Related Materials of Charles Edward Ives 1874–1954* (Library of the Yale University School of Music, New Haven, 1960), 60; cited in J. Philip Lambert, "Interval Cycles as Compositional Resources in the Music of Charles Ives," *Music Theory Spectrum* 12/1 (1990), 46–47.

[18] Although Seeger identified movements three and four of the String Quartet as "assignments" from him, Crawford did not indicate that she considered them assignments or that they were co-authored by him. She did acknowledge Seeger's imprint on pieces written under his direction – she called the four *Diaphonic Suites* "ours" and dubbed a sketch for an orchestral work their "child" (JT-RCS, 156–57).

Example 3.1 Crawford, String Quartet 1931, fourth movement

Example 3.1 (*cont.*)

Example 3.1 (*cont.*)

18

Example 3.1 (*cont.*)

Example 3.1 (*cont.*)

Example 3.1 (*cont.*)

Example 3.1 *(cont.)*

The first violin remains steadfastly independent of the second violin, viola, and cello throughout the piece. In her analysis of the movement, Crawford refers to the first violin as "Voice I" and to the lower three instruments as "Voice II," a designation I shall also employ. Voice II, in contrast, acts as an unyielding mass of authority which remains united in opposition to Voice I's passionately stated beliefs. My reading of the piece characterizes the fundamental interaction of the two voices as conflicting, opposed, and gendered. For Crawford, many of the professional barriers she faced were posed by men because of her sex – the nature of her portrayal of two voices in conflict can thus be understood as gendered, with Voice I and Voice II representing a female and a male persona, respectively.

Joseph Straus offers an alternative narrative for the quartet movement – that of gendering Voice I as male and Voice II as female – and suggests that this narrative is equally plausible:

One might argue that the serial voice, with its rational, orderly patterning, lines up with the first term in each of the familiar of male/female, reason/emotion, stable/unstable oppositions. One might argue equally plausibly, I think, that the free melody in the first violin asserts a striving, autonomous individuality against the cyclical melody shared communally by the other instruments, and thus that the free melody should be lined up with the first terms in the dualities. It is unprofitable, then, to imagine Crawford's music as lining up in any straightforward way with a network of philosophical dualities.[19]

I am not convinced that these two readings of the quartet are interchangeable and equally persuasive. The reading which designates Voice I as the male party does not take into account the psychological contexts of the quartet – that is, Crawford's dissatisfaction with her diffident manner and her anger about women's lack of freedom. Composing the quartet movement may well have allowed her to confront a weakness she perceived in her manner and to reverse traditional gender roles. The texture of a solo, unmuted voice confronting a group of three muted voices strengthens the reading that characterizes Voice I as embodying Crawford herself challenging a body of authority which was assuredly gendered male.[20]

In arguing that the two voices are gendered in this way, I am not suggesting that the musical material of each voice constitutes a "feminine" or "masculine" essence, neatly fitting into a list of gendered dualities. Indeed, my feminist account of the voices' relationship *contradicts* the stereotype in which female identity is equated with passive, weak, and timid, while male identity is equated with aggressive, strong, and confident – in the movement's opening and closing, Voice I is the more forceful and commanding of the two. Furthermore, because Voice II plays *con sordino* throughout and Voice I is never muted, the force of Voice II's statements is considerably weakened despite the difference in texture.

Voice I starts boldly, *ffz*, secure of what she says. Throughout the piece, the two voices employ very different styles of communication. Voice I's speech is initially choppy and irregular, later becoming more flowing with longer phrases as the dialogue moves toward its midpoint at mm. 57–60, which Crawford called its "Turning Point."[21] In contrast, Voice II's speech starts out inarticulately with a soft stream of pitches that becomes louder, shorter, and more defined as it proceeds toward the work's midpoint.[22] Voice I initiates the dialogue with a single pitch, Ab3,

---

[19] JNS-MRCS, 224.

[20] Seeger later described Crawford as an "ardent feminist" because of her firmly held beliefs in the equality of the sexes (interview with Seeger by Ray Wilding-White, 17 September 1976; cited in JTS-RCS, 86). As discussed in Chapters 2 and 5, several women greatly furthered Crawford's composition career – most prominently Djane Lavois Herz, Blanche Walton, and Marion Bauer. Although some men certainly supported Crawford's career, others obstructed her career at several turns.

[21] Noted on Crawford's score (SC-LC). In her analysis, she also called the E in m. 57 a "foreign tone" and a "turning-tone" (SC-LC; repr. in JT-RCS, 359).

[22] Straus's analysis of this movement asserts that while the two voices differ on the surface, they are also subtly linked through pitch elements (JNS-MRCS, 179–82); Straus shows that linear presentations of certain trichords also occur as simultaneities between the two voices.

played for the duration of an eighth note. Her next utterance contains two notes, G3 and A3, which are accented and played *détaché*; the subsequent utterance contains three notes, also accented and played *détaché*, and so forth. The length of each successive utterance increases by one note until m. 57, where Voice I has amassed a phrase twenty-one notes in length.

Voice II responds by using a contrasting dynamic, articulation, and phrase length. In mm. 3–5, the three instruments mutter amongst themselves, ***pp***, with a flurry of slurred eighth notes, none of which receives an accent or a *sforzando*. The pitch material of Voice II is derived from the ten-tone row that begins in m. 3 with D4 and ends with C5 in m. 4. (For the sake of consistency, I shall identify Voice II's pitches by referring to the second violin's part.) In m. 4, the row is rotated to start on E4, which is the second note of the row, and ends in m. 5 with D4, the first note of the row. After a rest in m. 6, the row is rotated a second time, this time to begin in m. 7 on F4, the third note of the row, and it concludes in m. 8 with E4, the second note of the row. Voice II's notes continue to cycle through successive pitches of the row in this fashion, sometimes completing the row after a rest: for example, the third rotation of the row begins in m. 8 on E♯4, the fourth note of the row, and continues to the E5 at the end of the phrase in m. 9, which is the second note of the row. After a rest, the row is completed in m. 10 with the entrance of F5, the third note of the row, which initiates a new phrase. The fourth rotation begins with F♯4 in m. 10.

In addition to these rotations of the original row, Voice II proceeds by presenting each successive phrase decreased in length by one eighth note until a phrase consisting of only a single sustained pitch remains in m. 57. As each phrase decreases in length, the length of the rest separating one from the next also decreases, from two full measures (= sixteen eighth rests) in mm. 1–2, to one-and-a-half measures (= twelve eighth rests) in mm. 5–6, to eleven eighth rests in mm. 9–10, to ten in mm. 13–14, and so forth, until the shortest rest between statements is reached in mm. 30–31, three eighth rests. As the length of phrase continues to decrease in the next statement, from eleven to ten notes, the length of rests now begins to *increase* to eight eighth rests in mm. 33–34, ten in mm. 36–37, twelve in mm. 39–40, and so forth, until the longest rest between statements – twenty-three eighth rests – is reached in mm. 60–62.[23]

Voice I proceeds similarly. Starting in m. 3, as each successive phrase is increased in length by one eighth note up to the piece's midpoint, the length of the rests separating one phrase from the next decreases, from twenty-eight eighth rests in mm. 3–6, to twenty-two and one third in mm. 6–9, to twenty-one in mm. 10–12, and so forth, until the shortest rest between statements – one eighth note – is reached in m. 31. As the length of phrase continues to increase in the next statement, in mm. 31–34, to thirteen notes in length, the length of rests also begins to *increase*, to two eighth rests in m. 34, to three in mm. 37–38, to four in m. 40, and five in m. 43. At

---

[23] Judith Tick notes that if the eighth-note and quarter-note rests in mm. 30–31 are regarded as a midway point, then the rests between Voice II's entrances can be divided into two sets of ten, a feature she links to the ten-tone pitch organization (JT-RCS, 220).

m. 46, the length of rest again decreases to four eighth rests, then to three in m. 49, to two in m. 52, to one in m. 55, and finally to no rest in m. 60. A further aspect of this movement's rhythmic organization is, in Crawford's words, that "[r]hythmic fluidity is sought after in Voice I through use of varied divisions of the half-measure – groups of 3 and 5 alternating with 4. In voice 2 the 8th note is constant, but irregular rhythmic patterns are obtained through bowing."[24]

Starting in m. 60, Voice I plays the pitches of the first half of the piece in their original rhythm, but in retrograde and transposed up a semitone. Starting in m. 63, Voice II does the same, concluding in mm. 112–14 with a phrase twenty notes long. By having both voices retrace their previous material, Crawford maintains a distinct identity for each.[25]

Melodic line is crucial to Crawford, particularly to the music she composed between the years 1930 and 1932.[26] Her "longing for a line"[27] and desire for "clarity of melodic line"[28] are evident not only in the quartet, but also in other of her works from this period.[29]

Contour theory offers a useful way to address the melodic structure and rhetoric in this piece. The formal component of my analysis draws upon recent studies of musical contour as the basis for the narrative that I am proposing. This narrative is situated within the work's "contour space," or the musical space that, in Robert Morris's words, "consists of elements, called c-pitches (cps) [that] are numbered in order from low to high."[30] An explanation of the methodology I shall employ in analyzing the movement follows.

I shall classify each phrase according to its melodic contour, or its basic shape. A contour is an ordered set of n contour pitches (cps), or pitches whose salient feature is their position relative to one another in contour space; a contour with n pitches has cardinality n. The distance between cps is not measured.[31] For a contour of cardinality n, its contour segment, or "cseg," is found by listing its contour pitches in order according to relative height, with 0 assigned to the lowest pitch and $n-1$ to the highest pitch. For example, Voice I's statement in m. 6, B♭3–A3–B3, has a cardinality of three. Example 3.2 shows that the lowest pitch of the phrase, A3, is assigned 0; the second lowest pitch, B♭3, is assigned 1; and the highest pitch, B3, is assigned $n-1$ or $3-1 = 2$. The cseg for this phrase is thus <102>.[32]

---

[24] Crawford (Seeger), "Analysis of 4th Movement/String Quartet 1931," SC-LC.

[25] Alternatively, the voices could have exchanged material after reaching the midpoint, with the first violin taking up the serialized eighth notes, and the instruments in Voice II playing the freer material.

[26] Tick identifies these years as constituting Crawford's second style period (JT-RCS, 201). Straus explores numerous features of Crawford's melodies, relating certain aspects to Seeger's theoretical ideas (JNS-MRCS, 5–48).

[27] Letter to Seeger, 30 January 1931; quoted in Tick, "Dissonant Counterpoint," 420.

[28] Letter to Varèse, 22 May 1948, quoted in MG-RCS, 213.

[29] *Piano Study in Mixed Accents*, *Diaphonic Suites 1–4*, *Three Chants for Women's Chorus*, *Two Ricercari*, and *Three Songs to Poems by Carl Sandburg*.   [30] Morris, *Composition with Pitch-Classes*, 26.

[31] In contrast to Morris's work, Michael Friedmann's theory of contour takes into account the distance between pitches in contour space. See Friedmann, "A Methodology for the Discussion of Contour," 223–48.

[32] Elizabeth West Marvin and Paul Laprade provide a detailed explanation of how to classify contours in "Relating Musical Contours," 225–67.

Example 3.2 Cseg <102> in Voice I, m. 6

⟨1 0 2⟩

Example 3.3 Cseg <14203> in Voice I, m. 13

⟨1   4   2   0   3⟩

Example 3.3 shows the cseg for a phrase made up of five pitches. Voice I's state-ment in m. 13, B3–F♯4–C♯4–G3–D4, has a cardinality of five. The lowest pitch of the phrase is G3, which is assigned 0; the second lowest pitch, B3, is assigned 1; the third lowest pitch, C♯4, is assigned 2; the fourth lowest pitch, D4, is assigned 3, and the highest pitch, F♯4, is assigned $n–1$ or $5–1 = 4$. The cseg for this phrase is thus <14203>.

A useful analytical tool to apply to this movement is Morris's contour reduction algorithm, shown in Figure 3.1.[33] It pares a contour down to a more basic, skeletal profile by reducing cps that are less salient in their relative height and relative posi-tion. The algorithm allows a listener to compare contours of varying lengths like those in Crawford's composition. Morris justifies the use of his algorithm by invok-ing the principles of Gestalt psychology, which suppose that the boundaries or out-lines of an object are perceptually prominent.[34] In this movement, playing or listening to the relatively lengthy phrases provides a convincing illustration of Morris's assertion. At a tempo of "*Allegro possibile,*" it is likely that listeners will per-ceive the boundaries of relatively long phrases, such as the statement in mm. 2–5, more immediately than the exact note-to-note contour of the twenty-pitch chain, much less the serial ten-tone rotation scheme. The skeletal version of a contour, called a "prime contour," consists of its first and last pitches as well as its maximum and minimum pitches (the maximum and minimum can be the first or last pitches).

To demonstrate how one applies the algorithm to the quartet, Example 3.4 reduces the cseg <14203>, which was found to be the cseg for Voice I's statement in m. 13, B3–F♯4–C♯4–G3–D4. Example 3.5 reduces a longer contour, Voice II's first statement in mm. 3–5, cseg <245369871t4536987102>, to prime <1201>.

Morris notes that the prime of each contour may be easily found by inscribing it within a rectangle.[35] For example, in mm. 3–5, the first, tenth, nineteenth, and

[33] Morris, "New Directions," 212.

[34] *Ibid.*, 218–19. James Tenney and Larry Polansky have also developed an algorithm based on Gestalt principles in their "Temporal Gestalt Perceptions in Music," *Journal of Music Theory* 24/2 (1980), 205–41.

[35] Morris, "New Directions," 218.

Definition: *Maximum pitch*: Given three adjacent pitches in a contour, if the second is higher than or equal to the others it is a *maximum*. A set of maximum pitches is called a *maxima*. The first and last pitches of a contour are maxima by definition.

Definition: *Minimum pitch*: Given three adjacent pitches in a contour, if the second is lower than or equal to the others it is a *minimum*. A set of minimum pitches is called a *minima*. The first and last pitches of a contour are minima by definition.

Algorithm: Given a contour C and a variable N:

step 0: Set N to 0.

step 1: Flag all maxima in C; call the resulting set the *max-list*.

step 2: Flag all minima in C; call the resulting set the *min-list*.

step 3: If all pitches in C are flagged, go to step 9.

step 4: Delete all non-flagged pitches in C.

step 5: N is incremented by 1 (i.e., N becomes N+1).

step 6: Flag all maxima in max-list. For any string of equal and adjacent maxima in max-list, either: (1) flag only one of them; or (2) if one pitch in the string is the first or last pitch of C, flag only it; or (3) if both the first and last pitch of C are in the string, flag (only) both the first and last pitch of C.

step 7: Flag all minima in min-list. For any string of equal and adjacent minima in min-list, either: (1) flag only one of them; or (2) if one pitch in the string is the first or last pitch of C, flag only it; or (3) if both the first and last pitch of C are in the string, flag (only) both the first and last pitch of C.

step 8: Go to step 3.

step 9: End. N is the "depth" of the original contour C.

The reduced contour is the prime of C; if N=0, then the original C has not been reduced and is a prime itself.

Figure 3.1 Morris's contour reduction algorithm

twentieth pitches, D4–C5–C4–D4, are the pitches that would meet the lines of a rectangle circumscribing the phrase; the other sixteen pitches would be contained within the rectangle.

An exception to this principle of rectangle inscription for finding primes occurs when a cseg has a cardinality of four and all four pitches are flagged by step 3, at which point one is directed to go to step 9. For example, the prime contour of <3021>, which was found to represent Voice I's statement of E♭4–B♭3–D4–C♯ in mm. 9–10, is <3021> according to step 3; if the algorithm did *not* direct one to proceed to step 9, the D would be pruned in step 6 ("Flag all maxima in the max-list"), since D is a passing tone rather than a maximum pitch at this stage. The D would be the only pitch of the four pitches in the cseg *not* inscribed within a rectangle. For these exceptional cases which occur only in mm. 9–10 and mm. 107–108

Example 3.4 Contour reduction algorithm applied to cseg <14203>

Let C = <14203>.
Steps 1 and 2. Flag all maxima and minima using upper and lower beams.

Steps 3 and 4. Not all pitches are flagged. Delete C♯4, which is not flagged.

Step 5. N = 1. Steps 6 and 7. Flag all maxima in max-list and minima in min-list.

Step 8. Go to Step 3.
Step 3. All pitches are flagged. Go to Step 9.
Step 9. End. The prime of cseg <14203> is <1302>; its depth is 1.

in the piece, I shall use the method of rectangle inscription, which results in primes of three pitches rather than four pitches.

Figure 3.2 lists the prime contours of both voices throughout the piece. By comparing entries in the two columns, we find that Voice I's brief three-note statement in m. 6, B♭3–A3–B3, shares the prime contour of <102> with Voice II's lengthy nineteen-note string in mm. 6–9, whose pitches that bound the prime rectangle are F4–E♭3–E5.[36] Having introduced the technical basis for my analysis, I shall return to an account of its drama.

Reducing each phrase to its prime contour reveals a deeper level at which the voices are opposed. In mm. 1–12, the first four exchanges between Voice I, which

---

[36] Each melodic string can also be heard as a chain of substrings. For example, Voice I's statement in mm. 26–67 can be broken down into three smaller <10> substrings. I have reduced each continuous phrase to a single prime rather than to a series of primes because the phrase grouping in this piece is unambiguous: each statement constitutes a single unit. It should be noted that in some cases, such as in Voice I's sequence of three <10> primes, the substrings may be heard as reinforcing the larger background contour of <10> at a more local level; in others, such as in Voice I's statement of mm. 16–17, the substrings may present an additional way to parse the components of a larger unit.

Example 3.5 Contour reduction algorithm applied to cseg <245369871t4536987102>

Let C = <245369871t4536987102>.

Steps 1 and 2. Flag all maxima and minima using upper and lower beams.

Steps 3 and 4. Not all pitches are flagged. Delete unflagged pitches.

Step 5. N = 1. Steps 6, 7, 8, 3, and 4. Flag all maxima in max-list and all minima in min-list. Delete unflagged pitches.

Step 5. N = 2. Steps 6, 7, 8, 3, and 4. Flag all maxima in max-list and all minima in min-list. Delete unflagged pitches.

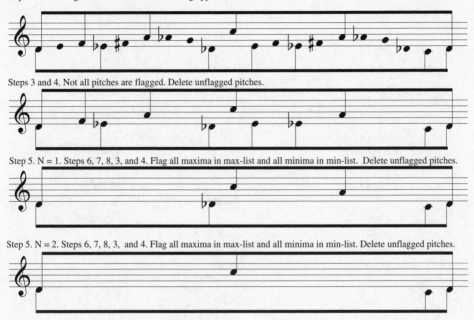

Step 5. N = 3. Steps 6 and 7. All pitches are flagged. Step 8. Go to Step 3.
Step 3. All pitches are flagged. Go to Step 9.
Step 9. End. The prime of the cseg is <1201>; its depth is 3.

constitutes the female voice, and Voice II, which constitutes the three male voices, are relatively polite. Each waits for the other to complete its statement before responding. This initial willingness to cooperate is reinforced by their prime contours: after Voice I plays B♭3–A3–B♮3 in m. 6, which forms cseg <102>, Voice II responds in mm. 7–9 with a nineteen-note phrase whose prime contour, derived using Morris's algorithm, is also <102>.

In mm. 9–10, this relationship becomes more strained. Voice I gives a statement that reduces to prime <201>, which is the retrograde of <102>. This retrograde relationship, which presents the voices as opposed, continues in the next four phrases: in mm. 10–12, Voice II's phrase takes the form of prime <2031>; in m. 13, Voice I immediately offers <1302>, a retrograde of her previous prime contour. In mm. 14–16, Voice II presents another <102> prime, which Voice I answers with prime <201> in mm. 16–17.

Measures 10–12 raise a critical theoretical point: for some contour strings, the first and last pitch of the prime contour lie close together and the inner pitch or pitches of the prime contour are comparatively distant – for example, Voice II's

measure(s)	Voice I	Voice II
2	<01>	
3–5		<1201>
6	<102>	
7–9		<102>
9–10	<201>	
10–12		<2031>
13	<1302>	
14–16		<102>
16–17	<201>	
17–19		<1032>
19–20	<1032>	
20–21		<201>
21–23	<102>	
22–24		<1032>
24–25	<1032>	
25–26		<1302>
26–27	<10>	
27–28		<1032>
28–29	<10>	
29–30		<1302>
30–31	<120>	
31–33		<102>
31–34	<021>	
34–36		<10>
35–37	<021>	
37–38		<021>
38–40	<2031>	
40–41		<102>
41–43	<2031>	
43–44		<01>
44–46	<120>	
46–47		<10>
46–49	<2301>	
49		<021>
49–52	<2301>	
52		<102>
52–54	<102>	
54		<01>
55–60	<10>	

Figure 3.2 Prime contours of Voices I and II in Crawford, Quartet, fourth movement

measure(s)	Voice I	Voice II
60–62	<01>	
63		<10>
63–65	<201>	
65		<201>
65–68	<1032>	
68		<120>
68–71	<1032>	
70–71		<01>
71–73	<021>	
73–74		<10>
74–76	<1302>	
76–77		<201>
77–79	<1302>	
79–80		<120>
80–82	<120>	
81–83		<01>
83–86	<120>	
84–86		<201>
86–87	<021>	
87–88		<2031>
88–89	<01>	
89–90		<2301>
90–91	<01>	
91–92		<2031>
92–93	<2301>	
93–95		<2301>
94–96	<201>	
96–97		<102>
97–98	<2301>	
98–100		<2301>
100–101	<102>	
101–103		<201>
104	<2031>	
105–107		<1302>
107–108	<102>	
108–110		<201>
111	<201>	
112–114		<1021>
115	<10>	

Figure 3.2 (*cont.*)

eighteen-tone statement in mm. 10–12 has a prime contour of <2031>, which is formed by F5–C4–A5–E5. Because some listeners might perceive this statement as prime <1021> rather than as prime <2031> since the pitches that flank the phrase lie only a semitone apart, I want to emphasize the importance of hearing each statement in its larger contexts rather than as an independent melodic entity.

Comparing the second statement of the second violin, viola, and cello in mm. 10–12 with their previous statement in mm. 7–9 and with their subsequent statement in mm. 14–16 strengthens a hearing of prime <2031> over <1021>. The first pitch of this phrase, F5 in m. 10, is heard as higher than the E5 that concludes the second statement in m. 9, and the E5 that concludes the phrase in m. 12 is heard as lower than the F5 which begins Voice II's fourth statement. A listener attentive to the adjacent phrases of the same voice and of the opposing voice surely would not accept the bookend pitches as equivalent, even in the absence of perfect pitch. Furthermore, the F5 that opens Voice II's phrase lies sixteen semitones higher than the C♯4 in m. 10 that concludes Voice I's preceding phrase, which forms interval class 4. The E5 that concludes Voice II's phrase lies seventeen semitones higher than the B3 in m. 13 that begins Voice I's subsequent phrase, which forms interval class 5. Hearing the phrase in question as prime <1021> would either require that the first F be an E, which would create interval class 3 with the preceding C♯, or that the final E be an F, which would create interval class 6 with the subsequent B.

Starting in m. 16, the exchange between the two gets more heated. The male voices scramble up at the end of their phrase to a higher register, first reaching C6 and then accenting D6. Now more stirred up, Voice I enters in m. 16 before they complete their statement. This act in turn rouses them to speak more loudly in mm. 17–19, crescendoing *poco a poco* to m. 60.

In response, Voice I attempts to regain her composure: in m. 19 and m. 22, she tries to speak in a more measured way, stressing each syllable with triplet quarter notes against Voice II's steady eighth notes. The prime contour of Voice I's phrase reinforces this idea of pulling back: rather than to continue to present the retrograde contour of Voice II's preceding phrase, she reiterates Voice II's <1032> prime in mm. 19–20.

But this moment of reconciliation is only temporary. Voice II's next phrase, in mm. 20–21, reduces to prime <201>, and as before, Voice I gives her retrograde in mm. 21–23. In mm. 24–25, Voice I repeats Voice II's prime uttered in mm. 23–25, but since the voices now overlap at both the beginning and the end of their phrases, neither can clearly hear what the other is saying.[37]

This situation agitates both parties. In mm. 21–30, Voice I rapidly rises upward. In mm. 22–23, she leaps eleven semitones from G3 to F♯4 and another eleven semitones up to F5; in m. 24, seven semitones between D♭5 and A♭5; in m. 25, eleven

---

[37] In m. 24, Voice II is missing the pitch class E, which should conclude the phrase according to Crawford's system. In her annotated score, Crawford identifies this moment as a "loose thread in Persian rug"; in m. 94, which begins the corresponding phrase in the second half of the piece, the F is also absent. The presence of the E in m. 24 would result in a prime contour of <1023> rather than <1032>.

semitones from B♭4 to A5; and in the phrases that begin in mm. 26 and 28, she places herself in a high register at the very beginning, on D♭6 and E6, respectively. Similarly, the other three instruments begin in m. 3 by playing in their lowest register of the piece and gradually work their way up to their highest register in m. 32, which requires each instrument to play on its uppermost string and thus increases their strained quality.

Wanting desperately to be heard, Voice I attempts to remedy the situation by using both contour and rhythm. In mm. 26–27, the prime contour of Voice I's phrase is <10>, a contour that she repeats with her next phrase in mm. 28–29 as if to underscore her point. Voice I continues to reinforce her statements by giving prime contours in pairs three more times, in mm. 31–37, 38–43, and 46–52. Voice II, in contrast, does not repeat any prime contours, which suggests a less clearly defined position.

Having steadily moved up in register, both parties have literally raised their voices, arguing with increased emotion, passion, and commitment. But it seems that they are no longer listening to each other; neither waits for the other to finish; their phrases continue to collide and overlap. The male voices contribute to this situation by sustaining their last note in m. 32. Rather than ending the phrase with an eighth note, as in each of their previous statements, they tie the eighth note F♯ to a half note which is, in turn, tied to another half note in m. 33. By sustaining the last pitch of the phrase in this manner, Voice II opposes Voice I for a longer duration.

Voice II's next four phrases continue to lengthen the final pitch by tying the eighth note, adding a *fz* to the initial attack for emphasis. In mm. 35–36, the F♯ is sustained for a half note tied to a quarter note; in m. 38, the E is sustained for an eighth note tied to a half note; in m. 41, the A is sustained for a half note; and in m. 44, the A♭ is sustained for a dotted quarter note. In m. 47, the final pitch returns to an eighth note, a duration maintained for the remainder of the movement. The decreasing length of the final pitch in Voice II's phrases from mm. 32–33 to m. 47 – from nine eighth notes to six to five to four to three to one – counterbalances the increasing length of rests between phrases after the "midway" rest of three eighth notes in mm. 30–31, noted previously.

In m. 32, Voice I lengthens the initial note of her phrase, delaying her more active pitches – the eighth notes and quarter-note triplets – only well after the male voices have played the last note of their phrase. This strategy works to some degree: in mm. 40–46, Voice II remains silent until the conclusion of Voice I's statements. In m. 49, however, Voice II interrupts her once again.

Hoarse from all this talk, Voice I has already faded from her assured opening *ff* to, in m. 44, a mere whispered *p*. While she has more and more to say, her energy and confidence with which to say it are being rapidly depleted.

Voice II, in contrast, has less and less to say, but says it with greater conviction. In m. 52, the three instruments state the three notes of their phrase firmly, *fortissimo*, over the final three notes of Voice I's nineteen-note phrase, played *piano*, effectively silencing them. In m. 54, they do exactly the same thing with their two-note entry, stating these notes over the last two notes of Voice I's phrase and with an emphatic *ffz*. In mm. 55–57, Voice I manages to articulate one last three-octave, twenty-one-note-long *pianissimo* plea, while Voice II triumphantly reaches E4. Voice I warily joins Voice II a minor third above on a tied G3, considering the terms of the agreement.[38]

Yet at the midpoint of the discussion, the voices cannot come to terms. Voice II does not tie the E in m. 60 to a half note, which would make the length of rests following the E twenty eighth rests long (as was the length of rests preceding the E). Instead, Voice II cuts the E short, holding it for only an eighth note in m. 60, which makes the sustained pitch in mm. 57–60 a total of twenty-one eighth notes rather than the expected twenty-four. As a result, Voice II's midpoint falls on the eleventh eighth note (the seventh eighth note beat of m. 58), while Voice I's midpoint occurs later, on the barline between mm. 58 and 59.

After Voice II cuts the E short, for the remainder of the movement Voice I repeats what she has just argued, but backwards and a semitone higher. The three opposing instruments respond by simply restating what they just said, also a semitone higher and in retrograde. Mirroring the first half of the composition, Voice I states four of her prime contours twice in succession in mm. 65–71, 74–79, 80–86, and 88–91; the piece ends with the voices presenting primes with a retrograde relationship in mm. 94–97, 100–103, 104–107, and 107–10 to emphasize the oppositional nature of their relationship one last time.

For the second half of the piece, then, the female protagonist retraces her previous argument, having failed to come to agreement with Voice II but maintaining the integrity of her own position. Rather than joining the collective male voice in intoning the row, she clings to her original assertion (transposed up a semitone) and the movement concludes as it started: after the lower three instruments grumble a string of twenty pitches, the first violin resolutely attacks a single note and so gets the last word.

The last movement of Crawford's quartet thus establishes a relationship of fundamental disagreement between the two voices, one that is present on the music's surface through the elements of pitch, dynamics, phrase length, and rhythm, and is also submerged at a deeper level through the piece's contour structure. Using events in Crawford's biography as a stimulus for my analysis, I have drawn the relationship of the voices into a reading that involves two distinct musical personae: a female voice in the music of the first violin, who is independent, assertive, and daring in the course of her interaction with the masculinist Voice II, with which it does not reach common ground by the movement's end.

By instituting a principle of conflict between the two voices, the fourth movement of Crawford's quartet differs markedly from its third movement, which I

---

[38] In her analysis of this movement, Crawford describes the turning point as a moment in which "both voices settle on a single tone" (repr. in JT-RCS, 358).

characterized in Chapter 2 as being produced by the communal labor of four instrumental voices. However, both movements can be heard as structures through which Crawford communicated aspects of being female, which for her often required battling traditional attitudes about appropriate activities for women. Composing allowed her to create musical spaces that expressed her own social condition, thus affording her the opportunity to feel the "great freedom" that she described with such longing in her diary and to write her voice, which would have otherwise been muted, into sound.

4

THE POLITICS OF CONTOUR IN CRAWFORD'S "CHINAMAN, LAUNDRYMAN"

San Francisco sleeps as the dead—
Ended license, lust and play:
Why do you iron the night away?
Your big clock speaks with a deadly sound,
With a tick and a wail till dawn comes round.
While the monster shadows glower and creep,
What can be better for man than sleep?

–Vachel Lindsay, "The Chinese Nightingale"

Being a laundryman is no life at all. I work fourteen hours a day and I have to send home almost all my wages . . . People think I am a happy person. I am not. I worry very much. First, I don't like this kind of life; it is not a human life. To be a laundryman is to be just a slave. I work because I have to. If I ever stop working, those at home stop eating.

–A Chinese laundry worker, ca. 1930

Experiencing the Depression in New York was an important catalyst in the decision of Ruth Crawford and Charles Seeger to take up the cause of folk music, which during the 1930s they would come to believe possessed more social relevance than modernist composition.[1] Seeger's desire to explore music that was pertinent to society led to his involvement with the Composers' Collective, a group of approximately twenty-four composers whose leftist political beliefs brought them together each week for the purpose of composing choral music whose texts expressed Communist sentiments.[2] Seeger's political stance was by no means unique: many others were also passionately committed during the 1930s to the work of writing

---

[1] The following publications chronicle Charles Seeger's shift from his rejection of folk music in the 1920s as an area of musical interest to his later hearty support of it beginning in the 1930s through his participation in the Composers' Collective: David K. Dunaway, "Charles Seeger and Carl Sands: The Composers' Collective Years," *Ethnomusicology* 24/2 (May 1980), 159–68; Dunaway, "Unsung Songs of Protest: The Composers' Collective of New York," *New York Folklore Quarterly*, 5/1–2 (Summer 1979), 1–19; Ann M. Pescatello, *Charles Seeger: A Life in American Music* (Pittsburgh: University of Pittsburgh Press, 1992), 109–19; Robbie Lieberman, *"My Song is My Weapon": People's Songs, American Communism, and the Politics of Culture, 1930–1950* (Urbana: University of Illinois Press, 1989); and MG-RCS, 95–103. Barbara A. Zuck's *A History of Musical Americanism* (Ann Arbor: UMI Research Press, 1980) presents a comprehensive portrait of this period in the chapter "Americanism Takes a Left Turn," 103–38.

[2] Seeger was a member of the Collective from 1931 through 1935. The Collective's minutes record that Crawford attended only two of its meetings. Pescatello notes that during these years Crawford had the added duties of

music "for the people," including Henry Cowell, Aaron Copland, Norman
Cadzen, Jacob Schaeffer, Marc Blitzstein, Elie Siegmeister, Wallingford Riegger,
Janet Barnes, and Earl Robinson, to give a partial list of the Collective's members.
The means by which Crawford would negotiate her feelings about how best to
employ her musical talents for the social good – in ways that might even somehow
contribute to the humanizing of society – is manifested in her decision to take up
the work of writing original piano accompaniments to folk tunes and of transcribing folk music, a project to which she would devote considerable energy during the
next two decades.

But Crawford's dedication to leftist political ideals is evident also in a pair of art
songs she composed in 1932 for a commission from the Society of Contemporary
Music in Philadelphia, entitled *Two Ricercari*.[3] Their texts, based on poems written
by H. T. Tsiang, address pressing concerns of the immigrant laborer in the United
States during the 1920s.[4] Crawford's songs respond to these concerns while remaining squarely within the atonal art music idiom in which she composed her other
works of the time. The first song, "Sacco, Vanzetti," is based upon the infamous
execution of two Italian anarchists in Massachusetts after whom the song is named;
the second song, "Chinaman, Laundryman," grapples with the capitalist exploita-
tion of an immigrant Chinese laundry worker.[5]

In a 1934 essay Seeger described what he envisioned as "proletarian music."[6]
Believing music to be a cultural medium through which a dehumanized society
might become more compassionate, Seeger argued that music composed specifically for the proletariat, defined as "the propertyless members of modern industrial
society," would make such humanizing possible.[7]

In his essay, Seeger set forth three stages in the evolution of proletarian music: a
first stage in which music draws upon a "bourgeois" musical style;[8] a second stage in

caring for her children Michael, born in 1933, and Peggy, born in 1935 (Pescatello, *Charles Seeger*, 111). Judith
Tick suggests that the critical atmosphere of the Collective may not have appealed to Crawford (JT-RCS, 196). It
is noteworthy that in April 1931, Crawford wrote to Seeger that she "could almost become a Communist
herself." Quoted in Judith Tick, "Ruth Crawford's *Proletarian Ricercari*," *Sonus: A Journal of Investigations into Global
Music Possibilities* 15/2 (Spring 1995), 55.

[3] Tick suggests that Crawford called these songs ricercari not from any relation they might have to the sixteenth-
century form of instrumental composition but from their concern with pre-compositional methods (*ibid.*, 60).

[4] The poem "Chinaman, Laundryman" was published in the Communist paper *The Daily Worker* (15 August 1928)
and in Tsiang's *Poems of the Chinese Revolution*, English edn (New York: Liberal Press, 1929), 7–8. H. T. [Hsi-
Tseng] Tsiang was a student at Columbia University in 1928; in his prefatory statement to *Poems of the Chinese
Revolution*, Upton Sinclair notes that American authorities sought to deport Tsiang to China (3).

[5] An incident recorded in a 1929 diary entry hints at Crawford's political beliefs, which resonate with her attraction to Tsiang's text a few years later: in response to Carl Ruggles's dismissal of the "god-damned Ellis Islanders"
and his suggestion that composers of non-European descent did not have the right to identify themselves as
American, Crawford declared that "You are American if you're American in spirit . . . Amalgamation will be a
great thing. Out of all the races will spring the true American" (RCd-LC, 5 December 1929; quoted in JT-RCS,
111).

[6] Charles Seeger, "On Proletarian Music," *Modern Music* 11/3 (March–April 1934), 121–27. Seeger also presented
his ideas about proletarian music in articles he published in *The Daily Worker* – see, for example, 31 January 1934
and 6 March 1934.   [7] Seeger, "On Proletarian Music," 121–22.

[8] Seeger does not define the term "bourgeois music" in his essay but mentions Schoenberg, Hindemith, and
Stravinsky as examples of composers of bourgeois music (*ibid.*, 124).

which music employs both proletarian content and the revolutionary techniques of art music; and a final stage which constitutes a new category of music "comparable to the grand styles of Plainsong, the Gothic, Renaissance, Rococo and Romantic periods."[9] As for what the music in this final stage would actually comprise, Seeger's article is more speculative than analytical.

Crawford's "Chinaman, Laundryman" was premiered by Radiana Pazmor and Elie Siegmeister at the MacDowell Club in New York on 12 March 1933; it was performed again at the Mellon Gallery for the Society of Contemporary Music in Philadelphia on 27 March 1933, and at the City College Auditorium in New York for the First American Workers' Music Olympiad on 21 May 1933.[10] This song, in my opinion, illustrates the second phase of proletarian music that Seeger describes: the music expresses revolutionary content through modernist experimental compositional techniques. The score is given as Example 4.1.

Although "Chinaman, Laundryman" is not an example of the mass-song style that the Composers' Collective was instrumental in developing during the 1930s, Crawford's song recalls a few of its characteristic features: the text is given primacy in order to emphasize its message, and its setting is syllabic.[11] But with its serial piano accompaniment given in octaves throughout, "Chinaman, Laundryman" does not share other traits of mass-song style, including a homophonic texture and a bass containing many octaves and fifths, elements that would have made the songs more suitable for performance by a workers' chorus.

"Chinaman, Laundryman" is politically significant not only for its choice of text, which portrays the oppressive working conditions of the immigrant ethnic laborer, but also for its musical setting. The structure of the composition comments on ways the laundry worker's race and gender shape his existence and underscores an optimistic narrative present in Tsiang's poem. More specifically, through her use of musical register, Crawford depicts a transformation in the relationship between the two figures in the poem, one in which the launderer eventually emerges from being dominated by the boss to becoming independent of him and self-affirming.[12]

The song's text cuts against the common contemporaneous stereotypes of Chinese men and of male Chinese launderers in particular that were circulating in the United States at this time; it instead portrays the laundry trade as it was experienced by many Chinese. Figure 4.1 presents Crawford's adaptation of

[9] *Ibid.*, 125–26.

[10] David K. Dunaway's interview with Charles Seeger about the Olympiad is published in "Charles Seeger and Carl Sands." (The 1935 date Dunaway cites for the Olympiad is incorrect.) A second Olympiad was reviewed by Ashley Pettis in "Second Worker's [*sic*] Music Olympiad," *New Masses* 11/8 (22 May 1934), 28–29.

[11] Carol J. Oja discusses mass-song style in "Marc Blitzstein's *The Cradle Will Rock* and Mass-Song Style of the 1930s," *Musical Quarterly* 73/4 (1989), 450.

[12] John Kuo Wei Tchen argues that the terms "launderer," "laundry worker," or "laundry man" avoid the negative ethnic connotations of the single word "laundryman," a term coined "in an era when a gender tag was appended to ethnic identifications, as in 'Irishman' or 'Chinaman,' and blue collar trades, as in 'postman' or 'washerwoman'." My terminology follows his example. Tchen's discussion appears in his introduction to Paul C. P. Siu, *The Chinese Laundryman: A Study of Social Isolation*, ed. John Kuo Wei Tchen (New York: New York University Press, 1987), xxxv.

Example 4.1 Crawford, "Chinaman, Laundryman"

Chinaman, Laundryman

1

Voice and Piano

Duration : *ca.* 3´

H. T. Tsiang   Ruth Crawford

*An accidental affects only the note it precedes.

All Rights Reserved
Printed in U.S.A.

International Copyright Secured
This edition published 1976

Example 4.1 (*cont.*)

Example 4.1 (*cont.*)

Example 4.1 (*cont.*)

Example 4.1 (*cont.*)

Example 4.1 (*cont.*)

Example 4.1 (*cont.*)

Example 4.1 (*cont.*)

Example 4.1 (*cont.*)

Example 4.1 (*cont.*)

Example 4.1 (*cont.*)

11

Example 4.1 (*cont.*)

12

95

press   with the iron!   Wash!

97

Brush!   Dry!

99

Iron!   Then we   shall have   a   clean——   world!

"Chinaman!" "Laundryman!"
Don't call me "man!"
I am worse than a slave.

Wash!— Wash!—
Why can I wash away the dirt of others' clothes
but not the hatred of my heart?
My skin is yellow,—
Does my yellow skin color the clothes?
Why do you pay me less for the same work?

Clever boss!
You know how to scatter the seeds of hatred
among your ignorant slaves.

Iron!— Iron!—
Why can I smooth away the wrinkle of others' dresses
but not the miseries of my heart?
Why should I come to America to wash clothes?
Do you think Chinamen in China wear no dresses?
I came to America three days after my marriage.
When can I see her again?
Only the almighty dollar knows!

Dry!— Dry!—
Why do clothes dry, but not my tears?
I work twelve hours a day, he pays fifteen dollars a week.

My boss says:
"Chinaman, go back to China, if you don't feel satisfied!
There, unlimited hours of toil:
two silver dollars a week, if you can find a job."

Thank you, boss,—for you remind me.
I know bosses are robbers ev'rywhere!

Chinese boss says:
"You Chinaman, me Chinaman, come work for me,—
work for your fellow countryman!
By the way, you 'Wong', me 'Wong',
do we not belong to same family?
Ha! Ha! We are cousins!
O yes! You 'Hai Shan', me 'Hai Shan',
do we not come from same district?
O come work for me;—I will treat you better!"

Get away from here!
What is the difference when you come to exploit me?
Chinaman! Laundryman!

Figure 4.1 Text of Crawford, "Chinaman, Laundryman"

Don't call me "Chinaman!"
Yes, I am a "Laundryman!"
The working man!
Don't call me "Chinaman!"
I am the worldman!

"Chinaman!" "Laundryman!"
All you working men!
Here is the brush made of study.
Here is the soap made of action.
Let us all wash with the brush!
Let us all press with the iron!
Wash! Brush! Dry! Iron!
Then we shall have a clean world!

Figure 4.1 (*cont.*)

Tsiang's poem, which passionately expresses its sympathies with the oppressed worker.

The poem begins by describing in the first person the harsh working conditions experienced by a Chinese launderer and his unhappiness with his present situation, and concludes with the launderer exhorting his fellow men to work for a better world.

When Crawford began composing "Chinaman, Laundryman" in 1932, such a declaration of sympathy with Asian immigrant workers would have been both radical and timely: in 1933, the New York City government proposed taxing Chinese launderers $1,000 and also fingerprinting workers in Chinese laundries; the Chinese Hand Laundry Alliance successfully prevented the passage of both of these proposals.[13] The political import of Crawford's compositional setting can be more fully understood when examined within the virulent anti-Asian and specifically Sinophobic sentiment that abounded in the United States during this period.

The first law in the United States that excluded immigrants on the basis of race or nationality was directed specifically at the Chinese: this was the 1882 Chinese Exclusion Act, which halted the immigration of Chinese skilled and unskilled laborers for a period of ten years.[14] Amended versions of the bill, which was renewed in 1892, 1902, and 1904, prevented women still in China from immigrating to join their male relatives who were already working in the U.S. When combined with the anti-miscegenation laws that prohibited marriage between Chinese

---

[13] "Chinese Hand Laundry Alliance," in *Dictionary of Asian American History*, ed. Hyung-Chan Kim (New York: Greenwood Press, 1986), 196.

[14] The Chinese Exclusion Act, from *The Statutes at Large of the United States of America, from December, 1881, to March, 1883, and Recent Treaties, Postal Conventions, and Executive Proclamations* (Washington, D.C., 1883) 22, 58–61; quoted in Andrew Gyory, *Closing the Gate: Race, Politics, and the Chinese Exclusion Act* (Chapel Hill: University of North Carolina Press, 1998), 261–64.

and non-Chinese, this added feature of the Exclusion Act prevented Chinese men from marrying *anyone*, and thus also had the effect of limiting the population of Chinese in the U.S.[15] This brand of anti-Asian legislation continued with the Immigration Act of 1924, which severely restricted the numbers of Asians who were permitted to immigrate, including Koreans and Japanese as well as Chinese.[16]

While lawmakers were actively minimizing the Asian presence in the United States, cultural representations were simultaneously being circulated that depicted Chinese persons as evil, servile, greedy, crafty, grotesque, and depraved. John Kuo Wei Tchen has called the process of engraving these collective images upon the American psyche "yellowface acculturation."[17] These portrayals of the so-called "Yellow Peril" took the form of newspaper caricatures, political cartoons, dime novels, films, pulp magazines, and the music of Tin Pan Alley.[18] Chinese women were represented in them as sexually exotic, but the real threat to the dominant white male consciousness in the domain of sexuality consisted of Chinese males' potential linkages with white women.[19] One response to this threat was to represent Chinese men as either asexual or feminine, perhaps in hopes of diminishing their attractiveness to white women.[20]

[15] Gyory notes that the Chinese Exclusion Act "set the precedent for . . . broader exclusion laws and fostered an atmosphere of hostility against foreigners that would endure for generations. It also fostered a bleaker atmosphere of racism, a racism that swiftly led to Jim Crow legislation in the 1880s, *Plessy v. Ferguson* in the 1890s, and decades of state-sponsored segregation in the 1990s" (Gyory, *Closing the Gate*, 1–2). Useful resources for information on anti-Asian sentiment and legislation in the United States are two volumes edited by Hyung-chan Kim: *A Legal History of Asian Americans, 1790–1990* (Westport, CT: Greenwood Press, 1994) and *Dictionary of Asian American History*. Benjamin B. Ringer provides a more general history of racially discriminatory legislation in *We the People and Others: America's Treatment of its Racial Minorities* (New York: Tavistock Publications, 1983).

[16] The provision of the Immigration Act of 1924 that restricted immigration of the wives of citizens was repealed in 1930. See Ronald Takaki, *Strangers from a Different Shore: A History of Asian Americans* (Boston: Little, Brown and Company, 1989), 235.

[17] John Kuo Wei Tchen, "Believing is Seeing: Transforming Orientalism and the Occidental Gaze," in *Asia/America: Identities in Contemporary Asian American Art* (New York: The Asia Society Galleries/New Press, 1994), 13.

[18] William Wu discusses stereotypes of Chinese Americans in fiction in *The Yellow Peril: Chinese Americans in American Fiction, 1850–1940* (Hamden, CT: Archon Books, 1982). Judy S. Tsou documents stereotypical representations of Asians in American popular song of the early twentieth century in "Gendering Race: Images of Chinese in American Popular Music," *repercussions* 6/2 (in press). One example of an anti-Chinese cartoon appeared in *Punchinello*, 23 July 1879, under the caption "Yan-ki vs. Yan-kee. Showing the Descent of Celestial Crispins upon the Shoemakers of the Bay State, and How They Robbed the Native Cobbler of his *All*"; reprinted in Gyory, *Closing the Gate*, 49.

[19] In *Strangers from a Different Shore*, Takaki notes that in nineteenth-century America, Chinese men were viewed as "sensuous creatures, especially interested in white women" (101). In 1880, anti-miscegenation legislation was enacted in California to prevent marriage specifically between whites and Chinese, who, like blacks, were regarded as threats to white racial purity. See Megumi Dick Osumi, "Asians and California's Anti-Miscegenation Laws," in *Asian and Pacific American Experiences: Women's Perspectives*, ed. Nobuya Tsuchida (Minneapolis: Asian/Pacific American Learning Resource Center and General College, University of Minnesota, 1982), 1–37.

[20] Siu discusses the sex lives of Chinese male launderers in Chicago during the 1930s, including their relations with white women and the phenomenon of intermarriage in *The Chinese Laundryman*, 250–71 and 279–88.

Example 4.1 shows the notation that Crawford devised to project a type of *Sprechstimme*. It appears first in m. 4.[21] To notate approximate rather than exact pitch, she employs an arrow notehead and a wavy line drawn between two pitches to indicate a portamento. In an explanatory note to "Sacco, Vanzetti," the first of her *Two Ricercari*, she writes: "It is essential that the audience understand the words. If the effort to secure the pitches as written should interfere with the clear rendition of the words, those pitches should then be regarded as general rather than as specific indications."[22] Crawford's emphasis on approximate rather than exact pitch in these songs makes relevant the application of contour theory to the vocal part. Contour theory also reveals crucial structural aspects of the piano's music, whose pitches are not approximated and are serialized.

As in several of Crawford's other pieces composed during the 1930s, the piano's pitch material in the song is strictly ordered.[23] The piano's music is based on a process of rotation similar to that in the fourth movement of her quartet. When the piano enters in m. 4, it plays a stream of notes in octaves, G–G♭–F–E♭–C–E–D–B–C♯, that give the prime form of a nine-tone row, T_0. Measure 5 begins on the second pitch of T_0, G♭, and ends on its first pitch, G♮; this statement can be considered rotation 1. Measure 6 begins on the third pitch of the prime form of the row, F, and ends on its second pitch, G♭. This process continues through m. 12; each subsequent measure rotates the row once to begin on a new pitch of T_0.

In m. 13 the row is then transposed a semitone down to begin on G♭; as before, subsequent measures begin on successive notes of this new transposition for the next eight bars. In m. 22, the row is transposed to begin on F, and the process of rotation is repeated. The transpositions of the row presented thus far – G, G♭, and F – are the first three pitches of T_0; Crawford continues to use each subsequent pitch of T_0 in turn for the remaining transposition levels. After T_0 has been rotated and transposed nine times, the piece presents in m. 91 one final statement of T_0; mm. 92–99 give its eight rotations. Example 4.2 summarizes the piece's serial organization.

The organization of the piano's melodic contour is perhaps more immediately perceptible than this serial plan of pitch or its rhythm structure, which is also strictly ordered. Figure 4.2 shows the three rhythmic patterns that organize the nine notes of the row: they are identified as A, B, and C.[24] With a few exceptions, these three rhythmic patterns are played as some permutation of (ABC) before any one pattern

---

[21] Another member of the Composers' Collective, Elie Siegmeister, employs *Sprechstimme* in his solo cantata *Strange Funeral in Braddock*, which was published in 1936. Its text was written by Michael Gold, a spokesman for the American Communist Party and an editor of *New Masses*.

[22] Ruth Crawford, "Sacco, Vanzetti" (Merion Music, 1973).

[23] These works include her *Piano Study in Mixed Accents* (1930), the *Diaphonic Suite* No. 1 for Flute or Oboe, mvt. 3 (1930), and her String Quartet, mvt. 4 (1931). Joseph Straus describes a number of structural and textual features of "Chinaman, Laundryman," including rotational serialism, rhythm, and motive (JNS-MRCS, 8–9, 75–76, 82–83, 117–18, and 150–51).

[24] Joseph Straus identifies these three rhythms as x, y, and z (JNS-MRCS, 117–118).

Example 4.2 Pitch organization of piano

Exceptions:
m. 15: substitutes C for B
m. 39: substitutes A for G
m. 50: substitutes G for A
m. 65: substitutes D♭ for D♮
m. 66: substitutes A for G
m. 77: substitutes B♭ for G♭
m. 78: substitutes A for B

Pattern   A   B   C

♫♫♫ ³♫♫♫ ♫♫   ♫♫♫ ⁵♫♫♫ ♫♫   ♫♫♫ ♫♫ ³♫♫♫

4 + 3 + 2   5 + 2 + 2   4 + 2 + 3

m. 1 2 3 4 5 6 7 8 9 10 11 12 13 14 15 16 17 18 19 20 21 22 23 24
      A B C A C B C A B C B A B C A B A C| A B C

25 26 27 28 29 30 31 32 33 34 35 36 37 38 39 40 41 42 43 44 45 46 47 48
A C B C A B C B A B C A B A C| A B C ★C C B C ★C B

49 50 51 52 53 54 55 56 57 58 59 60 61 62 63 64 65 66 67 68 69 70 71 72
C B A B C ★C B A C| A B C A C B C A B C B ★C B C A

73 74 75 76 77 78 79 80 81 82 83 84 85 86 87 88 89 90 91 92 93 94 95 96
B / / / A C| A B C A C / / / B C A B C B A B C A

97 98 99
B A C

Explanatory notes
___ Marks a complete presentation of the three rhythmic patterns
| Marks a complete presentation of the six possible permutations of (ABC)
★ Indicates a break in pattern
/ Indicates a rest

Figure 4.2 Rhythmic organization of piano

is repeated. These short chains of three-bar rhythmic patterns are in turn organized
into six groups of six.[25]

    In contrast to the piano's systems of pitch and rhythm, the register in which each
pitch class of the row is realized is not so predictable. Figure 4.3 gives a graphic representation of the piano's music in mm. 10 and 28 in the form of csegs. Both contours carry out rotation 6, but at different transposition levels of the row.

    As Figure 4.3 shows, the contours of the two statements are not identical. The
pair's corresponding contour pitches are in the same relative positions except for cps
4 and 5, which are given in reverse order. This change in two cps affects three internal contours of the cseg – the melodic directions between cps 3 and 4, 4 and 5, and
5 and 6 are inverted or reversed.

    Figure 4.4 identifies each of these contours in a manner introduced by Michael
Friedmann, as an ordered series of pluses and/or minuses within brackets to indi-

---

[25] Like the pitch organization in the piece, the rhythm occasionally does not follow the established pattern: the
three-bar rhythmic presentations that begin mm. 43, 46, 52, and 67 withhold rhythmic pattern A, instead
giving two statements of C.

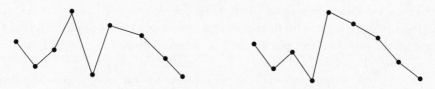

Figure 4.3 Graphic representation of piano, mm. 10 and 28

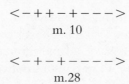

$$< - + + - + - - - >$$
m. 10

$$< - + - + - - - - >$$
m.28

Figure 4.4 CASs of piano, mm. 10 and 28

cate the change of direction between adjacent contour pitches. A plus sign indicates ascent and a minus sign indicates descent; this series of pluses and minuses is known as the Contour Adjacency Series (CAS).[26]

Comparing corresponding positions of the two series in mm. 10 and 28, we can observe that the third, fourth, and fifth symbols are dissimilar, which indicates an inversional relationship between corresponding contours – that is, an ascending gesture replaces a descending gesture and vice versa.

In my analysis, I have chosen to examine the piano's music in units of one measure because each contains a distinctive and audible rhythmic grouping – sixteenth notes or pentuplet sixteenth notes followed by two groups of eighth notes or triplets. Dividing the piece into ten sections – one to a transposition level – which are shown in Table 4.1, we can identify sections 1 and 2 as the prototype, or "normative state," for sections 3 and 4. For sections 5 through 10, the prototype is section 1 alone (after section 4, Crawford does not continue to use the contour prototype established in section 2).

To measure precisely the degree to which a given contour is modified from the prototype contour, we can count the number of inversions. The contour of m. 28 (see Figure 4.4) would be assigned the number three, since three internal contours are affected. I shall call this change in the contour of a row from its corresponding form in the prototype its "contour deviance value," which is simply the number of deviations in the CAS of a given contour from the CAS of its prototype.[27]

Table 4.1 gives the following data about the piano's music. The first column gives

[26] Friedmann, "A Methodology for the Discussion of Contour," 223–48. Friedmann's CAS is equivalent to Marvin and Laprade's Int_1, which is described in their article "Relating Musical Contours," 231.

[27] Eric J. Isaacson has introduced a similarity measure that is somewhat analogous to my contour deviance measure. In his article "Similarity of Interval-Class Content between Pitch-Class Sets: The IcVSIM Relation," *Journal of Music Theory* 34/1 (Spring 1990), 1–28, Isaacson measures the similarity of the interval content of two

the measure number. The second column lists the nine–note cseg for that measure, denoting the lowest pitch by 0, the second lowest pitch by 1, and so forth; the highest of the nine contour pitches (cps) is denoted by 8. For example, in m. 4, <G5–G♭5–F5–E♭5–C5–E5–D5–B4–C♯5> translates into cseg <8 7 6 4 1 5 3 0 2>. (For the sake of consistency, I shall identify the piano's pitches by referring to the left-hand part.) For each cseg, the third column lists its prime contour, or the skeletal version of a contour which may be calculated using Robert Morris's contour reduction algorithm, given in Figure 3.1.[28] (To demonstrate the application of Morris's algorithm to "Chinaman, Laundryman," Example 4.3 calculates the piano's nine-note contour in m. 4.[29]) The fourth column lists the corresponding text, giving the boss's text in italics, and the fifth column measures the contour deviance value for each measure. Each transposition level of the row is also labeled and given a section number.

As Table 4.1 shows, section 1 contains T_0 and its eight rotations; section 2 contains T_{11} and its eight rotations. Section 3, which begins in m. 22, transposes the nine contours of section 1 down two semitones, resulting in the same CAS's; section 4, which begins in m. 31, similarly transposes the contours of section 2 down two semitones.

In order to present the contour deviance values succinctly, Figure 4.5 shows the local contour of both voice and piano graphically.[30] The two lines that move in parallel motion trace the piano's movement, and the independent line traces the movement of the voice. Time is measured on the x axis in measures; pitch height is measured on the y axis.[31] Underneath the row of measure numbers, I have recorded the contour deviance values of each of the piano's contours. Figure 4.6 gives Figure 4.5 as a single graph, omitting the deviance values.

Footnote 27 (cont.)

pitch–class sets by calculating the difference between corresponding entries in their interval vectors. My contour deviance tool measures the similarity of the "contour content" of two csegs by comparing the changes in direction of corresponding cps.

In their article "Relating Musical Contours," Marvin and Laprade propose another way of measuring contour similarity, the contour similarity function (CSIM). CSIM measures the similarity between two csegs of the same cardinality by comparing their matrices. Although CSIM could be applied to the piano's music in Crawford's song, it would measure the similarity of direction between corresponding non-adjacent cps as well as between adjacent cps, which would be more comprehensive than is necessary for my purposes. In comparison, the contour deviance tool measures change of direction only between adjacent cps, which I find more immediately perceptible than all possible pairs of cps in a ten–note phrase.

[28] Morris, "New Directions in the Theory and Analysis of Musical Contour," 212.

[29] Morris also identifies each prime with a number measuring its "depth," which indicates how many levels of pruning are required to reach the prime. In this song, there is little variation in the depth values (the depth of the piano primes is either 2 or 3).

[30] As Figure 4.5 shows, I hear the singer's voice in the notated register rather than an octave lower as a male singer might perform the song. The premiere of *Two Ricercari* in 1933 with contralto Radiana Pazmor and Elie Siegmeister at the piano supports such an interpretation; the desire to situate myself in the position of the narrator by placing the vocal part within my own "natural" singing register is also a factor in my analytical decision.

[31] Where Crawford indicates approximate rather than exact pitch, the graph shows the pitch approximated by the arrow noteheads.

Table 4.1 *Contour data for piano in Crawford, "Chinaman, Laundryman"*

Explanatory note: The boss's text is italicized.

Meas.	Cseg	Prime contour	Text	Deviance
Section 1 – T$_o$				
1	[rest]		*"Chinaman!"*	
2	[rest]		*"Laundryman!"*	
3	[rest]		[rest]	
4	<8 7 6 4 1 5 3 0 2>	<2 0 1>	Don't call me "man!" I am	[norm]
5	<7 6 4 1 5 3 0 2 8>	<1 0 2>	worse than a slave.	
6	<6 4 1 5 3 0 2 8 7>	<1 0 3 2>	Wash! – Wash! –	
7	<5 2 6 4 1 3 0 8 7>	<1 0 3 2>	Why can I wash away the	
8	<2 6 4 1 3 0 8 7 5>	<1 0 3 2>	dirt of others' clothes but	
9	<6 4 1 3 8 0 7 5 2>	<2 3 0 1>	not the hatred of my heart?	
10	<5 2 4 8 1 7 6 3 0>	<1 2 0>	My skin is yellow, – Does my	
11	<4 6 3 2 1 8 5 0 7>	<1 3 0 2>	yellow skin color the clothes?	
12	<7 4 3 2 8 6 1 0 5>	<2 3 0 1>	Why do you pay me less	
Section 2 – T$_{11}$				
13	<4 3 2 8 6 1 0 5 7>	<1 3 0 2>	for the same work?	
14	<1 8 7 4 0 6 3 5 2>	<1 3 0 2>	Clever boss!	
15	<7 6 4 0 5 3 4 2 1>	<2 0 1>	You know how to scatter the	
16	<7 4 0 6 3 5 2 8 1>	<2 0 3 1>	seeds of hatred among your	
17	<8 3 1 7 0 6 5 4 2>	<2 0 1>	ignorant slaves.	
18	<2 0 6 8 5 4 3 1 7>	<1 0 3 2>	Iron! – Iron! –	
19	<0 6 8 5 4 3 1 7 2>	<0 2 1>	Why can I smooth away the	
20	<0 1 5 4 3 8 6 2 7>	<0 2 1>	wrinkle of others' dresses but	
21	<8 6 5 4 2 7 3 1 0>	<1 0>	not the miseries of my heart?	[norm ends]
Section 3 – T$_{10}$				
22	<8 7 6 4 1 5 3 0 2>	<2 0 1>	Why should I come to America to	0
23	<7 6 4 1 5 3 0 2 8>	<1 0 2>	wash clothes? Do you think	0
24	<6 4 1 5 3 0 2 8 7>	<1 0 3 2>	Chinamen in China	0
25	<5 2 6 4 1 3 0 8 7>	<1 0 3 2>	wear no dresses?	0
26	<2 6 4 1 3 0 8 7 5>	<1 0 3 2>	I came to America	0
27	<6 4 1 3 8 0 7 5 2>	<2 3 0 1>	three days after my marriage.	0
28	<5 2 4 1 8 7 6 3 0>	<1 2 0>	When can I see her again? Only the	3
29	<4 6 3 2 1 8 5 0 7>	<1 3 0 2>	almighty dollar knows!	0
30	<7 4 3 2 8 6 1 0 5>	<2 3 0 1>	Dry! – Dry! –	0
Section 4 – T$_8$				
31	<4 3 2 8 6 1 0 5 7>	<1 3 0 2>	Why do clothes dry, but	0
32	<0 8 6 3 7 5 2 4 1>	<0 2 1>	not my tears?	2
33	<8 6 3 7 5 2 4 1 0>	<1 0>	I work	2
34	<7 4 0 6 3 5 2 8 1	<2 0 3 1>	twelve hours a day,	0
35	<8 3 1 7 0 6 5 4 2>	<2 0 1>	he pays	0
36	<2 0 6 8 5 4 3 1 7>	<1 0 3 2>	fifteen dollars a week. *My*	0
37	<0 6 8 5 4 3 1 7 2>	<0 2 1>	*boss says:*	0
38	<0 1 5 4 3 8 6 2 7>	<0 2 1>	[rest]	0
39	<8 6 5 4 2 7 3 1 0>	<1 0>	*"Chinaman,*	0

Table 4.1 (*cont.*)

Explanatory note: The boss's text is italicized.

Meas.	Cseg	Prime contour	Text	Deviance
Section 5 – T₅				
40	<8 7 6 4 1 5 3 0 2>	<2 0 1>	*go back to China, if you*	0
41	<7 6 4 1 5 3 0 2 8>	<1 0 2>	*don't feel satisfied!*	0
42	<6 4 1 5 3 0 2 8 7>	<1 0 3 2>	*There, un-*	0
43	<3 0 4 2 8 1 7 6 5>	<1 0 3 2>	*limited*	4
44	<8 3 1 7 0 6 5 4 2>	<2 0 1>	*hours of toil:*	5
45	<1 7 5 0 4 3 2 8 6>	<1 0 3 2>	*two silver dollars a week,*	4
46	<0 5 7 4 3 2 1 6 8>	<0 1>	[rest]	5
47	<4 6 3 2 1 8 5 0 7>	<1 3 0 2>	*if you can find a job."*	0
48	<3 0 8 7 5 2 6 4 1>	<2 0 3 1>	[rest]	4
Section 6 – T₉				
49	<8 7 6 4 1 5 3 0 2>	<2 0 1>	Thank you, boss, –	0
50	<7 6 4 0 5 3 1 2 8>	<1 0 2>	for you remind me.	0
51	<3 1 7 2 0 6 8 5 4>	<1 0 3 2>	I know	4
52	<2 8 3 1 7 0 6 5 4>	<1 3 0 2>	bosses are robbers	6
53	<7 2 1 6 0 5 4 3 8>	<1 0 2>	ev'rywhere!	6
54	<0 5 2 4 1 8 7 6 3>	<0 2 1>	*Chinese boss says:*	4
55	<6 3 5 2 1 8 7 4 0>	<1 2 0>	[rest]	1
56	<4 6 3 2 1 8 5 0 7>	<1 3 0 2>	*"You Chinaman,*	0
57	<6 3 2 1 8 5 0 7 4>	<2 3 0 1>	*me Chinaman,*	2
Section 7 – T₇				
58	<8 7 6 4 1 5 3 0 2>	<2 0 1>	*come work for me*	0
59	<0 7 5 2 6 4 1 3 8>	<0 1>	*work for your fellow countryman!*	1
60	<7 5 2 6 4 1 3 0 8>	<1 0 2>	*By the way,*	2
61	<4 1 5 3 0 2 8 7 6>	<1 0 3 2>	*you 'Wong', me 'Wong',*	2
62	<0 4 2 8 1 7 6 5 3>	<0 2 1>	*do we not belong to same family?*	4
63	<0 7 4 6 3 2 1 8 5>	<0 2 1>	*Ha! Ha!*	4
64	<7 4 6 3 2 1 8 5 0>	<1 2 0>	*We are cousins!*	3
65	<2 4 0 1 8 6 3 7 5>	<1 0 3 2>	*O yes!*	5
66	<3 1 0 7 5 4 6 4 2>	<2 0 3 1>	*You 'Hai Shan', me 'Hai Shan',*	4
Section 8 – T₄				
67	<8 7 6 4 1 5 3 0 2>	<2 0 1>	*do we not come from same district?*	0
68	<7 6 4 1 5 3 0 2 8>	<1 0 2>	*O come work for me; –*	0
69	<5 3 0 4 2 8 1 7 6>	<1 0 3 2>	*I will treat you better!"*	2
70	<2 8 3 1 7 0 6 5 4>	<1 3 0 2>	[rest]	6
71	<1 5 3 0 2 8 7 6 4>	<1 0 3 2>	Get away from here!	2
72	<8 6 3 5 2 1 0 7 4>	<2 0 1>	What is the difference when you	3
73	<7 4 6 3 2 1 8 5 0>	<1 2 0>	come to exploit me?	3
74	[rest]		[rest]	—
75	[rest]		*"Chinaman!"*	—
76	[rest]		*"Laundryman!"*	—
77	<3 5 2 1 0 6 4 7 1>	<2 0 3 1>	Don't call me "Chinaman!"	2
78	<1 5 6 5 3 7 4 2 0>	<1 2 0>	Yes, I am a "Laundryman!"	5

Table 4.1 (*cont.*)

Explanatory note: The boss's text is italicized.

Meas.	Cseg	Prime contour	Text	Deviance
Section 9 – T$_6$				
79	<8 7 6 4 1 5 3 0 2>	<2 0 1>	The "working man!"	0
80	<7 6 4 1 5 3 0 2 8>	<1 0 2>	Don't call me "Chinaman!"	0
81	<5 3 0 4 2 8 1 7 6>	<1 0 3 2>	I am the worldman!	2
82	<2 8 3 1 7 0 6 5 4>	<1 3 0 2>	[rest]	6
83	<6 1 0 5 7 4 3 2 8>	<1 0 2>	[rest]	4
84	[rest]		[rest]	—
85	[rest]		*"Chinaman!"*	—
86	[rest]		*"Laundryman!"*	—
87	<0 6 3 5 2 1 8 7 4>	<0 2 1>	All you working men!	2
88	<5 2 4 1 0 8 6 3 7>·	<1 0 3 2>	Here is the brush	2
89	<0 1 6 5 4 2 7 3 8>	<0 1>	made of study.	3
90	<0 5 4 3 8 7 2 1 6>	<0 2 1>	Here is the soap	1
Section 10 – T$_0$				
91	<8 7 6 4 1 5 3 0 2>	<2 0 1>	made of action.	[return to norm]
92	<7 6 4 1 5 3 0 2 8>	<1 0 2>	Let us all	
93	<6 4 1 5 3 0 2 8 7>	<1 0 3 2>	wash with the brush!	
94	<5 2 6 4 1 3 0 8 7>	<1 0 3 2>	Let us all	
95	<2 6 4 1 3 0 8 7 5>	<1 0 3 2>	press with the iron!	
96	<6 4 1 3 8 0 7 5 2>	<2 3 0 1>	Wash!	
97	<5 2 4 8 1 7 6 3 0>	<1 2 0>	Brush!	
98	<4 6 3 2 1 8 5 0 7>	<1 3 0 2>	Dry!	
99	<7 4 3 2 8 6 1 0 5>	<2 3 0 1>	Iron!	
100	[rest]		Then we shall have a clean	
101	[rest]		world!	

Example 4.3 Reduction of piano, measure 4, to cseg <2 0 1>

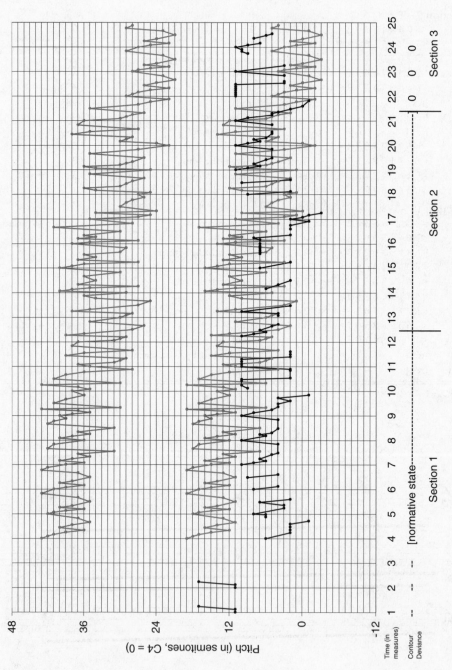

Figure 4.5 Local graph of piano and voice

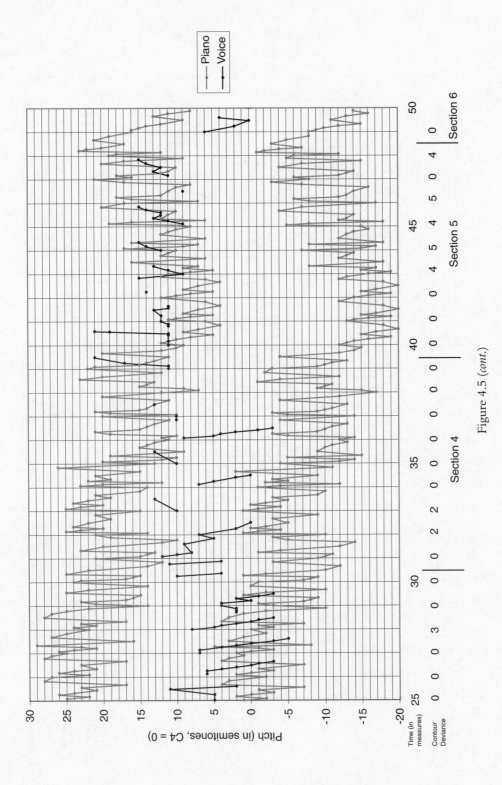

Figure 4.5 (cont.)

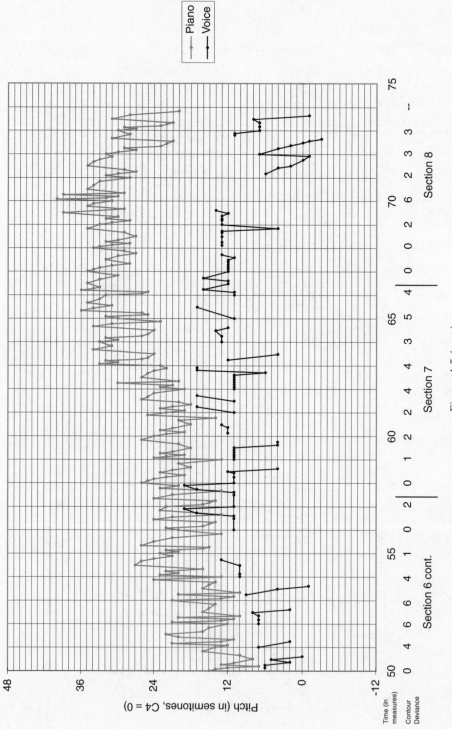

Figure 4.5 (*cont.*)

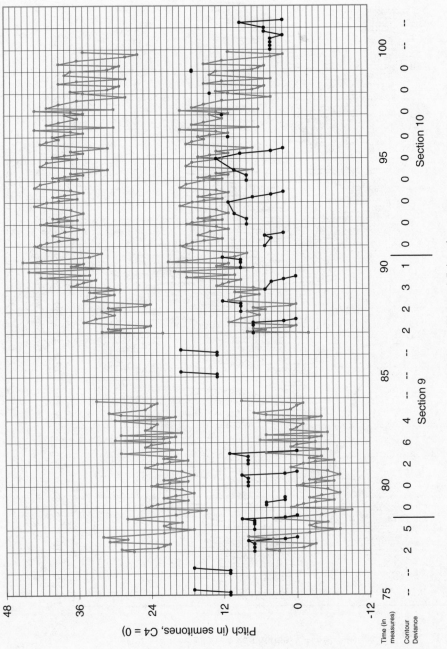

Figure 4.5 (*cont.*)

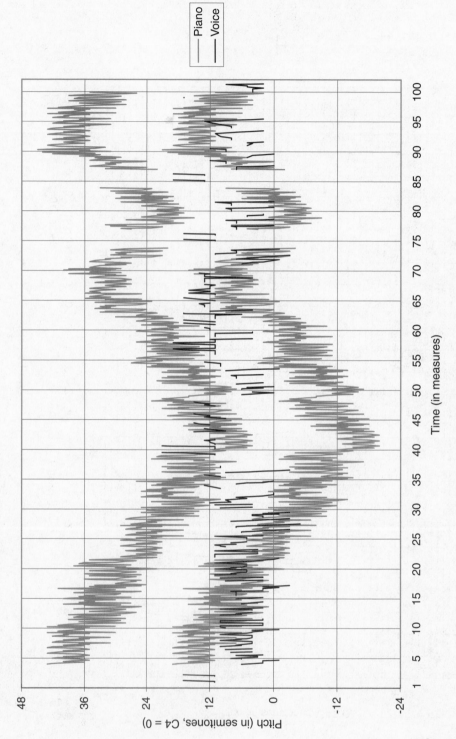

Figure 4.6 Large-scale graph of piano and voice

As one can see from Figure 4.5, a progression of gradual increase and decrease of the row's contour deviance emerges starting with section 3, a progression analogous to the "degree of twist" voice-leading process in Crawford's String Quartet, third movement, discussed in Chapter 2. Each process, of twist and of contour deviance, proposes a norm (either a relative registral ordering of instrumental voices or a particular realization of a row form in pitch space) and then measures the deviation from that norm through the entire piece.[32]

As Figure 4.5 shows, the piano contours in sections 3 and 4 vary minimally from the corresponding contours in sections 1 and 2, giving only briefly the contour deviance values of 3 and 2, respectively. Beginning in sections 5 and 6, these values rise sharply, to 5 and 6, respectively, and contour deviance occurs much more frequently. In section 5, the values are 0–0–0–4–5–4–5–0–4, and in section 6, the values are 0–0–4–6–6–4–1–0–2.

The beginning of section 6 (mm. 49–57) marks the midpoint of the song; here, both piano and voice begin their ascent back to their initial registers. This section also marks the point at which the piano abandons the two-section contour norm given in sections 1–2 (mm. 4–21); section 6's prototype is section 1 (mm. 4–12), as is the case for all subsequent sections.

Sections 7, 8, and 9 reach relatively high contour deviance values of 5 and 6: in section 7, the values are 0–1–2–2–4–4–3–5–4; in section 8, the values are 0–0–2–6–2–3–3–2–5; and in section 9, the values are 0–0–2–6–4–2–2–3–1. The final section, section 10, restates T_0, leaving all of the original contours of section 1 intact.

Although the piano's fixed systems of pitch and rhythm seem to represent the unyielding nature of the world of work the worker describes, this third element of structure, the registral deployment of each pitch class in a row form, alters this characterization.[33] As the declamation unfolds, the piano's melodic contour begins a regular process of departing from and then returning to the prototype, thereby restructuring what was initially a rigid and uncompromising system.

Moreover, as this musical system is dismantled, the relationship between the launderer and his boss goes through a transformative process. The launderer initially describes his unhappiness with his working conditions by merely asking a series of rhetorical questions about his condition, but later emerges from being dominated by his boss, addressing him more sharply, and by the end of the song comes to ignore him completely.

When first addressed by the boss in mm. 1–2 ("Chinaman! Laundryman!"), the launderer responds with the first of eight rhetorical questions, asking "Why can I wash away the dirt of others' clothes but not the hatred of my heart?" He ends in

---

[32] The idea of comparing various musical states to a norm is one that I also use in Chapter 5, which presents an analysis of Bauer's Toccata from *Four Piano Pieces*.

[33] Straus argues that the launderer is depicted through the free vocal melody, and the cruel world in which he is trapped is represented in the strict rotational-transpositional scheme of the piano (JNS-MRCS, 75–76). My analysis shares this premise, but divides the vocal line into two speakers and adds the element of contour.

mm. 31–32 with "Why do clothes dry, but not my tears?" The launderer also describes the degrading nature of his work in mm. 4–5 ("I am worse than a slave").

When the boss speaks a second time in m. 39 using the same words, the launderer departs from this mode of self-questioning to remark angrily in mm. 52–53, "I know bosses are robbers ev'rywhere!"; notably, this moment occurs when the piano's contour deviance reaches the highest level of 6.

Sections 8 and 9 reach their local high contour deviance value of 6 when the piano plays alone, in mm. 70 and 82. This high contour deviance value occurs in m. 70 after the boss promises "I will treat you better." Because the voice is silent, the piano's contour deviance is more audible and this gives the launderer an opportunity to reflect. Subsequently, in his next statement he becomes increasingly forceful, directly challenging the boss in m. 71 with the line "Get away from here!".

The piano's pattern of departure from the original contours of T_0 parallels the launderer's increased resistance to his situation, which climaxes in his statement of self-affirmation ("I am the worldman!").[34] Finally, when the boss once again repeats his familiar cry in mm. 85–86, the launderer does not respond to him at all, taking up instead the more important task of uniting his fellow "working men."

One can understand the piano to have a dual function: it represents the labor system that is being splintered, and it prompts the launderer to take a more active role in changing his situation. In m. 91, the piano returns to playing its initial set of contours from the opening, having successfully prodded the launderer from merely articulating his dissatisfaction with his situation to gathering his fellow workers to take action.

This metamorphosis of the launderer's actions is reflected also in the variation of his vocal contour. Morris's contour reduction algorithm, which I applied in Chapter 3 to the final movement of Crawford's quartet, makes it possible to compare contours of different lengths, such as those shaping the singer's vocal line, more systematically.

In the song's opening, the worker begins by singing in the voice of the boss, who summons the launderer with the cry of "Chinaman! Laundryman!" His two pitches, B4 to F5, form his signature interval, an ascending tritone, which has cseg <0 1>.

Being called the derogatory term "Chinaman" provokes the launderer.[35] In response, he immediately resists the affront by singing the vocal line in m. 4, whose first pitch is the highest of the phrase and whose final pitch is the lowest. Since all intervening pitches lie between these boundary pitches, they are considered "passing tones" and are subsequently pruned by Morris's algorithm; the launderer's response is thus labeled prime <1 0>; the launderer's contour <1 0> is the inver-

---

[34] This swell toward the final cadence recalls the rhetorical structure of mass songs of the 1930s, which were designed to leave the audience stirred by the spirit of revolution. See Oja, "Marc Blitzstein's *The Cradle Will Rock*," 446.

[35] A variant on the appellation "Chinaman" is "John Chinaman." Other pejorative terms for Chinese people are listed in *Dictionary of Asian American History*, 199.

sion of <0 1>, the contour that accompanies the boss's statements. (The inversion of contour <a b c> is defined as <*n*–a *n*–b *n*–c>, where *n* is one fewer than the cardinality of the cseg.)

The prime contour for each vocal phrase is given in Table 4.2; text phrases determine the boundaries of vocal contours.

As Table 4.2 shows, all of the boss's statements in mm. 1–2 and 36–47 that are reducible to two-note primes are characterized by contour <0 1>. (I am regarding the introductions to the boss's statements as the boss's text.) In mm. 4–36, nineteen of the launderer's twenty-one statements that are reducible to two-note primes are characterized by prime <1 0>. There is thus a clear division between the launderer and the boss, based on the contour of their two-note primes; by drawing this basic distinction between boss and worker, Crawford underlines the opposition between them.

Reducing vocal contours to their primes by using Morris's algorithm makes concrete the intuition that the voices of the two narrative personae are distinguished by ascending or descending contour, and provides a way of formally linking the vocal phrase of m. 4, which comprises a single downward gesture, with the phrase of m. 7, which comprises two downward gestures connected by an ascending semitone.

Table 4.3 gives a more precise account of this division between the two voices. It lists the number of times that the boss and the launderer sing each prime. Table 4.3 records that the launderer sings prime <1 0> relatively frequently, a total of thirty-one times in fifty-seven total phrases, while the boss sings it only three times. In contrast, the boss sings <0 1> a total of twenty-one times out of twenty-nine total phrases, compared to the launderer who sings it only seven times.

Of these seven times, five occur in the final section of the text, in which the launderer entreats the working class to take up the "brush of study" and the "soap of action" to improve the world. The launderer's ability to sing both the upward <0 1> contour that is characteristic of the boss and his own downward <1 0> contour with equal ease for the first time in the piece demonstrates a change in him. By the end of the song, he is able to enter what formerly had been the preserve of the boss: he sings in the highest vocal register of the piece, one that had been previously accessible only to the boss; and in mm. 96–99, he outlines the boss's trademark tritone and sings contour <0 1>.

This idea of making the two narrative voices distinct by means of the simple marker of up or down is one that is carried throughout the piece for three-note primes of the vocal line, as well as for contours <0 1> and <1 0>. As Table 4.2 shows, the contour of the launderer's statements that are reducible to three-note primes takes the form of cseg <1 2 0> more often than any other: m. 13, which accompanies the cadence of the lines "Why do you pay me less / for the same work?" is one of the sixteen total occurrences of <1 2 0>. The first and last pitches of this contour retain the downward gesture of the launderer's previous statements. The boss, in comparison, sings <1 0 2>, the three-note prime that has an overall upward gesture, three times, in contrast to the launderer, who never sings this

Table 4.2 *Prime contours of voice in Crawford, "Chinaman, Laundryman"*

meas.	prime	text phrase
1	<0 1>	*"Chinaman!"*
2	<0 1>	*"Laundryman!"*
4	<1 0>	Don't call me "man!"
4–5	<1 2 0>	I am worse than a slave.
6	<1 0> <1 0>	Wash! – Wash! –
7	<1 0>	Why can I wash away
7–8	<0 1 0>	the dirt of others' clothes
8–9	<1 2 0>	but not the hatred of my heart?
10	<1 2 0>	My skin is yellow, –
10–11	<0 1 0>	Does my yellow skin color the clothes?
12	<1 0>	Why do you pay me less
13	<1 2 0>	for the same work?
14	<1 0>	Clever boss!
15	<1 0>	You know
15–16	<1 2 0>	how to scatter the seeds of hatred
16–17	<1 0>	among your ignorant slaves.
18	<1 0> <1 0>	Iron! – Iron! –
19	<1 0>	Why can I smooth away
19–20	<0 1 0>	the wrinkle of others' dresses
20–21	<1 2 0>	but not the miseries of my heart?
22	<1 0>	Why should I come to America
22–23	<0 1 0>	to wash clothes?
23–24	<1 2 0>	Do you think Chinamen in China
25	<1 2 0>	wear no dresses?
26	<1 0>	I came to America
27	<1 0>	three days after my marriage.
28	<1 0>	When can I see her again?
28–29	<1 2 0>	Only the almighty dollar knows!
30	<1 0> <1 0>	Dry! – Dry! –
31	<2 0 1>	Why do clothes dry,
31–32	<1 2 0>	but not my tears?
33	<0 1>	I work
34	<1 0>	twelve hours a day,
35	<0 1>	he pays
36	<1 0>	fifteen dollars a week.
36–37	<0 1>	*My boss says:*
39	<0 1>	*"Chinaman,*
40	<0 1>	*go back to China,*
40–41	<0 1 0>	*if you don't feel satisfied!*
42	<2 3 0 1>	*There, unlimited*
44	<0 1>	*hours of toil:*
45	<0 1>	*two silver dollars a week,*
46–47	<0 1>	*if you can find a job."*
49	<2 0 1>	Thank you, boss, –
50	<1 0>	for you remind me.

Table 4.2 (*cont.*)

meas.	prime	text phrase
51	<1 0>	I know
52–53	<1 2 0>	bosses are robbers
53	<1 0>	ev'rywhere!
54	<0 1>	*Chinese boss says:*
56	<0 1>	*"You Chinaman,*
57	<0 1>	*me Chinaman,*
58	<1 2 0>	*come work for me*
59	<1 0>	*work for your fellow countryman!*
60	<0 1>	*By the way,*
61	<0 1> <0 1>	*you 'Wong', me 'Wong',*
62	<1 0 2>	*do we not belong to same family?*
63	<1 0>	*Ha! Ha!*
64	<1 2 0>	*We are cousins!*
65	<0 1>	*O yes!*
66	<0 1> <0 1>	*You 'Hai Shan', me 'Hai Shan',*
67	<1 0 2>	*do we not come from same district?*
68	<1 0>	*O come work for me;—*
69	<1 0 2>	*I will treat you better!"*
71	<1 0>	Get away from here!
72	<1 0>	What is the difference
73	<1 0>	when you come to exploit me?
75	<0 1>	"Chinaman!"
76	<0 1>	"Laundryman!"
77	<1 2 0>	Don't call me "Chinaman!"
78	<1 2 0>	Yes, I am a "Laundryman!"
79	<1 0>	The working man
80	<1 2 0>	Don't call me "Chinaman!"
81	<1 2 0>	I am the worldman!
85	<0 1>	"Chinaman!"
86	<0 1>	"Laundryman!"
87	<1 0>	All you working men!
88	<0 1>	Here is the brush
89	<1 0>	made of study.
90	<0 1>	Here is the soap
91	<1 0>	made of action.
92	<0 1>	Let us all
93	<1 0>	wash with the brush!
94	<0 1>	Let us all
95	<1 0>	press with the iron!
96–99	<0 1>	Wash! Brush! Dry! Iron!
100–101	<1 2 0>	Then we shall have a clean world!

Note:
The boss's text is italicized.

Table 4.3 *Number of occurrences of vocal prime*
contours sung by boss and launderer

	No. of occurrences	
	Launderer	Boss
2-note primes		
<0 1>	7	21
<1 0>	31	3
3-note primes		
<0 1 0>	4	1
<0 2 1>	0	0
<1 0 2>	0	3
<1 2 0>	16	2
<2 0 1>	2	0

contour. Thus the contours of three-note primes distinguish the two narrative voices and underscore the stark opposition between the capitalist boss and the exploited worker.

In mm. 36–37, the worker alters his characteristic descending vocal gesture when he sings an ascending melodic third, A♯–C♯. This change can be attributed to the change in function of the words he sings – here he introduces a change in voice with the words "My boss says." The boss's subsequent statement in m. 39, "Chinaman, go back to China / if you don't feel satisfied!" begins with his emblematic tritone, which reiterates the <0 1> prime of his initial statement.

The launderer's inability to improve his working conditions is symbolized further by his lack of pitch mobility. Each time that he sings <0 1 0> (in mm. 7–8, 10–11, 19–20, and 22–23, shown in Table 4.2), he asks a question; the downward cadential gesture accentuates the rhetorical nature of his statements. That this contour prime does not change serves as a musical manifestation of the worker's inability at this point in the poem to alter or to improve his condition.

The graphs in Figures 4.5 and 4.6 show that the relative registers of the voice and piano are unconventional – rather than being given harmonic support by the piano, the voice begins below the piano. In fact, the launderer *never* sings in the normative register above the piano; his vocal register is always either beneath or between the staves of the piano's music. He begins singing in the register about an octave below the pianist's left hand. Throughout the song, he remains suspended in this register. The only moment where the voice does ascend above the piano's upper staff occurs in mm. 40–41; significantly, this is a passage sung by the boss, who, as the graph shows, typically occupies a higher register than does the launderer.

The piano has much greater registral mobility than either vocal part. After entering in m. 4, where its highest and lowest pitches are G5 and B4, it makes a steady downward trajectory through m. 42, descending three octaves; here its highest pitch is C5 and its lowest pitch is E2. The music begins its about–face in m. 43, where its minimum pitch moves up a semitone from the previous bar to F2 and its maximum up four semitones to E5; the piano's music then ascends in mm. 44–99, returning to the registers in which it originated.

Since the voice's register remains more or less constant, the piano first collides with the voice during its downward plunge and then passes over it. The voice and piano intersect first in m. 11 – the voice's four B♭s followed by three Ds twist through the music played by the pianist's left hand. From m. 11 to m. 18, the piano's and voice's lines alternately meet and move apart; by m. 19, the musical space traversed by the voice is firmly enclosed within the musical space bounded by the pianist's hands.

As the worker enumerates the various unjust practices of his boss, the space bounded by the piano's two melodic lines surrounds the vocal line, suggesting the launderer's immobility. The piano's ability to move easily from the octaves of C5 and C7 in section 1 to the octaves of C2 and C4 in section 6 while rolling over the launderer's limited melodic space in the process can be read as indicating the system's utter disregard for his situation; he is completely subject to the actions of the labor machine of which he is merely a cog.

The piano's ascent in the second half of the piece is, however, not nearly so steady as its descent. As the graph in Figure 4.6 shows, brief passages break up the larger V-shaped framework with smaller descending motions in mm. 71, 78, and 94. Like the measure-to-measure contours which deviated from the prototype, the piano's large-scale contour similarly fractures a musical process for the second half of the poem.

While the contour of the launderer's local statements is predominantly downward, his pitches form chromatic ascending lines over several phrases. Measures 5–7 form a chromatic chain of F♯–G♮–G♯–A–B♭; the B♭ is then repeated in the next six bars as the highest pitch, through m. 13. The F♯ in m. 14 initiates another stepwise line, one that reaches a higher endpoint than did the one in mm. 7–13, a B♮ in m. 19 which is repeated through m. 25.

After reporting his long workday with little compensation, in mm. 36–47 the worker quotes the boss, who tells him that it would be worse for him in China. When the piano reaches its lowest point in m. 40, the boss is singing; during his entrance, the voice clings to the melodic ceiling of the right hand rather than remaining either positioned below both hands or poised between them. The boss again sings a tritone, now from D♯ to A, to "un-lim-" (mm. 42–43) or from A to D♯, to "-limited hours of toil" (mm. 43–44), "two silver dollars a week" (m. 45), and "if you can find a job" (mm. 46–47).

This is the moment in which the song comes closest to employing a "traditional" distribution of voices supported by the piano in a lower register. The boss's music, then, might be understood to have the function of interrupting the launderer's ascending chromatic line and of acting as the agent that inflects the piano to ascend again.

In the final fifteen measures (mm. 87–101), the launderer turns from outlining the details of his miserable situation to imploring his fellow workers to unite forces. This is the passage in which he instead sings <0 1> and <1 0> in alternation.

As well as commenting upon the launderer's circumstances brought about by both his class and race, Crawford's use of register pertains also to gender. If we consider David Lewin's idea that register can function as a gendered domain with relatively low and high registers traditionally signifying male and female identities, respectively, then Crawford's positioning of the male launderer in a mezzo-soprano register can be understood to comment upon how his gender is socially constructed.[36] The sight and sound of a woman performing a text written from a man's perspective, as in the song's premiere in 1933, invests the performance with a tension that might be understood as a statement about how gender was constructed for Asian American men at this time. Doing laundry has been understood to be a prototypical form of "women's work," but it has also been a task tradition-ally done by hand laundry establishments run by Chinese men.[37] The redistribu-tion of this stereotypically female type of labor to men does not disrupt assumptions of gender normativity, however, but rather reinforces them: since Asian men were represented at this time as having "weaker" characteristics and have been constructed to be more stereotypically feminine than white men, Asian men doing "women's work" would have been considered appropriate rather than odd and emasculating.[38]

Through its meticulous use of register, Crawford's setting thus makes it possible for a listener to perceive how, in the early twentieth century, a Chinese American laundry man's existence was marked by gender, sexuality, race, and class – not as inherent, immobile systems but as socially constructed ones that were alterable. The analytical technique I have applied to this song – measuring contour deviance from a prototype – makes evident a subtle parallel between the song's transformation of two systems, one musical and one social. By means of register, Crawford succeeds in composing an example of the "proletarian music" of which Seeger and other leftist theorists wrote, by bringing to a text with obtrusive political sentiment these more sophisticated compositional methods.[39] In weaving this serial tapestry, Crawford recognizes the nexus of difficulties that a Chinese American male laborer endured during the early decades of this century; in composing a song in which the worker is able to alter his initially unyielding musical environment, Crawford makes a musical statement of compassion, and of hope.

[36] David Lewin, "Women's Voices and the Fundamental Bass," *Journal of Musicology* 10/4 (Fall 1992), 464–82.
[37] Ellen Lupton, "Love, Leisure, and Laundry," in *Mechanical Brides: Women and Machines From Home to Office* (New York: Cooper-Hewitt National Museum of Design/Princeton Architectural Press, 1993), 16. In contrast to my reading of the song's racialized gender politics, Tick proposes that "Ruth Crawford might have addressed the issue that oppression could be female, composing music for a female singer about symbolic women's work" (JT-RCS, 192).
[38] In *The Yellow Peril*, Wu documents the feminization of Asian men in American literature during the 1920s and 1930s.
[39] In contrast to my reading, Straus writes that "Crawford's politics did not impinge in any deep way on her music," noting that she still composed the piano part of "Chinaman, Laundryman" and "Sacco, Vanzetti" in the "ultra-modern idiom," as it was then called (JNS-MRCS, 211).

GENDER, SEXUALITY, AND PERFORMANCE IN MARION BAUER'S TOCCATA

[Marion Bauer] asks me to lunch on Tuesday. After lunch she plays some of her preludes. I am bewildered by the strangeness of the experience. We are close kin. We – you might call us affinities. Our manner of building, our feeling very strongly the spirit of our work, our strengths and weaknesses – in all these, tho we are individuals, yet we are very close. Tho we have only just met, yet our spirits have been friends for years. We are strangers, and yet we long have been friends. It is beautiful and very strange.

Ruth Crawford, 12 August 1929

A significant figure to enter Ruth Crawford's life in 1929 was Marion Bauer. Their close friendship began at the MacDowell Colony that summer and continued in New York into the fall. As a fellow composer and older woman prominent in new music circles of this period, Bauer quickly became both mentor and companion to Crawford, who wrote admiringly about Bauer to Gene Shuford, a poet with whom she was having a romantic relationship at the MacDowell Colony: "You would find her real. She is human. She is sincere. Her humility . . . And yet she has great confidence too. Genuine. She has suffered. She has loved and has suffered, and she is radiant."[1] At the MacDowell Colony, Bauer helped Crawford to overcome "a final week of torture when I decide I have no talent, no fire, no feeling, no ear, no fire, no poetry. Nothing. I am a shell. I am ice that isn't even sensitive enough to melt."[2] After Bauer firmly told Crawford to "Work! You have a great talent. You *must* go ahead. I don't mean that you must not marry. But you *must* not drop your work," Crawford completed her five Sandburg songs, declaring to Shuford: "Marion Bauer. She has freed me. I am writing again . . . Glory and vision and poetry have come back. And I can make songs."[3]

In New York, Bauer contributed greatly to Crawford's musical growth and her professional visibility: she gave her free tickets to numerous musical events, which they attended together; published a glowing review of a private concert of Crawford's music in *The Musical Leader*; introduced her to prominent musical figures, including Gustave Reese (then an editor at G. Schirmer), pianist Harold

---

[1] RCd-LC, excerpt from letter to Gene Shuford, 12 August 1929; quoted in JT-RCS, 98.
[2] RCd-LC, August 1929; quoted in JT-RCS, 98–99. [3] RCd-LC, 16 August 1929.

Bauer, composer Carlos Salzedo, and *Christian Science Monitor* critic Winthrop Tryon; and programmed her music on a League of Composers Concert.[4]

Crawford warmly described their relationship in her diary: "My dear wonderful Marion Bauer . . . Our Peterboro friendship has grown more and more beautiful. We feel like sisters. She has been a marvelous friend to me."[5] She recorded an intimate moment after a concert in the late summer of 1929:

I go to the chair beside Marion Bauer. She draws me very close to her and kisses me . . . my head is on Marion Bauer's shoulder and her arm is about me and her hand on my arm, and my hand in hers. I have found a beautiful, a sincere, a warm friend. I am deeply stirred.[6]

The diary entry continues by registering Crawford's feelings about this incident and about her relationship to Gene Shuford:

At home I sob dry sobs of sad joy. Life is rich. That is a grand vista. I fear to love this exultation, this ecstasy, as I go to sleep I think of Gene. I feel him near. It would be sweet to have his head there on the pillow. I imagine my hands on his face on his neck, in his hair. It would be peace to have him there.

I sleep. I dream. I am kissing a very young girl, a child of fifteen or sixteen. I have her in my arms as she lies there in bed and kiss her often. She is slight, tiny. I am not satisfied. I hold her, but there seems nothing there to satisfy my grip. I think of Gene as I dream, the strength of his grip, his vigor.

Strange, that dream. If it were not for that last thought, I should wonder if it were [from] hearing . . . Miss Bauer's suggestion regarding Gene: You want to be sure your love for him is not a mother love for him rather than a sister's love. Also another thing I have been wondering. Is that fact that I was not really physically moved a sign that I do not love him? . . . Do I love him? I answer again & again, yes, I do, I do. And then there came those wonderings. Is it his work, his thoughts, I love? But isn't he his work, his thoughts? And O the beauties of Gene, the exquisite song of him. He is a song. Many songs. I do love you Gene.

Like her feelings about Gene Shuford, Crawford's feelings about Bauer shifted during the course of their relationship: in a letter to Charles Seeger, Crawford

---

[4] JT-RCS, 108, 106–107, 113, 157. Bauer also assisted Crawford's career in later years: in the first edition of her book *Twentieth Century Music* (1933), she mentioned Crawford's "interesting experimental work in dissonant counterpoint and dissonant rhythm combinations" and declared that "we may expect splendid things from this highly individual thinker and student" (MB-TCM, 287); in the revised edition of *Twentieth Century Music*, published fourteen years later, she noted Crawford's accomplishments in the realms of art music and folk music and mentioned her marriage to Seeger (MB-TCM, 1947 edn, 352); and she programmed Crawford's music, arranging for a performance of two of the five Sandburg songs in 1936 and one of the piano preludes in 1941; see JT-RCS, 234 and 313.   [5] RCd-LC, 17 October 1929; quoted in JT-RCS, 107.

[6] RCd-LC, 16 August 1929. Crawford attributed her "revulsion against physical attraction" to her "puritanical upbringing" in which "a kiss was a duty performed once or twice a year," and observed that "I cannot sincerely give him what he wants. It seems to have been left out of my make-up. I have not the craving" (RCd-LC, 26 July 1929 and 27 July 1929; quoted in JT-RCS, 96). Judith Tick notes that when Shuford left the MacDowell Colony at the end of July 1929, Crawford was still a virgin (JT-RCS, 96). Less than two weeks after his departure, Bauer arrived at the MacDowell Colony. One evening, after hearing Bauer's piano preludes, Crawford told her new friend about her recent romance and about her aversion to having intercourse (RCd-LC, 12 August 1929; quoted in JT-RCS, 97). Bauer told Crawford that there was nothing wrong with opposition to a sexual relationship, and that "anyone who writes music like [yours] must be warm, and will want it when the time comes" (RCd-LC, 16 August 1929; JT-RCS, 97).

characterized her friendship with Bauer as being "like mad falling in love" and that their "close constant friendship could not continue in the intensity in which it began."[7] Crawford believed that their relationship at one time verged on becoming a sexual one, which she identified as "Lesbian."[8] When both women were in Liège in September 1930, having arrived separately to attend the International Festival of Contemporary Music, Bauer reserved a hotel room for them, which made Crawford quite uncomfortable.[9] Crawford preferred to characterize Bauer's affection for her that developed in New Hampshire and later in New York as one of "sisterly–motherly love":[10]

I am Marion's child. Gnome, gypsy, monkey, she calls me. I am not young enough to be her child, in years, and yet – I am. But strange . . . I wonder if she knows that often I feel very much as tho she were my child, and feel that I really am the older one?[11]

Of Bauer's personal life, little has been published. It is known that she never married, that she was supported by her sister Emilie until Emilie's death in 1926, and that in the same year she and her sister Flora began to live together in New York, an arrangement that continued until Flora's death in the early 1950s.[12]

Remarks by two additional people who knew Bauer, as a colleague and as a teacher, are evocative in light of Crawford's depictions of her relationship with Bauer. Martin Bernstein, a former chair of the music department at New York University who knew Bauer for over twenty-five years, stated that to his knowledge she did not have any romantic relationships with men, and moreover that he believed that she was not interested in them.

Marion was a . . . well . . . she had no . . . she didn't . . . as a female, she had very little interest in *men* . . . At least if she had any romantic liaisons with men, we don't know about it.[13]

When asked in an interview about his former teacher at NYU (then Washington Square College), Milton Babbitt commented that

Marion Bauer was one of the dearest, most wonderful creatures in the world. The only thing was that her basic orientation was [Nadia] Boulanger. She had studied with Boulanger. She was very French oriented, very much in the Boulanger tradition, except she wasn't that kind of personality. She was a dear lady from Walla Walla; she wasn't a stern lady

---

[7] Letter to Seeger, (14) February 1931; quoted in JT-RCS, 107. Seeger disliked Bauer, writing in a letter to Crawford that "I don't know how reliable M.B. is or whether she can speak legitimately in so authoritative a way [about programming Crawford's *Diaphonic Suite No. 1* on a League of Composers Concert]. But she does seem to be a good friend of yours and I am trying to be nice to her." (Letter to Crawford, 1 February 1931, collection of Mike Seeger; quoted in JT-RCS, 157).   [8] JT-RCS, 107.

[9] JT-RCS, 141 and personal communication with Tick, 7 April 1995.

[10] RCd-LC, October 1929; quoted in JT-RCS, 107.

[11] RCd-LC, 17 February 1930; quoted in MG-RCS, 196.

[12] NLS-SPM, 30–31, 76. Marion and Emilie Bauer are buried in a twin grave in Valhalla, New York; see Pickett, "Why Can't We Listen to Marion Bauer's Music?".

[13] Interview with Martin Bernstein, 22 March 1994. Bauer and Bernstein began teaching in the music department of New York University in 1926; Bauer retired in 1951 and Bernstein in 1972. For biographical information on Bernstein, see Edward H. Clinkscale, Introduction to *A Musical Offering: Essays in Honor of Martin Bernstein*, ed. Edward H. Clinkscale and Claire Brook (New York: Pendragon Press, 1977), vii.

from France. And she was very much a . . . let's simply say unmarried. But she was an absolute dear.[14]

Although Crawford's writings and Bernstein's and Babbitt's remarks do not definitively establish Bauer's sexual orientation, they do suggest the possibility that Bauer was a lesbian.

Suzanne Cusick's description of her relationship to music usefully informs a reading of Bauer's Toccata, the third of her *Four Piano Pieces*, op. 21. Cusick describes the various ways she positions herself to particular pieces of music that allow her to vary whether it is she or the music which is "on top" – that is, whether the music becomes "the active force which generates pleasure, which leads one body and soul into an alternate reality . . . into intimacy" or whether the relationship is reversed; that is, when she as a performer "love[s] [music] in return . . . when, attending to its messages with ears, heart, and mind, I [use] my own body to release those messages again into the air, for the pleasure of my own ears and mind." In Cusick's relationship with music, she and the music take turns being "on top."[15]

She characterizes this relationship as lesbian not only from its analogy with physical expressions of sexuality, which she defines as "a way of expressing and/or enacting relationships of intimacy through physical pleasure shared, accepted, or given," but also – more relevant to Bauer's particular case in which her rejection of traditional heterosexual relationships has been alluded to but not verified – as suggestive of a possible psychological relationship between women.[16]

If women are constructed to be non-dominating in some social situations, then a relationship between two women can be understood to take place between two selves who are what Cusick calls "non-power":

With her, a self who is also non-power is more likely to create a relationship based on non-power – that is, a relationship in which a porous boundary exists at all moments . . . allowing for a flow of power in both directions. No one in the relationship has been formed to be the power figure, although all can play at it.[17]

Cusick's essay suggests an approach to the Toccata that takes into account the issue of Bauer's sexuality. My analysis of the Toccata explores the relationships between music and gender that exist within the dimension of performance and describes a fundamental aspect of its structure, the relationship of the performer's hands.

Example 5.1 gives the score. Both hands begin by playing in the same register. In

---

[14] Interview with Milton Babbitt in Duckworth, *Talking Music*, 62. Babbitt transferred from the University of North Carolina to Washington Square College because of Bauer: "[T]here was a wonderful woman there named Marion Bauer who had just written a book called *Twentieth Century Music*. It was the first American book in which there were actually musical examples from Schoenberg's and Stravinsky's works. I said, 'That's for me!'" Quoted in Rosenberg and Rosenberg, *The Music Makers*, 41–42.

[15] Cusick, "On a Lesbian Relation with Music," 74, 77. Fred Everett Maus explores the gendered roles of dominant and non-dominant positions in musical experience in "Masculine Discourse in Music Theory," *Perspectives of New Music* 31/2 (Summer 1993), 264–93.   [16] Cusick, "On a Lesbian Relation with Music," 70.

[17] *Ibid.*, 72.

Example 5.1 Bauer, Toccata

TO RUTH CRAWFORD

FOUR PIANO PIECES

III

TOCCATA*)

Marion Bauer, Op. 21, № 3

*) *Accidentals apply to individual notes only; they are not effective through the measure*

C. C. P. 2

Gendering Musical Modernism

Example 5.1 (*cont.*)

Example 5.1 (*cont.*)

m. 1, the left hand plays C4–E4 and the right hand plays D♭4–G♭4. The lower notes of these two dyads, C4 and D♭4, played by the left and right hands, respectively, lie one semitone apart; their upper notes, E4 and G♭4, lie two semitones apart.

Because the notes played by the lower fingers of the left and right hands lie so close together, separated by the slimmest of intervals, the pianist's hands touch one another. Furthermore, given the particular pitches that are played, the right hand lies on top of the left. In m. 1, after the right hand strikes its initial dyad of D♭4–G♭4, the left hand moves up from C4–E4 to D4–F4, a motion that places its dyad squarely within the right hand's dyad, D♭4–G♭4, which the right hand immediately strikes a second time.

This relationship between the two agents of its performance, the pianist's hands, varies throughout the piece. The question of "who's on top" indeed motivates the entire composition: the initially clear-cut relationship of inequality between the hands that occurs in m. 1 – that is, right-hand dominance – is subsequently shifted back and forth in later sections of the piece in a persistent state of reversal. When directed toward a pianist's performance, the question of "who's on top" is also a question of which hand constrains and contains the other.[18]

My reading of Bauer's Toccata suggests that the exchange of power can be understood as a primary organizing force in the work. In its particular musical manifestation in this piece, power is not wielded by only one party as a means to control a weaker party, but flows in both directions. The pursuit of one hand by the other becomes a game, and reinforces the work's playful quality suggested by its *Allegro scherzando* indication. If a relationship between women can be understood as one of a "continuous circulation of power," then the relationship between the pianist's hands in the Toccata – a composition on which Bauer worked at the MacDowell Colony during the summer she met Crawford and one that she dedicated to her – might thus be heard as expressive of a relationship between women.[19]

---

[18] Hand crossing in piano compositions certainly does not originate with Bauer – examples by male composers (e.g., Debussy's "Mouvement" from *Images* and Bartók's "Syncopation," no. 133 from *Mikrokosmos*, vol. 5) also exist. In Bauer's Toccata, however, the hand crossing occurs in a systematic way within a specific narrative framework which can in turn be usefully contextualized in terms of Bauer's gender and sexuality. The structural aspects that I am examining in Bauer's music – as well as in Crawford's and Gideon's – are inextricable from the historical and biographical contexts within which I am placing each work. My argument should not be misconstrued as claiming that *any* piece with hand crossing or black-and-white key contrast has a gendered, sexualized, or symbolic dimension; one must take into account the composer's particular circumstances. In the case of Bartók's "Syncopation," for example, I would not claim that the hand crossing signifies a same-sex sublimated relationship.

[19] The technique of hand crossing has a gendered history within the genre of keyboard compositions by male composers, enabling male pianists to have direct physical contact with female performers. One example is Wilhelm Friedrich Ernst Bach's "Das Dreyblatt" for pianoforte, six hands. The composer's instructions stipulate that the male pianist should sit in the middle, just behind the two female performers, and further specify that "[the ladies] have to hold their arms above his, and the restricted space makes it necessary for the three persons to sit somewhat closely together." Moreover, the male performer's music is written in the outermost registers, which ensures that his arms surround the two women. The physical aspects of performance in this work are unambiguously related to both gender and power. "Das Dreyblatt" appears in *Music of the Bach Family: An Anthology*, ed. Karl Geiringer (Cambridge, MA: Harvard University Press, 1955), 231–36. My thanks to David

Bauer's *Four Piano Pieces* were premiered in April 1930 at a League of Composers Concert in New York by Harrison Potter, a faculty member in the music department at Mount Holyoke College. Potter continued to perform them at recitals in New England and New York over a twenty-year span, up through the 1950s.[20] By the time Bauer composed this set of pieces, she had published at least seven compositions for solo piano.[21] Her first published piano works, *Arabesque* and *Elegie*, appeared in 1904; by 1930, she had completed numerous songs with piano accompaniment as well as a violin sonata and a string quartet.[22]

As a solo keyboard work characterized by sweeping melodic gestures, continuously active eighth notes, and a somewhat improvisatory flair, Bauer's piece merits its designation as a toccata; the origin of the word "toccata," from the Italian "toccare" ("to touch"), is suggestive in the context of Cusick's account of musical experience. Also typical of a toccata is the composition's relatively free form. Bauer's Toccata comprises seven sections, distinguished by texture, pitch, and rhythm. Nearly all of the sections increase their dynamic levels throughout.

Section I (mm. 1–22) opens with alternating dyads, one to an eighth note, that continue until the performer's hands join at m. 23 to play the heavy *forte* chords that begin the next section. Throughout Section I, the left hand's pitches are drawn exclusively from the white keys and are centered upon C, while the right hand's pitches are drawn from the black keys and are centered on G♭; the hands' relative positioning makes the right hand dominant over the left. Neither hand dominates in the next three sections: in Section II (mm. 23–33), each hand plays three- and four-note harmonies made up of both black and white notes and based primarily on the intervals of a fourth and fifth; both hands play on the same beats rather than on alternate beats. In Section III (mm. 34–43), the left hand strikes the downbeat of each of the first five bars, taking a momentary leadership role, but by the section's conclusion, it joins with the right hand in presenting the fourth- and the fifth-based harmonies once again.

In contrast, Section IV (mm. 44–59) begins by separating the duties of the hands,

Lewin for mentioning this work. A second example is John Field's early nineteenth-century "Duet on a Favorite Russian Air" for pianoforte, composed for Field's female students; in the seventh, eleventh and twelfth measures, the hands of the performers cross. See Nicholas Temperley, Introduction to *A Selection of Four-Hand Duets Published between 1777 and 1857*, vol. 19, *The London Pianoforte School, 1766–1860* (New York: Garland, 1986), 6.

[20] Performances of *Four Piano Pieces* include concerts at the Harvard Musical Association on 10 April 1931; a recital given on 24 November 1931, which was part of a series on twentieth-century music given by Bauer and Potter at the homes of various women in New York City; a Works Progress Administration Music Project concert on 22 January 1936; a concert at the National Gallery in Washington, D.C., on 3 December 1944; and a concert at Pratt Music Hall, Mount Holyoke College, on 14 February 1954. Programs for these concerts are housed in the Library Archives, Mount Holyoke College.

[21] A complete listing of Bauer's compositions has not yet been compiled. A partial chronology appears in NLS-SPM, 83–89.

[22] Bauer's Violin Sonata was published by G. Schirmer in 1928 under the title *Fantasia quasi una Sonata*; her String Quartet remains unpublished.

giving the left hand a brisk staccato accompaniment and the right hand a more melodic line. Section V (mm. 60–79) presents the two parts working together to form a composite line, a situation that is overturned when the right hand again assumes the dominant position. This section again divides the white- and black-key material between the hands until m. 75, but without the dyadic organization of Section I. The right hand moves away from the left hand through the first beat of m. 72, and then chases it back down again.

Section VI (mm. 80–101) opens with the hands apart: the right hand maintains an eighth-note pulse while playing a mixture of black and white keys; the left hand plays black keys in half notes for three bars. Beginning in m. 81, the left hand moves on top of the right hand with its black-note B♭2–B♭3 octave, reversing Section I's right-hand dominance. After retreating in m. 82, the left hand again moves atop the right hand in m. 83, this time with a white-note octave, C♭3–C♭4. Measures 84–85 present the same situation: in m. 84, the left hand sinks back to the lower octave, and then in m. 85 leaps to the higher octave, to D♭3–D♭4 on beat 1, followed by E♭3–E♭4 on beat 2. After a playful struggle between the hands starting in m. 88, the passage drives to the composition's climax in mm. 98–100. Section VII (mm. 102–20) begins as Section I did, with alternating dyads played on white and black keys, and so repeats the situation of right-hand dominance; the piece briefly surges up to a second, smaller climax in mm. 115–16 just before the final cadence in which the hands separate.

A closer look at Section I shows that while the principle of alternating dyads organizes both the upper and lower parts, it is applied in different ways for each hand. Throughout this section, which ends in m. 22, the left hand is confined to the white keys of the piano. This hand plays a stream of parallel thirds, each of which is connected to the next by either a step or a third. As the first and last bass note in Section I, pitch class C functions as a framing structural point. In contrast to the left hand, the pitches of the right hand are drawn entirely from the black keys of the piano: this hand's pitch center is G♭, heard as the uppermost pitch in the opening four bars; and this note returns as an upper pitch in m. 15 to dominate the final eight bars of the section.[23]

In Section I, the hands are further distinguished by size of interval. All of the left hand's harmonic intervals are thirds, while the right hand's dyads comprise intervals larger than a third – initially a fourth, then a fifth, sixth, seventh, and, by m. 21, an octave. In intervallic space, the right hand, then, may be construed more generally as differing from the left hand in two ways: its dyads are relatively large (that is, larger than a third) and its intervals can be characterized by their tendency to

[23] In *Generalized Musical Intervals* David Lewin discusses the structural contrast between the performer's hands in Bartók's "Syncopation," no. 133 from *Mikrokosmos*, vol. 5. This contrast is established by the white-note versus black-note distinction and by the different modes to which each hand's music belongs (225–26). In *Musical Form and Transformation: 4 Analytic Essays* (New Haven: Yale University Press, 1993), Lewin further explores the idea of a contrast between black-note and white-note material, in Debussy's "Feux d'artifice" (97–159).

Example 5.2 Position of hands, m. 1, beat 1

RH

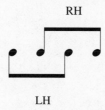

LH

change, whereas the left hand projects a single, relatively small interval that is kept constant for nearly all of the section.

Rhythm further differentiates the music each hand plays in Section I. The hands never play at the same time; instead, dyads are dispensed either to the strong eighth-note beats of the bar or to its weak beats, a distribution that switches three times from hand to hand – for example, in the opening bar the left hand plays on the first and third eighth notes in a 2/4 meter while the right hand plays on the second and fourth eighth notes. In m. 6 this arrangement changes – the right hand moves into the first eighth note position, occupying the strong beats while the left plays on the weak beats. Measure 9 reverts to the original rhythmic organization via the left hand's successive attacks on the second and third eighth notes, and m. 10 returns the right hand to its original position of playing second and fourth eighth notes. When the right hand plays successive eighth notes over mm. 12–13, the rhythm is reversed once again, and after this moment, the right hand's leadership role in playing each measure's strong beats is maintained through the rest of the section, which concludes in m. 22. This rhythmic contest between the hands in Section I adds a further dimension to the dominance issue established by the physical placement of the hands – this idea is developed in Sections V and VII, two particularly crucial sections in terms of the narrative that unfolds.

Example 5.2 gives a model for the first four-note grouping in m. 1, beat 1. From left to right, the pitches played by the left hand are represented by the first and third notes, which are beamed together; the pitches played by the right hand are represented by the second and fourth notes, which are also beamed together. (The beams indicate which hand plays the notes grouped; they do not indicate traditional rhythmic values.) Example 5.2 clarifies the aspect of contour in my analytical model, which considers the position of the notes relative to one another rather than their exact pitches. It also tracks the positions of the hands relative to each other throughout the passage in the following way.

Figures 5.1 and 5.2 illustrate the method by which I shall label these positions. By assigning "0" to the finger of the left hand that plays the lower note of its dyad, "1" to the finger that plays the upper note of the left-hand dyad, "2" to the finger of the right hand that plays the lower note of its dyad, and "3" to the finger that plays the upper note of the right-hand dyad, we can label the situation in Example 5.2 as

0   1   2   3

Figure 5.1 Numerical way of labeling a hand position with four cps

0 1 2   3 4 5

Figure 5.2 Numerical way of labeling a hand position with six cps

<0213>. From left to right, the first number indicates which finger plays the lowest note of the cluster of four notes, the second number tells which finger plays the second lowest note, and so forth.[24]

In m. 1, the left hand's ascent from C–E to D–F alters the initial <0213> relationship between the hands. Example 5.3 illustrates this second two-dyad grouping. Using the numerical notation introduced above, we can identify this new relationship as <2013>. As the model shows, this notation describes the situation in which the pitches in the upper staff flank the pitches in the lower staff, a position in which the right hand's notes encompass the left hand's notes.

Example 5.4 lists the six possibilities for the four-note configurations in this model. As in my analyses in Chapters 2 and 4 of the third movement of Crawford's String Quartet and her song "Chinaman, Laundryman," my method calculates the contours of musical situations with the same cardinality and compares each of these situations to a norm in order to formalize a narrative of the piece. For each bar in Section I, Table 5.1 lists the four patterns that are formed between consecutive pairs of dyads between the two staves (i.e., dyads 1–2; 2–3; 3–4; and 4–1 of the next bar).[25]

Table 5.2 lists the total number of occurrences of each configuration in Sections I, V, and VII, the three sections in which hand crossing is prominent. (The hand positions for each combination of successive dyads in Sections V and VII are given in my subsequent discussions of those sections.)

The frequency of <0213> and <2013> is evident from the listing; the other patterns occur infrequently.[26] The total number of occurrences of <0213> and

---

[24] This method of numbering contours starting with zero is consistent with the system of contour labeling established by Robert D. Morris in *Composition with Pitch-Classes*; it is also employed by Friedmann, "A Methodology for the Discussion of Contour," 223–48; and Marvin and Laprade, "Relating Musical Contours," 225–67.

[25] When two dyads are stated successively in one hand (e.g., mm. 5–6), no pattern is listed.

[26] <2031> occurs thrice in m. 4 because the dyad in each hand is repeated.

Example 5.3 Cseg <2013>

Example 5.4 Six possibilities for four-note csegs

<2013> is 56 + 18 = 74 out of 84 four-note patterns, or 88 percent of all hand posi-
tions in Section I.

Several additional significant pieces of information about Section I are summarized in Table 5.2. First, <0123>, the position in which the hands do not cross,
occurs rarely – in only five of the eighty-four four-note groups in the section's
twenty-two bars. Second, the pattern occurring most frequently, <0213> (the
pattern of the opening bar), occurs fifty-six times. This position may be thus
understood to be the "standard" or normative relationship between the hands in
this section. Third, there is a notable disparity between the two models given in the
fifth and sixth rows of Table 5.2, <0231> and <2013>. In these three sections,
<0231> is never asserted, in contrast to its inversion, <2013>, which is stated rela-
tively frequently – a total of eighteen, thirteen, and thirteen times in Sections I, V,
and VII, respectively.

The patterns that occur most frequently in Section I, <0213> and <2013>,

Table 5.1 *Hand positions in Section I (mm. 1–22)*

Meas.	Position	Meas.	Position	Meas.	Position
1a	<0213>	9a	<0213>	17a	<0213>
1b	<2013>	9b	—	17b	<0213>
1c	<2013>	9c	<2013>	17c	<0213>
1d	<0213>	9d	<0213>	17d	<0213>
2a	<0213>	10a	<0213>	18a	<0123>
2b	<2013>	10b	<0213>	18b	<0213>
2c	<2013>	10c	<0213>	18c	<0213>
2d	<0213>	10d	<0213>	18d	<0213>
3a	<0213>	11a	<2013>	19a	<0213>
3b	<2013>	11b	<2013>	19b	<0123>
3c	<0213>	11c	<0213>	19c	<0123>
3d	<2013>	11d	<0213>	19d	<0213>
4a	<2031>	12a	<2013>	20a	<0213>
4b	<2031>	12b	<2013>	20b	<0213>
4c	<2031>	12c	<0213>	20c	<0213>
4d	<0213>	12d	—	20d	<0213>
5a	<0213>	13a	<2013>	21a	<0213>
5b	<2031>	13b	<2013>	21b	<0213>
5c	<2013>	13c	<0213>	21c	<0213>
5d	—	13d	<0213>	21d	<0213>
6a	<0213>	14a	<0213>	22a	<0213>
6b	<0213>	14b	<0213>	22b	<0213>
6c	<2013>	14c	<0213>	22c	<0213>
6d	<0213>	14d	<2013>	22d	—
7a	<0213>	15a	<2013>		
7b	<0123>	15b	<2031>		
7c	<0213>	15c	<0213>		
7d	<0213>	15d	<0213>		
8a	<0213>	16a	<0213>		
8b	<0213>	16b	<2013>		
8c	<0213>	16c	<2013>		
8d	<0123>	16d	<0213>		

require that the right hand be placed over the left. If the key domains were reversed so that the right hand were assigned the white keys and the left hand the black keys – for example, by transposing m. 1 up a tritone, which would result in the left hand playing two black notes, (F♯4–A♯4) and the right hand playing two white notes (G4–C5) – then the left hand would be dominant. That is, patterns <0213> and <2013> could theoretically be played with either the right or the left hand on top. But because of their position on the keyboard in these passages, the distribution of white and black keys to each hand ensures that these situations result in right-hand dominance.

This division of black and white keys between the hands serves the following

Table 5.2 *Number of occurrences of hand positions in Sections I, V, and VII*

	Section I	Section V	Section VII
<0123>	5	7	2
<2301>	0	0	0
<0213>	56	32	25
<2031>	5	0	3
<0231>	0	0	0
<2013>	18	13	13

purpose. Not only does it strengthen the characterization of the hands as opposed agents, but it ensures that one hand will be dominant. Only by later appropriating black-key material for itself will the left hand have any chance to become the dominant hand; it does this during stretches of Section VI, as I shall discuss later.

After the first four bars, which establish the fundamental opposition between the left and right hands (white keys vs. black keys, alternating dyads vs. constant dyads, thirds vs. fourths, strong beats vs. weak beats), m. 5 introduces a crescendo accompanying the right hand's first change of intervallic size, from a perfect fourth to a perfect fifth. In m. 6, where the crucial rhythmic modification mentioned previously commences, the right hand strikes two dyads in succession, resulting in an inversion of the previous rhythmic ordering – from m. 6 through m. 8, the right hand's dyads now fall on strong beats, and the left hand's dyads on weak beats.

What this rhythmic inversion accomplishes is significant: by pushing past the left hand into the first eighth-note beat position of m. 6, the formerly rhythmically subordinate right hand seizes the dominant role and gets to occupy the strong beats. The right hand's striking of the G♭4–D♭5 dyad immediately after the E♭4–B♭4 dyad is a physical gesture felt by the performer which is also visible to the audience, not only to those with a clear view of the pianist's hands, but in certain performative gestures that might be made at the moment of weak-to-strong conversion – e.g., a nod or a firm downward motion made with the right side of the body.

Measure 7 begins the second crescendo of the piece with which both hands ascend to their highest dyads of this section: in m. 9, the right hand moves to G♭5–E♭6 and the left hand to F5–A5. After playing F5–A5 on the second eighth note beat, the left hand immediately strikes a second dyad, E5–G5, and regains the strong beats. The right hand's second dyad in m. 9, E♭5–D♭6, closes around the left hand's E5–G5 dyad in an attempt to check its movement; the left hand resists the right hand by dropping lower still, continuing its stepwise descent on the white keys by thirds, from F5–A5 in m. 9 to B4–D5 in m. 11. During this passage, the right hand continues to shadow the left by inching down after it.

In m. 11, the right hand again encloses the left hand's pitches and pursues it down the keyboard in a string of <0213> and <2013> hand positions. The right hand regains its dominant rhythmic role here, last held in mm. 6–9, by capturing the downbeat position via the successive dyads D♭5–G♭5 to A♭4–G♭5 in mm. 12–13. After this successful rhythmic incursion into strong-beat space, the right hand retains the dominant rhythmic position for the remainder of the section. In m. 15, <2031> occurs in a right-hand dominant position between the left hand's E4–G4 and the right hand's D♭4–G♭4.

Measure 17 initiates this section's final descent toward the cadence in m. 22. Over these six bars, the right hand's intervals expand to their largest yet – to the octaves in mm. 21–22. The last three bars of Section I give a steady stream of <0213> patterns, eleven in all. The left hand continues to sound its diatonic thirds, and then in mm. 21–22 plays larger intervals – still on white keys – of a fifth, seventh, and sixth. But because the right hand's G♭3–G♭4 dyad is relatively large and is played on the black keys, the left hand remains the non-dominant hand.

Sections II, III, and IV mark an abrupt change in this imbalanced situation. Beginning in m. 23, the hands are drawn apart into distinct registers, a situation that continues until Section V. In addition, pitch material is now shared between the two parts; each hand partakes of both black and white keys.

Measure 23 launches Section II. The right hand remains in the register in which it concluded Section I, while the left hand dives down to a lower register to free itself from being pinned underneath the right hand as it was for most of Section I. Both hands abandon the dyad texture: the left hand plays two Bs an octave apart and divided at the fifth by F♯, while the right hand's G♭ octave is converted into an F♯ octave, divided at the fourth by B. The enharmonic respelling of G♭ as F♯ marks the shift to Section II and the hands' reorientation from a state of being opposed to one of working together.

The double statement of B and F♯ in both staves emphasizes the balance between them. Both hands play the same pitch classes; the distinction between the hands as a performer of either white-key or black-key material has temporarily dissolved. Furthermore, the harmonies in both parts are based upon the intervals of a fourth or a fifth: for example, in m. 24 the left hand moves up from B1–F♯1–B2 to D2–A2–D3 and the right hand moves down from F♯3–B3–F♯4 to E3–A3–E4.

In mm. 24–26, the hands enter into a comfortable whole-step relation: the left hand's D3 and the right hand's E3 approach each other in contrary motion and politely step away. In mm. 27–28, the right hand leaps away from the left hand, from G3–D4–G4 to C4–E4–F♯4–B4 at the same time that the left hand moves closer to the right hand with its leap from A1–E2–B2 in m. 27 to A2–E2–B3 in m. 28. The left hand's leap brings it within a semitone's reach of the right hand's lowest pitch, C4, in m. 28, a situation that occurs again in m. 29.

Measure 34 introduces Section III, which returns to the cooperative effort by the two parts. As in Section II, the hands keep to their separate registers. However, the left hand again takes the initiative to move closer to the right hand – in m. 34 its uppermost voice moves up from B3 to D4, a second away from the right hand's E4, and in m. 36 it leaps up a major ninth from B2 to C♯4 to land four semitones from the right hand's F4. Beginning in m. 37, the roles of pursuer and pursued continue: the left hand follows the right hand upward, but the right hand quickly avoids capture, moving higher still to seek refuge in m. 43's D6–G6–D7. Again, the piano's pitch material, based upon fifths and fourths, is shared by the hands.

In m. 44, which begins Section IV, the left hand first plays pairs of ascending major ninths, the interval it used in the previous section to climb rapidly upwards. The right hand remains in its high register, keeping its distance from the left hand, which now assumes a more accompanimental role. Beginning in m. 47, the left hand moves up once again toward the right hand: on the last eighth note of m. 49, the left hand's C♯5 comes within a semitone of the right hand's D5. But this time, the right hand answers the left hand's incursion with its descending gesture in m. 50, and rather than risk being positioned again under the right hand, the left hand beats a hasty retreat in mm. 51–52, thus reversing the established roles of pursuer and pursued. In mm. 53–59, the right hand continues to approach the left hand, which manages to keep a safe distance of at least four semitones between them.

Measure 60, the first bar of Section V, returns to the earlier distribution of white and black keys. Initially, the two parts work together to present a composite line comprising the two ninths (E2–F♯3–B2–C♯4) that the left hand presented in mm. 44–45; the left hand plays the first and third eighth-note beats, and the right hand plays the second and fourth eighth-note beats.

This situation does not last long: the right hand begins to dominate the left in mm. 62–63, with the same hand position that characterized Section I, <0213>. Table 5.3 lists the patterns that are formed between each pair of dyads in Section V. For the situations in which one hand plays successive dyads on the second and third eighth-note beats (for example, in m. 62), I have measured the hand position between the dyad struck on the first eighth-note beat and each dyad on the inner eighth-note beats (e.g., for m. 62, I list <0213> between G3–B3 and A♭3–D♭4 and <0213> between G3–B3 and B♭3–E♭4). For simultaneous four-note clusters such as those in m. 71, I calculate the hand position for the simultaneity rather than for a nonsimultaneous, diagonal grouping as I did previously.

In mm. 62 and 63, the right hand plays successive eighth notes, as it did in Section I, which reinforces its attempt to regain the role of leader in the rhythmic domain. Dominance through hand position is achieved again in m. 65 with the <2013> that occurs between the third and fourth eighth notes; the right hand again plays strong beats in an attempt to overtake the left hand. <0213> and <2013> continue in mm. 66 and 67, as do the successive eighth notes. These two bars lead to the right hand's momentary rhythmic victory in m. 68, in which it plays the first and third eighth notes. The left hand regains its rhythmic footing in mm. 70–71, but quickly loses to the right hand in mm. 72–75. The four final bars of Section V, mm. 76–79, give four more instances of right-hand dominance <2013>; while both hands share the strong beats in mm. 76–77, the left hand also plays weak beats in mm. 78–79.

In Section VI, the issue of hand dominance from sections I and V comes again to

Table 5.3 *Hand Positions in Section V (mm. 62–79)*

Meas.	Position		
62a	<0213>	73a	<0213>
62b	<0213>	73b	<0213>
62c	<0213>	73c	<0213>
63a	<0213>	73d	<2013>
63b	<0213>	74a	<2013>
63c	<0213>	74b	<2013>
64	<0213>	74c	<0123>
65a	<0213>	75a	<0123>
65b	<0213>	75b	<0123>
65c	<2013>	75c	<0123>
65d	—	75d	<0123>
66a	<0213>	76a	<0213>
66b	<0213>	76b	<2013>
66c	<2013>	77a	<2013>
66d	—	77b	<2013>
67a	<0213>	78	<2013>
67b	<0213>	79	<2013>
67c	<2013>		
67d	<0213>		
68a	<0213>		
68b	<0123>		
68c	<0213>		
68d	<0213>		
69a	<0213>		
69b	<2013>		
69c	<0213>		
69d	<0213>		
70a	<0213>		
70b	<2013>		
70c	<0213>		
70d	<0213>		
71a	<0213>		
71b	<0213>		
71c	<0213>		
72a	<0213>		
72b	<0123>		
72c	<0213>		

Example 5.5 Registral transfer from cseg <0123> to <0231>

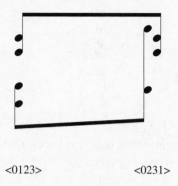

<0123>   <0231>

the fore. However, the left hand is no longer confined to the white-key world it inhabited in Section I; instead, it stations itself mostly on the black keys. Its new pitch domain thus makes possible a significant change in the musical narrative. The right hand's opening dyad, m. 80's D♭3–G♭3, recalls Section I, in which its first dyad was also D♭–G♭. The left hand begins the passage by playing B♭1 and B♭2 for the duration of a half note. The pianist's hands begin in the uncrossed <0123> position; after the left hand strikes the low B♭s in m. 80, the right hand responds with the three dyads in a register clear of the left hand's B♭s.

The relation of the hands, <0123>, is then transformed. In m. 81, the left hand reaches over the right to play the B♭s that lie an octave above its previous B♭ pairing of B♭1–B♭2, while the right hand remains in position, repeating the three dyads it played in m. 80.

Example 5.5 illustrates this registral transfer in contour space. The resulting four-note structure now formed by the hands is <0231>. As Table 5.2 shows, this position is one that did not occur at all in Sections I or V.

Measured according to the model of dominance presented earlier, this particular position, <0231>, is the one in which the left hand's dyad contains the right hand's dyad; it occurs here for the first time in the piece. With this measure, the left hand successfully inverts the right hand's dominance established earlier.

The novel situation of the right hand being immobilized by the left governs mm. 81–85. In m. 82, the left hand moves back to its original pair of B♭s, a move that uncrosses the hands and frees the right hand to ascend from D♭3–G♭3 to the next pair of black keys, E♭3–A♭3. In m. 83 the left hand responds by moving up an octave and a semitone, to C♭3 and C♭4, which again produces the <0231> position. As did mm. 80–81, these bars recall the three bars in which D♭–G♭ also moved up to E♭–A♭.

The next two-bar grouping, mm. 84–85, repeats this two-step gesture of uncrossing followed by enclosing. The left hand's motion constrains the right hand, causing it to reiterate its three-dyad statement from the previous bar while the left hand gains more freedom to move: in m. 85, it leaps up a tenth, from the B♭2–B♭3

Example 5.6 Relationship of the pitches in mm. 88–90, third eighth note beat

octave to D♭3–D♭4, and supplants its half notes with the more active quarter notes of m. 85. This new quarter-note rhythm incites the right hand also to move in quarter notes, as suggested by the diagonal line drawn in the score that joins m. 85's E♭s to the G♭s in m. 86 in the upper staff.

Measure 86 offers a momentary respite for the right hand; the hands are kept separate in the <0123> formation. Then, in m. 87, the left hand backs away from the right hand. Rather than maintaining the pattern of moving up an octave to enclose the right hand, the left moves *down* an octave, to strike B♭0 and B♭1, and the right hand plays its three dyads unimpeded by the left hand. As in m. 83, the left hand draws upon white keys as well as black keys in m. 87, playing D3–G3 followed by D♭3–G♭3. This statement mirrors the right hand's material: it plays a pair of dyads, C4–F4 followed by D♭4–G♭4, simultaneously with the left hand.

But this return to the original <0123> situation does not last long. In m. 88, the right hand continues upon a linear course of ascending octaves. Here it also presents an additional series of dyads of either a major third or perfect fourth that fills in the second eighth-note beat against the right hand's octaves in the upper voice.

After remaining silent on the downbeat of m. 88, the left hand enters again on beat two with A♭3–E♭4–A♭4. The chain of octave plus dividing fifths it plays in mm. 88–90 occupies the second quarter-note beat. In m. 89, it returns to its former task of stating octave B♭s for the duration of a half note while continuing to present this new series of three-note chords built from either a fifth plus a fourth or two fourths.

Measure 88, beat 2, presents a new, seven-note contour situation. The left hand's uppermost note, A♭4, wedges itself midway between the right hand's G♭4 and B♭4, bringing the left thumb over the right thumb; the left hand's E♭4 covers the right thumb's D♭4; and the contour situation shown in Example 5.6 results. This example depicts in contour space the interlocking nature of the pitches on the third eighth notes of mm. 88, 89, and 90. To classify these seven-note pitch configurations, I conflate the right hand's two highest pitches (between which no left-hand pitch is played) into a single contour pitch. If we modify our numerical method for labeling hand positions shown in Figure 5.1 to that shown in Figure 5.2 in order to accommodate six contour pitches, then we can classify the seven-note contour situations in mm. 88–90, beat 3, as <031425>.

As soon as the left hand strikes the three-note sonority on beat 2, which brings it closer toward recapturing its former role of covering the right hand, the right hand emphatically repositions itself. It moves up in m. 88 from D4–G♭4–B♭4–D5 to the octave G♭4–G♭5, which not only shakes it free of the left hand, but in fact reverses its position in relation to it: to play the lower pitch of its new octave, G♭4, the right hand places itself on top of the left hand, which is playing A♭4, so that the right hand now covers the left thumb, resulting in a right-hand dominant <0213> situation.

The right hand's determination to elude the left hand is evident in this gesture, which functions as an *échappée* in contour space rather than in pitch space. It is repeated twice, in mm. 89 and 90. Each time, the same three events take place: (1) on the second eighth note of the bar, the right hand plays the interval of a perfect fourth; (2) on the third eighth note, the left hand plays a three-note group in which its lower two pitches flank the right hand's lowest pitch, its upper two pitches surround the second lowest note played by the right hand, and the left thumb covers the right thumb; and (3) on the fourth eighth note of the bar, the right hand pries itself from under the left hand to play a new dyad, an octave, whose lower note lies between the upper two notes of the left hand's three-note sonority, so that the right hand now covers the left thumb.

Having had the tables turned, the left hand abandons in m. 91 the idea of encroaching into the musical space of the right hand. In mm. 91–92, the hands do not intersect; the closest they come in these two bars is the minor third in m. 92 between the right hand's G♭4 and the left hand's E♭4.

Measure 93 presents for the last time in Section VI an instance of hand crossing. On the first quarter note, the right hand's lower note, C5, appears between the left hand's A♭4 and D5; and on the second quarter note, the right hand's F5 appears between the left hand's D♭5 and G♭5. In both of these cases, a pianist would place the left hand over the right hand in playing the black keys forward on the keyboard.

As a response to being placed underneath the left hand for this brief moment, in mm. 94–100 the right hand darts up to the highest register of the piece, one unencumbered by the left hand. The hands do not cross in these seven bars but move in contrary motion. This passage occurs as the piece builds to m. 98's climactic eight-note chord, played *fff*, which is sustained for three half notes. This chord, which consists of B♭♭3–E♭4–G♭4–C♭5 in the left hand and G♭6–C♭7–E♭7–G♭7 in the right hand, suggests the left hand's ultimate failure: while the right hand has succeeded in clinging to pitch class G♭, the left hand's bass pitch has slipped down one semitone, from B♭3 to B♭♭3; it cannot continue to maintain its grip upon the crucial B♭. Even if the right hand had remained within reach of the left hand, the left hand's inability to remain on B♭ prevents it from regaining its former dominant position.

After a measure-long rest, the final section, Section VII, begins in m. 102. It restates the material from the opening of the piece but at a *presto* tempo. Throughout the section until the last six bars the left hand plays on strong beats

Table 5.4 *Hand positions in Section VII*
(mm. 102–12)

Meas.	Position	Meas.	Position
102a	<0213>	109a	<0213>
102b	<2013>	109b	<0213>
102c	<2013>	109c	<0213>
102d	<0213>	109d	<2013>
103a	<0213>	110a	<0213>
103b	<2013>	110b	<2013>
103c	<2013>	110c	<0213>
103d	<0213>	110d	<0213>
104a	<0213>	111a	<0213>
104b	<2013>	111b	<0213>
104c	<0213>	111c	<0213>
104d	<2013>	111d	<0213>
105a	<2031>	112a	<0123>
105b	<2031>	112b	<0213>
105c	<2031>	112c	<0123>
105d	<0213>		
106a	<0213>		
106b	<2013>		
106c	<0213>		
106d	<2013>		
107a	<0213>		
107b	<0213>		
107c	<0213>		
107d	<2013>		
108a	<0213>		
108b	<2013>		
108c	<0213>		
108d	<2013>		

while the right hand plays on weak beats; unlike Section I, the right hand does not strike any successive eighth notes, and accordingly the left hand remains rhythmically dominant.

Table 5.4 lists the patterns that are formed between each consecutive pair of dyads between the two staves in Section VII. In m. 106, Section VII diverges from the corresponding moment in m. 5; here both hands proceed up by step. As Table 5.4 shows, mm. 107–11 present only <0213> and <2013>, the two right-hand dominant positions that were prevalent in Section I. Beginning in m. 106, both hands clamber up to the top of the keyboard. Significantly, their rush to a higher register culminates with the left hand returning triumphantly to black-key material: in m. 113, it plays B♭5–E♭6–A♭6 while the right hand plays F6–B♭6–E♭7. Because the left hand is once again positioned on black keys and because the right hand's note that crosses the left hand's note falls on a white key (F6), m. 114 ends with one final <0213>; in this position, the *left* hand crosses over the right thumb, recalling mm. 88–90.

The Toccata concludes in mm. 117–20 with the hands withdrawing into separate registers. The hands together play the two six-note chords of the final cadence; the penultimate chord consists of all white-key notes based upon the now familiar principle of the octave divided at the fifth – the left hand plays G2 and G3 with D3 as its interior pitch, and the right hand plays A3 and A4 with E4 as its interior pitch – and the final chord comprises five black-key pitches, F4–Bb4–Eb5 in the right hand and Eb2–Bb2–Eb3 in the left. The piece ends with the hands separating into distinct registers, and thus with an equalizing of their relationship.

In her diary, Crawford described what happened after hearing Bauer play some of her piano preludes, the strange and bewildering experience from which she discovered that their "spirits [had] been friends for years":

I start to go and she kisses me. I kiss her then somehow the subject of Gene comes up. I had told her of Gene before. I say I wonder if I shall ever have intercourse, and that is one question in my mind to be decided.

But, I continue, I have always before argued that one does not need physical intercourse. I have argued that it can become a spiritual thing, coming forth in one's music or one's art.

Sublimation – you are right, you can sublimate, she says. I had a beautiful friend who taught me that. But the physical act can be accomplished in a beautiful way, as a symbol . . . .[27]

In light of Crawford's remarks on the nature of their relationship and Bauer's dedication of her Toccata to Crawford, the work may be heard to give musical expression to a psychological relationship that permits the flow of power from one party to the other and back.

The analytical approach I have introduced in this chapter proposes that the relationship between the pianist's hands in performance can be related to an aspect of the composer's life. The shifting relationship of the hands as measured by which is on top necessitates that one never exclusively controls the other; instead, power is passed between them. Heard in this way, Bauer's Toccata suggests that the act of composing might have provided a woman modernist with the means to fashion "a room of one's own" – not Woolf's physical space, but a psychological one – by giving her both the technical means and the aesthetic freedom to forge an innovative and subtle musical narrative.

[27] RCd-LC, 16 August 1929; SC-LC.

MUSICAL SUBLIMATION IN BAUER'S "CHROMATICON"

> The shift from a man's experiences and personality to its integration into the art work is one of the most fascinating spectacles in creation. Obviously it is not a problem that can be reduced to the precision of a mathematical equation. But we may certainly accept those leads which the artists themselves have given us when they showed how dominant traits in their disposition as well as their inner experiences became part and parcel of their artistic impulse.
>
> –Frederick Dorian, *The Musical Workshop*

> The greatest work of the composer is often sublimation, that is, the deflection of energies, thoughts, occurrences, psychological and physical reactions, into socially constructive or creative channels.
>
> –Marion Bauer

After quoting the above passage from Frederick Dorian's book *The Musical Workshop* in a set of notes for a book she planned to write, Marion Bauer added: "Sometimes composers give us clues when they write about art."[1] Bauer's own writings about music provide a starting point for relating her music and her social beliefs.

Bauer's book *Twentieth Century Music*, first published in 1933, takes a strong pro-modernist stance and a progressive view of modernism, as the following passage articulates:

We might successfully sum up the new music as an attempt to escape the obvious, to avoid time-worn combinations, to elide the unnecessary, to allow the mind to supply implied detail and to break down established boundaries . . .[2]

Bauer urges listeners to confront the "discomfort of unknown territory" and attributes the rejection of modern music to "intolerance and short-sightedness"; she also

---

[1] Frederick Dorian, *The Musical Workshop* (New York: Harper & Bros., 1947), 37. Quoted in Marion Bauer, "Working ideas for *Titans of Music*," n.d., 4 (in MBp-NYU).

[2] MB-TCM, 128. Milton Babbitt, a former student of Bauer at New York University, describes how important Bauer's book *Twentieth Century Music* was to him in the early 1930s, when he was unable to find other books in English giving examples of the twentieth-century music he wished to study. He also recalls that Bauer suggested that he consider studying composition with Edgard Varèse and Roger Sessions. See Duckworth, *Talking Music*, 62, 66.

asserts that listeners would do well to accept modern music, as it would benefit their individual development.[3]

Her beliefs about the organization of society are suggested in *Twentieth Century Music* and in other of her writings. Bauer consistently promoted music by women in her writings and lectures, and recognized the necessity of the category "women composers," co-founding the Society of American Women Composers in 1925 with Amy Beach and eighteen other composers.[4] *Twentieth Century Music* mentions a number of women composers – Ruth Crawford, Louise Talma, Germaine Tailleferre, Ethel Glenn Hier, Rosalie Housman, Miriam Gideon, Ulric Cole, Vivian Fine, Evelyn Berckman, and Dorothy James, among others.[5] Although Bauer does not knead a discussion of their music into the substance of the book, the fact that she includes them at all makes a significant statement about her personal stand on the importance of women's compositional contributions to twentieth-century art music.

An examination of books on twentieth-century music published within thirteen years of Bauer's reveals that *Twentieth Century Music* mentions women composers comparatively frequently: all twenty of Paul Rosenfeld's subjects in *Musical Portraits*, published in 1920, are men;[6] in Rosenfeld's *An Hour with American Music*, published in 1929, women are virtually absent, though he does mention Crawford in passing.[7] Few women are represented in John Tasker Howard's *Our Contemporary Composers*, published in 1941.[8] Its table of contents lists forty-one composers, including only one woman – Marion Bauer. In these publications, approval of compositions by women – as in the 1925 edition of Louis C. Elson's *The History of American Music*, which enthusiastically praises the music of Amy Beach – is the exception rather than the rule.[9]

In her paper "Contemporary Trends in Choral Composition," Bauer pointedly mentions music by several women (Amy Beach, Gena Branscombe, Mary Howe, Mabel Daniels, and Marianne Genet), and in a typescript entitled "American Piano Music," Bauer surveys the music of Beach, Crawford, and Talma.[10] She articulates her viewpoint on the status of women composers more directly in the following statement:

[3] MB-TCM, 4.

[4] Society of American Women Composers file, NYPL; cited in Adrienne Fried Block, *Amy Beach, Passionate Victorian: The Life and Work of an American Composer, 1867–1944* (New York: Oxford University Press, 1998), 246.   [5] MB-TCM, 287–88.

[6] Paul Rosenfeld, *Musical Portraits: Interpretations of Twenty Modern Composers* (New York: Harcourt, Brace and Howe, 1920).   [7] Paul Rosenfeld, *An Hour with American Music* (Philadelphia: J. P. Lippincott, 1929).

[8] John Tasker Howard, *Our Contemporary Composers: American Music in the Twentieth Century* (New York: Thomas Y. Crowell, 1941). One brief section addresses the topic of "women composers."

[9] Louis C. Elson, *The History of American Music* (New York: Macmillan, 1925 [1904]). In the chapter "American Women in Music," he provides an extended discussion of Beach (293–305).

[10] Marion Bauer, "Contemporary Trends in Choral Composition," lecture given for the New York Federation of Music Clubs, Binghamton, NY, 20–23 April 1938; and "American Piano Music," unpublished typescript, n.d., 9; both in MBp-NYU.

My early aspiration was not to listen to the sly remarks of intolerant men regarding women composers . . . if given a reasonable chance for development, an individual talent, regardless of sex, can progress and grow.[11]

Not only did Bauer vigorously advocate for the recognition of women composers, but her many references to modernist music by African American composers and her inclusion of jazz in her accounts of twentieth-century music bespeak the importance she placed on the contributions of black composers and musicians. In her writings from the 1930s, Bauer cited the music of R. Nathaniel Dett, William Grant Still, H. T. Burleigh, Hall Johnson, J. Rosamond Johnson, and Clarence Cameron White, testifying to her belief that African American composers deserved recognition alongside white composers.[12] Of the books on twentieth-century music discussed above, Howard's *Our Contemporary Composers* is notable for mentioning Burleigh, White, Dett, and Still; Paul Rosenfeld promoted the music of Still for several years during the 1920s, giving Still's 1924 *From the Land of Dreams* a favorable review and arranging for a performance of his "Dialect Songs" in 1927. With the publication of *An Hour with American Music* two years later, however, Rosenfeld wrote dismissively of Still's music.[13]

The following recollection by Fredric Stoessel (the son of Albert Stoessel, who founded the Department of Music at New York University) also casts light upon Bauer's social convictions:

Marion Bauer was one of the closest friends I had among my parents' circle. To me she was a boyhood friend, associate of my father's, a gifted composer and author of books on music, a welcome figure at holiday gatherings, and later an inspiring teacher when I was at N.Y.U. . . . [M]y most vivid memory of Marion is at a New England resturant [*sic*] one summer when I drove her back to Peterborough [New Hampshire]. She sat in silence in the car with her negro maid Ella refusing to go in because they would not serve negros [*sic*], while the rest of us, somewhat unchivalrously, munched coffee and a doughnut inside.[14]

Bauer's quiet protest against a policy of segregation recalled in this vignette makes apparent her belief in social equality.[15] Yet the fact that Bauer even employed a

---

[11] Irwin Bazelon, "Woman with a Symphony," *The Baton of Phi Beta Fraternity* 30 (March 1951), 6; quoted in NLS-SPM, 79.   [12] Bauer, "Contemporary Trends in Choral Composition," 11–12; MB-TCM, 323.

[13] Carol J. Oja examines Rosenfeld's changing views of Still and Still's reception within American musical modernist circles more generally, in "'New Music' and the 'New Negro': The Background of William Grant Still's *Afro-American Symphony*," *Black Music Research Journal* 12/2 (Fall 1992), 145–69.

[14] Fredric Stoessel, "In Memoriam Marion Bauer," n.d., MB-NYU.

[15] In her review of a performance of Marc Blitzstein's nine songs to texts by Whitman, published under the title of "A Furious and Outraged Audience, a Debasing Program," *The Musical Leader* 56 (3 January 1929), Bauer described two of the songs, "I Am He" and "Ages and Ages," as "incongruous and debasing" because of their use of a jazz idiom to set the poetry of Whitman (8). In "Reclaiming Walt: Marc Blitzstein's Whitman Settings," *Journal of the American Musicological Society* 48/2 (Summer 1995), 240–71, David Metzer writes: "By dismissing Blitzstein's songs with language employed to denigrate African American music, [Bauer and *New York Times* critic Olin Downes] sought to equate the two and to push the settings onto the 'Other' side of the racial/aesthetic divide, clearing the concert hall, and above all, the revered Whitman from such contamination" (251). Metzer's stern reading of Bauer's review as revealing a desire for musical segregation does not square with the sympathetic attitude to music by black Americans that she exhibits in other of her writings.

black woman as a maid can also be criticized as insensitive to the historically racialized politics of the labor practice. Bauer's objection to the restaurant's refusal to
serve the woman she employed as a maid can be understood to reveal a desire to
challenge racial inequity while accepting a traditional arrangement, or a clashing of
custom with progressive inclinations.[16]

Bauer's wish to establish equality between unequal groups provides the basis for
an analysis of "Chromaticon," the first of her *Four Pieces for Piano*, op. 21. Example
6.1 gives the score.[17]

The ascending triplet of m. 1 is established as the dominant musical element of
"Chromaticon." It undergoes repeated challenge by other triplet figures, and in a
central passage that builds to the climax of the piece, these competing triplets affix
themselves to the ascending dominant triplet. After a struggle, the original trichord
regains its position of authority, a situation that concludes the piece with an uneasy
unity. The primary motive thus successfully maintains its dominance, fighting off
repeated challenges by the other triplets, a narrative that sublimates what Bauer
observed and experienced.

To track this narrative more precisely, I shall identify the various triplet shapes
and their pitch content using two branches of post-tonal theory: contour theory
and set theory. The first triplet of m. 1, D4–F♯4–A♭4, establishes central musical
elements of the piece – its primary contour, contour segment or cseg <012>, and
its pitch-class set, set class 3-8 [026]. It also introduces the central pitch class of the
opening, D.

The left hand begins by playing D4 followed by F♯4, and the right hand com-
pletes the triplet with A♭4. An upward gesture carries D4 to F♯4, and a second
upward gesture carries F♯4 to A♭4. These two gestures comprise a melodic contour
that serves as a fundamental shape in Section I and indeed saturates each of the three
sections of the piece. Section I comprises mm. 1–16; Section II comprises mm.
17–34; and Section III comprises mm. 35–56.

As in Chapters 3 and 4, I shall label a melodic contour by listing its contour
pitches, or cps, in order of occurrence from lowest to highest, using the numbers
from 0 to $n-1$, where n is the cardinality of the pitches in the contour. Figure 6.1
sketches the piece's first triplet as cseg <012>.

In m. 2, the right hand plays a dyad on the last note of each triplet. Because each
note of the dyad is higher than cps 1 and 2, we can regard the dyad as a single
contour pitch, cp 3, and can also label this new type of contour cseg <012>. Figure
6.2 shows <012> with a dyad as its third cp.

With this new method to account for dyads, cseg <012> can be heard throughout mm. 1–2, and, in mm. 3–4, on beats 1 and 3. In mm. 3–4, beats 2 and 4, the
first beat of the triplet is now higher than the second, which are both lower than cp
3 on beat 3; accordingly, these triplets present cseg <102>. Since these two <102>

---

[16] David Mura's essay "Strangers in the Village" examines the practice of non-blacks hiring blacks as nannies, in
Multi-Cultural Literacy: Opening the American Mind, ed. Rick Simonson and Scott Walker (St. Paul, MN:
Graywolf Press, 1988), 135–53.   [17] A bass clef is missing in m. 35, lower staff.

Example 6.1 Bauer, Chromaticon

TO ALMA M. WERTHEIM

FOUR PIANO PIECES

I

CHROMATICON*)

Marion Bauer, Op. 21, № 1

*) *Accidentals apply to individual notes only; they are not effective through the measure*

Example 6.1 (*cont.*)

Example 6.1 (*cont.*)

Figure 6.1 Cseg <012>

Figure 6.2 Cseg <012> with dyad as third cp

contours in mm. 3–4 occur on relatively weak beats, and because beats 1 and 3 are further strengthened by sustained half notes on D3, cseg <012> can be understood as the governing contour for the first four measures of the piece.

In m. 5, the second and fourth triplets require a further adjustment to our model of contour analysis. Here, the first note of the triplet occurs in contour space between the notes of the dyad on the last beat of the triplet. Unlike mm. 2–4, these triplets have *two* ternary contours, one formed with each note of the dyad – that is, in m. 5, beat 2, G4–C4 plus the upper note of the dyad, E5, constitutes one contour, cseg <102>; G4–C4 plus the lower note of the dyad, F4, constitutes a second contour, cseg <201>. Figure 6.3 shows these two contours in m. 5, beat 2.

To summarize the narrative strategy in the first five measures : (1) in m. 1, <012> is asserted as the dominant contour; (2) in m. 2, a dyadic variant on cseg <012> enters; (3) a second contour, <102>, is introduced on the weak beats of mm. 3–4; and (4) in m. 5, a new arrangement of cps introduces csegs <201> and <102> simultaneously. By calculating csegs in this manner, we shall find that cseg <012> is established as the primary contour, after which other types of contours confront it, at first tentatively, and then with greater force.

After cseg <012> has been challenged by two other ternary contours, <102> and <201>, it reaffirms its presence in m. 6 on beats 1, 3, and 4, and then even more decisively in m. 7 with a strand of six additional <012> contours; measure 8 presents two additional <012> contours.

In m. 9, the triplets vigorously attempt to twist away from <012>: each of the contours in m. 9 resists <012>, in contrast to mm. 3–5, where only two of the four contours opposed the dominant contour. The left hand strikes a pitch on each beat that lies in the register between the second and third triplet eighth notes. This results in the succession of triplets whose contours are shown in Figure 6.4.

The chain of four triplets twists quickly back and forth from <102> to <120>.

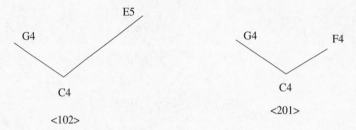

Figure 6.3 Contours in m. 5, beat 2

The left hand's reaching up to G4, in the highest register in which it has played thus far, draws additional attention to the departure from cseg <012>. The restatement of cseg <102>, coupled with the introduction of a new contour, <120>, seizes the listener's attention, as does the quickened rate of change – the contour type changes on every beat in contrast to the prior sustaining of <012> for two and a half measures in mm. 6–8.

Cseg <012> attempts to take command once again in m. 10, but its efforts are checked by the triplets on beats 2, 3, and 4, which form a <201>-<102> cseg hybrid, cseg <201>, and second <201>-<102> hybrid, respectively. Each of the next three measures, mm. 11–13, presents <012> on beat 1, but the contours on the three subsequent beats prevent <012> from spreading through these measures. Just before the section concludes, m. 14 strongly reaffirms cseg <012> in both hands, but in m. 15, the hands veer into opposite directions – the right hand continues to surge upwards while the left hand sinks downwards.

These triplets can be classified according to their pitch-class content as well as their melodic contour. The pitch classes of the first triplet, D–F♯–A♭, make up the primary pitch-class set of the piece, set class 3–8 [026]. Like cseg <012>, this set class dominates the piece and reasserts itself most strongly at the conclusion. The A♭ in m. 1, beat 1, is also the first pitch for another instance of 3–8 [026], A♭–B♭–D, which is formed by the pitches in the uppermost voice in m. 1, on the last triplet eighth notes of beats 1–3. The pitch classes on beat 4 of this measure, B3–D♯4–A4, present a third statement of set class 3–8 [026].

Calculating the set classes of the triplets with dyads reveals additional instances of the prevalent set class – for example, in m. 2, beat 3, set class 3–8 [026] occurs as A♭3–B♭3–D4, including the lower note of the dyad; in m. 2, beat 4, it occurs as G3–B3–C♯4 similarly; and in m. 3, beat 2, it occurs as A♯3 plus the E4–F♯4 dyad.

Unlike cseg <012>, however, set class 3–8 [026] is displaced early in the piece. The second triplet of m. 1, D♭4–F4–B♭4, constitutes set class 3–11 [037]. Using the method of contour labeling described previously which calculates each note of a simultaneous dyad as an individual pitch, a listener will find that [037] suffuses mm. 2–6. To cite some examples, [037] occurs in m. 2, beat 1, as C4–E♭4–G4, including both notes of the dyad; in m. 2, beat 2, as A3–C♯4–E4, including the lower note of the dyad on the third beat of the triplet, and as A3–C♯4–F♯4, including the upper

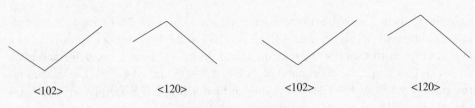

<102>   <120>   <102>   <120>

Figure 6.4 Csegs in m. 9

note of the dyad; in m. 3, beat 1, as D3–A3–E♯4 and as D3–A3–F♯4, including the upper and lower notes of the dyad in turn; in m. 4, beat 4, as B♭3–F4–D♭5 including both notes of the dyad; in m. 5, beat 1, as D3–B3–F♯4–D5; and in m. 6, beat 2, as F♯4–A3–D5, including the upper note of the dyad.

As befits a piece with such a title, chromatic lines serve as its melodic glue, helping the work to cohere while the primary triplet motive faces repeated challenge. By means of chromatic descent in the lowest voice over mm. 1–2, each triplet moves seamlessly to the next, urging the music constantly forward. The first note of each triplet in these bars contributes to a descending chromatic line which links the initial D4 to the G3 in m. 2, beat 4; G will also serve as a secondary pitch-class center for the piece. Chromatic lines pervade other voices as well: in m. 1, the middle voice contains a chromatic line leading from F♯4 to D♯4; this line breaks off to present two pairs of chromatically linked neighbors in m. 2, C4–C♯4 followed by B♭3–B♮3. Pairs of pitches a semitone apart also appear in m. 3 (E♯4–E4 and F4–E4), m. 4 (E♭4–D4–E♭4), and mm. 4–6 (F4–F♯4–F4–F♯4–F4–E4). The four-note chromatic descending lines return in m. 7 with C♯5–C♮5–B4–B♭4 in the bass voice on the first note of each triplet and G5–F♯5–F♮5–E5 in the middle voice on the second eighth note of each triplet.

Set class 3-8 [026] reappears to sound three times in succession in m. 5, beats 3 and 4 (D3–C4–F♯4 and G4–B3–F4) and in m. 6, beat 1 (D3–B♭3–E4). The last of these trichords also presents set class 3–4 [015] as D3–B♭3–E♭5, including the upper note of the dyad. [015] is played again two beats later, on beat 3, as an ascending perfect fifth plus ascending semitone, G3–D4–E♭4.

Set class 3–4 [015] begins to overtake set class 3–8 [026] smoothly while asserting its importance in the piece, returning in m. 8 as F3–C4–D♭4, a whole step lower than in m. 6, beat 3. In m. 9, beat 1, it reappears as F5–D♭5–C6 at the peak of a crescendo. A second string of three [026] triplets returns in m. 9, on the next three beats (E5–A♭5–B♭4; C5–A♭4–G♭5; and B4–F5–G4). All the pitches of the set class are now free-standing rather than part of a harmonic dyad. This reassertion of set class 3–8 [026] attempts to bring the music back to its original course, but in vain: in m. 10, [015] decisively puts the three [026] triplets in their place, with its *sforzando* C4–G4–A♭4 on beat 1 (including the lower note of the dyad in beat 1), followed by B4–G4–C5 on beats 2 and 4 (including the upper notes of the dyads), and m. 11's four successive statements of [015] (again including the upper notes of the dyads).

In m. 13, beat 3, [026] again reasserts itself via a C5–Gb4–Bb4 triplet, only to be answered by two [015]s on beat 4 (F4–Gb4–Bb4 and F4–Gb4–Db5). [026] makes a *forte* attempt in this section to regain control: in m. 14, beat 1, the left hand plays Ab3–C3–Gb4 while the right hand plays E4–Ab4–D5 and Ab4–Bb4/D5; on beat 2, the right hand plays F4–Cb5–Db5; and on beat 4, the left hand plays F3–Eb4–B4 (the reader will find others); but these instances of [026] are quickly swallowed up in the fierce drive toward the *fff* in m. 16.

The duties of each hand in mm. 15–16 are demarcated not only by contour, but also by the pitch-class content of the trichords. In mm. 15–16, the left hand plays a perfect fifth plus a minor or major sixth creating five [037] trichords. In m. 15, beat 1, the right hand plays a simultaneity built of two perfect fifths with a bass pitch of G4, creating a member of set class 3-9 [027]; on beat 2 a second simultaneity transposes the first simultaneity up a whole step; on beat 3 the right hand plays a minor sixth plus augmented fourth with a bass pitch of C5, giving a member of set class 3-8 [026]; and on beat 4 it plays another pair of stacked perfect fifths, D5–A5–E6, which is then transposed up a whole step in m. 16, beat 2, to E5–B5–F♯6. On the last three beats of m. 16, [026] is grandly reasserted, *fff*, as C2–E3–F♯6, within the larger six-note chord made up of C2–G2–E3 in the left hand and E5–B5–F♯6 in the right hand. The cadential chords are rolled in both hands in m. 16, beat 2 for a quarter note, *molto ritardando*, and then a second time for a half note; the fermata over the barline encourages the performer to linger over this moment. (The cadence to Section I foreshadows the return of the opening [026] sonority, D–F♯–Ab, in mm. 53–54, which will firmly declare [026] as the principal trichord.)

As if the climax of Section I had not even occurred, Section II begins serenely in m. 17 with the simple pair of <012> csegs heard once before, in m. 6. Having met much resistance in Section I, cseg <012> attempts to reassert its position at the outset of Section II, but is immediately foiled: on beat 3, the right hand plays a C♯ quarter note, and as a result, the left hand plays its triplet under a sustained melodic pitch, which generates the cseg <201> over <012>. Figure 6.5 shows this pair of contours.

Cseg <012> continues to be obstructed by these tied upper-voice quarter notes through m. 26. The basic strategy in the opening of this section is for a second cseg – in this case <201> – to attach itself to cseg <012> so that <012> must share the musical space with an alternate contour, and its power is thus diminished.

In the domain of pitch, G replaces D as the primary pitch-class center at the opening of Section II: it is the first pitch of the trichord in m. 17 and is struck eight times as a pedal in mm. 17–18 and 22–23. Set class 3–4 [015] continues to dominate, opening this section with three statements of G3–D4–Eb4 in the left hand. In the right hand, set class 3–11 [037] is heard as F♯4–A4–D5 three times in mm. 17–18 and as F4–Ab4–C5 in m. 18, beat 4. The left hand plays set class 3–8 [026] in the triplets of m. 19, beat 1 (D♯3–A3–B3) with the right hand's reinforcing of B; in m. 21, beat 1 (Ab2–D3–Gb3) with the right hand again doubling the highest pitch; and in m. 24 (D♯3–A3–B3) with another doubling. Yet these moments are fleeting

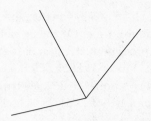

Figure 6.5 Csegs <210> and <012>

and isolated, preceding melodic trichords with three successive pitches that belong to set classes 3–7 [025], 3–3 [014], and 3–11 [037] in mm. 19 and 24, 3–10 [036] and 3–12 [048] in m. 21.

Set class 3–8 [026] also occurs in this section, but never as a melodic trichord: for example, in m. 20, beat 1, it sounds as A2 and D♯3 in the left hand and G4 in the right hand; in m. 21, beat 3, as D2 and A♭2 in the left hand and F♭4 in the right; in m. 25, beat 1, as G♭3 and B♭3 in the left hand and C4 in the right; and in m. 25, beat 4, as E♭4, G4, and A4 in the right hand. The more disguised form of these statements, as compared to the direct statements of [015] and [037], bespeaks the diminished capacity of [026].

The uppermost melodic line of m. 18 begins a gradual descent from F5 to land gently, *molto rallentando*, in m. 23, beat 3, on C4. It begins to ascend again in m. 24. This process of gradual descent and ascent is repeated, with turning points in mm. 26–27 and mm. 28–29. Measure 27's duple rhythm, played *forte*, provides a rhythmic transition from the continuous triplet texture into the quarter-note pulse of mm. 28–30.

In m. 28, the left hand presents a series of four harmonies consisting of a perfect fifth crowned by a perfect fourth. The first of these, F2–C3–F3, descends a whole step to E♭2–B♭2–E♭3 on beat 2, descends another whole step to D♭2–A♭2–D♭3 on beat 3, and then descends a minor third on beat 4, arriving on B♭1–F2–B♭2. This four-chord series is used in the two subsequent measures, mm. 29 and 30, and functions as a brief ostinato.

The right hand's first trichord of m. 28, G♭3–B♭3–F4, is a member of the familiar set class 3–4 [015], which destabilized [026] in previous passages. The right hand also plays trichords belonging to set classes 3–5 [016] and 3–7 [025] in mm. 28–30 – [016] in m. 28, beat 4, and in m. 30, beat 1; [025] in m. 28, beat 2, and in m. 29, beat 4 – which further destabilizes [026]. The left hand's sustained B♭1–F2–B♭2 simultaneity in mm. 30–32 provides a harmonic cushion for the right hand's dramatic **sƒƒƒ** [016] triplet in m. 31, beat 1 C7–G6–D♭6, presented in a decisive <210> contour. Of the five triplets in m. 31 and m. 32, beat 1, four also belong to [016] – only that in m. 31, beat 4, belongs to another set class, 3–9 [027].

Beginning in m. 32, the situation swiftly changes. Set class 3–8 [026] reclaims the passage on beats 2 and 4 as an <012> cseg, G4–B4–D♭5 and E4–G♯4–D5, respectively, and returns in mm. 33–34, which lead directly to Section III: m. 33 presents

E♭4–G4–A5 twice, on beats 1 and 3 of a 3/4 meter, and m. 34 presents this trichord again on beats 2 and 4 in common time. Of the eleven beats of mm. 32–34, only four are non-[026] trichords: [024] in m. 32, beat 3; [048] in m. 33, beat 2; [016] in m. 34, beat 1; and [048] in m. 34, beat 3. They fail to prevent the return to power of [026] in m. 35, just as the only two non-<012> cseg triplets – <210> in m. 32, beat 1, and m. 34, beat 1 – cannot stave off <012>, which returns with a vengeance (nine times out of eleven in mm. 32–34).

The last four bars of Section II, mm. 31–34, display in condensed form the central conflict of the contour narrative: in m. 31, beat 3, cseg <012> fights to maintain its position, but is strongly countered by cseg <210> on the next two beats. Cseg <210> is, in turn, overcome by the three <012> csegs that fill out m. 32. At the same time, set class 3-8 [026] reemerges, trumpeting its arrival in m. 32, beats 2 and 4. The trichordal types in m. 33, beats 1 and 3, and m. 34, beats 2 and 4, draw the music back in m. 35 to its starting point, the initial D4–F♯4–A♭4 triplet, *tempo primo*. The combination of set class 3-8 [026] and the return of <012> in mm. 31–34 fortifies the return in m. 35 of the original D–F♯–A♭ triplet figure and cseg <012>'s former dominance.

In the third and final section of the piece, the conflict between cseg <012> and other triplet contours is revisited. Measures 35–37 restate mm. 1–3, and the music turns a corner in m. 38, beat 3, to depart from section I. The left hand plays D3–B♭3, which the right hand answers with the harmonic dyad E4–E♭5, rather than D3–A3 followed by E♭4–D5 as in m. 4. Set class 3-8 [026] is present as D3–B♭3–E4 with the lower note of the dyad; Section I, in contrast, produced set class 3-5 [016] at the corresponding point, as D3–A3–E♭4 in m. 4. Measure 39 then repeats all but the last triplet eighth note of m. 17, substituting C5 for D5.

As in the opening three measures, set class 3-8 [026] saturates mm. 35–37. It returns again in m. 41, beat 1, as D♭3–G3–A3; in m. 43, beat 1, as F♯2–C3–E3; in m. 43, beat 3, as C2–G♭2 of the left hand and D4 of the right hand; and in m. 43, beat 4, as C4–G♭3–B♭3.

The D♭5 in the uppermost voice of m. 45 initiates the ascending chromatic line that leads into the climax of the piece. The climax contains the final struggle between the dominant <012> cseg and the csegs that attempt to displace it. From the starting point of D♭5 in m. 45, the line creeps up by semitone to B♭5 in m. 47, and then, stretching up by whole step, rises to C6 and lands on D6, a pitch that it repeats five times, through m. 49.

Beginning in m. 45 and continuing through m. 48, multiple contours simultaneously intertwine. In m. 46, beats 3 and 4, a third pitch is struck in the left hand along with the right hand's dyad. One way to analyze the contour for these triplets is to extend the approach developed for dyads to three-note simultaneities, calculating csegs for each three-note melodic contour by using each note of the three-note simultaneity in turn.

Figures 6.6a and 6.6b illustrate this method for m. 46, beat 3. They show that for each ternary contour grouping, four distinct contours, <021>, <012>, <210>,

Figure 6.6 Csegs for a triplet containing a three–note simultaneity, mm. 46–47

and <120>, result from the three possible contour paths that travel through each pitch of the trichord simultaneity in turn.

In Figure 6.6a, we can calculate csegs <012>, <012>, and <021> by grouping the first beat of the triplet with its second and third beats. In Figure 6.6b, we can calculate csegs <120>, <120>, and <210> by grouping the triplet's second and third beats with the first beat of the subsequent triplet.

These groupings for m. 46, beat 3, through m. 47, beat 1, are plausible for the following reason: because triplet beats 1, 2, and 3 have been grouped earlier in the piece, one's ear is immediately drawn to this rhythmic grouping. Triplet beat 2 asserts itself as an alternative starting point because of the upper voice's chromatic ascent and the gradual thickening of the texture on the second note of each triplet – the passage begins with two notes that are struck in mm. 45–46, increases to three notes in mm. 46–47, to four notes in mm. 47–48, and culminates in the five-note texture of m. 49.

Figure 6.7 shows the contours of the ternary groupings in mm. 47–48 that contain four-note simultaneities. Like Figure 6.6, Figures 6.7a and 6.7b show two sets of csegs. Figure 6.7a depicts the csegs that begin on the beat – for example, in m. 47, beat 2, the csegs shown start with G3, then travel through D4, B♭4, C5, and B♭5 in turn as the middle pitch, and end with F♭5–A♭5.[18] Figure 6.7b depicts the csegs that begin on the second beat of the triplet – for example, in m. 47, beat 2, the csegs start with D4, B♭4, C5, and B♭5 in turn as the first cp, proceed to F♭5–A♭5 as the second cp, and complete the cseg with F♯3 as the third cp.

As a comparison of Figures 6.6 and 6.7 shows, the same pairs of contours as produced by the ternary groupings result: <021> and <012>, and <210> and <120>. Heard in mm. 46–48, these four contours dissipate the force of the dominant cseg <012>. These measures contain the most successful effort yet in the piece so far to displace the dominant contour from its position of power.

To hear the four contours in this passage more readily, a listener can use m. 45, a bar that contains csegs <021> and <210>, as preparation for the <021> and <210> csegs in the outer voices of the subsequent three bars. By further conceiving

---

[18] As in m. 2, a dyad is considered to constitute a single contour pitch if no other cp in the cseg is positioned between the notes of the dyad – thus for m. 47, beat 2, F♭5/A♭5 constitutes a single cp.

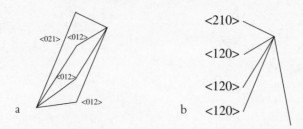

Figure 6.7 Csegs for a triplet containing a four-note simultaneity, mm. 47–48

of mm. 46–48 as having a three- and four-part texture, a listener will be able to separate the melodic note from the inner notes of the triplet's second eighth note. The
pianist can further bring out the contour formed by the inner notes by deemphasiz-
ing the upper line, which is already quite audible from its ascending chromatic
motion.

The climax's powerful effect, created by its increased dynamic and tempo,
upward registral sweep, and thickened texture, is intensified when heard within the
context of contour. Contained here is the composition's most crucial struggle,
between the formerly authoritative <012>, heard in the bass voice of m. 46, beat 3,
though m. 48, beat 4, and the three competing contours, <021>, <210>, and
<120>.

Like its cseg structure, the pitch content in this passage is also diverse. In m. 47,
beat 4, the pitches cease moving outward; they are locked into place in m. 48, and
are struck one last time as a simultaneity, *fortissimo*, in m. 49. Table 6.1 identifies the
set classes of the ternary contour groupings in m. 48.

Trichord types in Table 6.1 are calculated using the pitch class of the first triplet
eighth note (F); each of the four pitch classes of the tetrachord on the second triplet
eighth note (D♯, A, C, and D); and each pitch of the harmonic dyad (G and B) on
the third eighth note. For example, the first trichord listed in Table 6.1 is F–D–B,
pitch classes which occur on the downbeat, as the highest cp of the tetrachord on
the second triplet eighth note, and as the higher cp of the dyad on the third triplet
eighth note.

As Table 6.1 shows, of the eight trichords that can be calculated for this cluster of
pitches, two belong to set class 3-8 [026]. The remaining six trichords belong to
five additional set classes. The climax of the piece thus presents the original domi-
nating element as only one participant among many in a complex of ternary trichords.

The uppermost line, which had been steadily ascending from D♭5 in m. 45, stops
on D6, the pitch-class center introduced in m. 1. In m. 47, beat 4, through m. 49,
the left hand strikes three pitch classes, F, D♯, and A, which belong to the primary
trichord type that began the piece, set class 3-8 [026].

In m. 50, the right hand plays a trichord that immediately begins to ascend to the
highest register of the piece, each bar marking off an <012> contour, over three
quarter notes in a triple meter. In contrast, the left hand strikes a trichord in m. 50

Table 6.1 *Ternary set classes in m. 48*

Set class with B	Forte name	Prime form
F–D–B	3–10	[036]
F–C–B	3–5	[016]
F–A–B	3–8	[026]
F–D♯–B	3–8	[026]
Set class with G		
F–D–G	3–7	[025]
F–C–G	3–9	[027]
F–A–G	3–6	[024]
F–D♯–G	3–6	[024]

that descends in a series of <210> contours but, unlike Section I, rolls each chord from low to high as a rapid <012> gesture. The left hand's beat-to-beat <012> csegs against its measure-to-measure <210> csegs creates a conflict between these two contours one final time, as does the left hand's <210> descent against the right hand's <012> ascent.

Like the previous two sections, Section III closes with a string of six-note chords, three notes to a hand, which move out in contrary motion to the climactic *fff* chord in m. 54. The trichord content of the final closing chordal passage is similar to Section I's: from m. 50, beat 1, through m. 52, beat 2, the left hand plays a series of harmonies composed of a perfect fifth plus minor or major sixth, which are members of set class 3-11 [037]. Measure 52, beat 3, and m. 53, beat 1, present members of set class 3-9 [027], the only non-[037] chords in the left hand's quarter-note passage thus far. Another [037] is played in m. 53, beat 2. The right hand's final stretch to the cadence also begins in m. 50, beats 1 and 2 with C4–G4–D5 and D4–A4–E5, the sonority familiar from m. 15 of two perfect fifths. As in Section I, set class 3-8 [026] interrupts the [027] sequence on the third simultaneity with a minor sixth topped by a in m. 50, beat 3, with F4–D♭5–G5.

[026] returns with force: in m. 51, the right hand's two [027]s on beats 1 and 2 are tailed by a [026] on beat 3, C5–A♭5–D6; in m. 52, the [027] on beat 1, D5–A5–E6, is followed by a [026] on beat 2, F5–D♭6–G6; and in m. 53, [026] opens and closes the measure as C6–A♭6–D7 on beat 1 in the right hand, and as D3–A♭3–F♯4 on beat 3 in the left hand, reinforced by the right hand's F♯6, A♭6, and F♯7.

A tripled D closes the work in mm. 55–56, sealing the piece with the same pitch-class center with which it began. The conclusion thus folds the work back to its beginning, rather than escaping to a new pitch world or to an alternative set of contours – consequently, the possibility of overturning the musical world of the beginning dissolves.

This analysis has identified in "Chromaticon" a primary idea that undergoes challenge, is nearly overturned, is repositioned within a complex of contours and trichords, and then reinstates itself, in order to suggest that Bauer's music and her social beliefs may usefully be linked. This narrative of challenge and reinstatement is, of course, the basic tale of a great many compositions, tonal as well as post-tonal. I am not arguing, however, that this piece's narrative is unique. Rather, I wish to suggest that a possible relationship between Bauer's subjectivity and this piece exists. Her writings and actions recognized domination of one group by another and insist on inclusion of various kinds. I believe that this insistence may have been translated or sublimated into music.

By compelling a dominant musical element to relinquish its position of authority, "Chromaticon" can be heard to give musical expression to Bauer's interest in altering social situations in which one group is elevated over others. By ultimately reasserting the primary figure and reiterating a tonal center, "Chromaticon" stands not as a utopian musical narrative that realizes Bauer's ideal vision of society, but rather as one that mirrors a reality she might have more commonly experienced.

7

"A WOMAN'S WAY OF RESPONDING TO THE WORLD": MIRIAM GIDEON'S "NIGHT IS MY SISTER"

In a 1970 interview for *Dimensions in American Judaism*, Miriam Gideon was asked if she objected to the term "Jewish composer." She responded:

I don't object very much. In fact, I can see where it might prove to be of utmost importance to a certain type of composer as a form of symbolic reference. But if I am to be honest I would have to say that I do usually associate it with a kind of singling out – again like the term "woman composer" and as such implies in my mind, at least, some limitation.[1]

A decade later, in an interview with the *Baltimore Sun*, Gideon remarked that "for me to talk about the fact that women are discriminated against is unnecessary. They are and have been. But really, I didn't even know I was a woman composer until the movement in the 1960s."[2] When asked about being a woman composer, Gideon characteristically gave this response, and it has been widely circulated.

When invited to address the topic of "women composers" for a special issue of *Perspectives of New Music* in 1981–82, she submitted a statement which began with a version of her remark from the *Baltimore Sun* interview about having first learned she was a "woman composer" in the 1960s.[3] She repeated this comment in an interview with the *New York Times* in 1986, and the caption to an accompanying photograph of Gideon and Louise Talma reads "Miriam Gideon and Louise Talma, both celebrating 80th birthdays this month, still like writing music as much as ever but disdain the label 'woman composer.'"[4] Gideon's obituary in the *New York Times* in 1996 further solidified the public image she cultivated as a person uncomfortable with the label of "woman composer" when it reprinted the same comment, as did an article published later that year in the *Washington Post*.[5] And in his memorial tribute to Gideon delivered at the American Academy and Institute of Arts and Letters the year of her death, George Perle repeated the statement. After reminding his audience that Gideon was the first woman commissioned by a synagogue to

[1] Albert Weisser, "An Interview with Miriam Gideon," *Dimensions in American Judaism* 4/3 (Spring 1970), 39–40.
[2] Lesley Valdes, "Miriam Gideon among Most Honored," *Baltimore Sun*, 27 September 1981, D9.
[3] Miriam Gideon, Response to questionnaire from Elaine Barkin sent to women composers, *Perspectives of New Music* 20/1–2 (1981–82), 301.
[4] Tim Page, "Gideon and Talma at 80 – Composers and Neighbors," *New York Times*, 19 October 1986, H23.
[5] Allan Kozinn, "Miriam Gideon, 89, a Composer of Vocal and Orchestral Music," *New York Times*, 20 June 1996, D21; Tim Page, "Two Lives in Harmony: The Parallel Paths of Trailblazers Miriam Gideon and Louise Talma," *Washington Post*, 25 August 1996, G02.

compose a Sabbath service and the second woman composer to be elected to membership in the Academy, he added that "feminism, however, was not on her agenda."[6]

Because of these published remarks, Gideon has been understood to be largely unsympathetic to the category of "women composers." She also frequently made known her belief that concerts, broadcasts, and recordings should not be devoted only to music by women:

I think there's just one way that [women composers] *shouldn't* [organize], and that is by designing programs of all women's music. Nothing can convince me otherwise because I know what happens in my own case. I find myself unable to be judged as I want to be judged. We like to think of ourselves as *composers*, at least I like to think I am, and I'm sure that all women composers, I guess I would have to say, want to be judged as *composers*, not as *women* composers.[7]

According to Lucille Field Goodman, one of Gideon's former students at Brooklyn College, Gideon considered herself "a composer who happened to be a woman."[8] Goodman recalls that when she programmed Gideon's works on a concert of music by women composers, Gideon became quite angry.[9] Alexander Ewen, a grandson of Gideon's husband Frederic Ewen, also remembers Gideon's resistance to the label of "woman composer."[10]

Yet being a woman composer was not as irrelevant an issue to Gideon as has been suggested in the comments she made and in publications about her. Journals in which she recorded her thoughts, dreams, and events in her life reveal a private self that has not emerged in published writings about her. In contrast to the public persona she projected, of an independent composer who rejected the designation "woman composer" as a relevant rubric, in these journals Gideon in fact identified herself as a "woman composer."

In one entry, she observes that "I have a double image of myself: masc. & fem. – the masc. from adolescent assoc. – from my profession as woman composer (supposedly "unfeminine" – like mother's interest in teaching at that era)."[11] Because she recorded in several entries that she was considering the possibility of having children with Frederic Ewen, whom she met in the 1940s when both were on the faculty of Brooklyn College and whom she married in 1949, these writings probably date from the 1940s or the early 1950s at the latest – well before the women's

---

[6] George Perle, "A Tribute to Miriam Gideon," memorial statement read at the American Academy and Institute of Arts and Letters, 1996, typescript of remarks, 3. Gideon was commissioned by the Temple in Cleveland, Ohio to compose *Sacred Service* for Sabbath morning (1971) and by the Park Avenue Synagogue in New York City to write *Shirat Miriam L'Shabbat* for Sabbath evening (1974). See LePage, "Miriam Gideon," 130. The first woman composer to be inducted into the American Academy was Louise Talma, who became a member in 1974.

[7] Quoted in Ardito, "Miriam Gideon," 213. Gideon repeated versions of these remarks about the necessity to program music by women alongside music by men in LePage, "Miriam Gideon," 123, and Rosenberg and Rosenberg, "Miriam Gideon," 68.

[8] Telephone interview with Lucille Field Goodman, 21 December 1999.   [9] *Ibid.*

[10] Interview with Alexander Ewen, 17 December 1999.   [11] MGj-NYPL.

movement of the 1960s, the decade she reported first learning that she was a woman composer.

Gideon's journals rewrite the dominant image that has been established of her as an assured and successful artist who wholeheartedly rejects the category of "women composers" into that of a woman uncertain of her talent who contemplates her status as a female composer. In another journal entry – perhaps prompted by reading Freud's *Leonardo da Vinci and a Memory of his Childhood* – she writes: "Homosexuality equated with sacrifice (self destr.) thru art – do I feel that as a women [*sic*] composer there is a dest. element (as in Mme. Curie?)"[12] These writings contain her innermost thoughts – about tensions between her parents; about her often competitive relationship with her older sister, Judith Gideon; about her sympathies with her mother's struggles as a homemaker and mother – and a self-portrait surfaces of a woman not on equal professional footing with men, having successfully dodged the many barriers posed to female composers, but of a composer haunted by the self-questioning that has plagued many women composers, artists, and writers for centuries.[13]

In the 1960s, Gideon began to provide information about her professional activities to the composers' organization Broadcast Music, Inc. (BMI), of which she was a member. Her correspondence to BMI frequently highlighted her accomplishments specifically as a *woman* composer: in 1963, she noted that her scores, programs, photographs, and biographical sketches, along with materials of nine other composers whom she identified as "American women composers," were displayed at the New York Public Library in recognition of the seventy-fifth anniversaries of the International Council of Women and the National Council of Women in the United States;[14] after remarking in 1978 that a composer's brochure about her had still not been issued, she indignantly asked: "Isn't it about time that the only woman composer in BMI who has been elected to the American Academy and Institute of

---

[12] MGj-NYPL. In *Leonardo da Vinci and a Memory of his Childhood*, ed. James Strachey, trans. Alan Tyson (New York: W. W. Norton, 1964 [1910]), Freud argues that Leonardo sublimated his libido into art and scientific research rather than into relationships with other men: "A man who has won his way to a state of knowledge cannot properly be said to love and hate; he remains beyond love and hatred. He has investigated instead of loving. And that is perhaps why Leonardo's life was so much poorer in love than that of other great men, and of other artists" (23). Gideon quoted passages from Freud's essay for a paper that she authored in January 1945 entitled "Freudianism and the Arts," written for Philosophy 43 (143), Columbia University, (MGp-NYPL).

[13] Women including Fanny Mendelssohn Hensel and Clara Schumann wrote poignantly of their lack of confidence in their abilities as composers, doubts that can be attributed to cultural expectations of women. Clara Schumann wrote in a November 1839 diary entry: "I once thought that I possessed creative talent, but I have given up this idea; a woman must not desire to compose – not one has been able to do it, and why should I expect to? It would be arrogance, though indeed, my Father led me into it in earlier days." Quoted in Berthold Litzmann, *Clara Schumann: An Artist's Life, Based on Material Found in Diaries and Letters*, vol. 1, trans. Grace E. Hadow (New York: Da Capo Press, 1979), 259. See also Fanny Mendelssohn Hensel, letter of 24 November 1843, quoted in Eva Weissweiler, *Fanny Mendelssohn: Ein Portrait in Briefen* (Frankfurt am Main: Ullstein Taschenbuch, 1985), 154. Marcia J. Citron explores this issue of women composers' self-image in *Gender and the Musical Canon*, see particularly 44–79. For reactions by twentieth-century women composers to Elaine Barkin's questionnaire about being a woman composer, see "In response," *Perspectives of New Music* 20, 1/2 (1981–82), 288–330, particularly the response from "Anonymous" (294).

[14] Letter from Gideon to BMI News, 5 October 1963; in MGf-BMI.

Arts and Letters should have a brochure?"[15] That year she also noted that her elec-
tion to the American Academy was to a body whose membership numbered 250,
with only 39 composers, "2 of which are women."[16] Her notes for a 1983 recording
demonstrate that she believed it important to identify the "first woman" of a particular accomplishment: she wrote that Anne Bradstreet's Prologue to *The Tenth Muse*,
which she used as the text for the prologue to her 1981 song cycle *Spirit Above the
Dust*, "states with elegant irony [Bradstreet's] creed of woman's independence"; she
also noted that Bradstreet was the "first American woman poet to be published."[17]
Moreover, after acknowledging that she has allowed her music to be performed on
programs that presented only music by women, Gideon mused: "I have certainly
sometimes contradicted my own belief about all of this."[18]

The multifaceted nature of Gideon's stance on how to negotiate her identity as a
woman composer is further reflected in a remark she made in 1979:

It can't be denied . . . that women have suffered from less attention and recognition as composers. I never thought so in the past. For years people would ask me about the hardships of
being a woman composer, and I'd tell them, "*I've* never suffered from that. *I've* always had
my fair share of recognition." Now I realize that the kind of recognition we don't get is
something we very often don't know about. And since serving on many committees and
juries, I've come to sense that there is a subtle discrimination against women. It's almost
unconscious, but I've recognized it even in myself. When I'm being very honest, trying to
nab my prejudices as I come across them, I'm aware of a tendency to be more sceptical
about a woman composer than a man. Now if *I* feel that way, surely my male colleagues do,
too.[19]

In an interview published four years later, she again mentioned an "invidious attitude" on the part of competition judges and grant award committees, acknowledging bias against women "even in myself" when serving on juries.[20]

Gideon experienced great difficulty herself in obtaining a major fellowship or
composition prize. After a promising start to her career when she received the
Ernest Bloch Award in 1947 for her choral composition *How Goodly Are Thy Tents*
(Psalm 84), the major awards and fellowships in composition eluded her.[21] Milton
Babbitt wonders why "she never got a Guggenheim or the conventional breaks so
many of the rest of us got."[22]

---

[15] Letter to James (Roy), BMI, 25 March 1978; in MGf-BMI. When asked in 1991 about being the second
woman composer to be inducted into the American Academy, Gideon said, "I never thought about it that way"
(Ardito, "Miriam Gideon," 203).

[16] "Miriam Gideon: recent activities, events, etc.," April 1978; in MGf-BMI.

[17] Miriam Gideon, liner notes to *Spirit Above the Dust*, CRI SD 493, 1983; repr. in Miriam Gideon, *Music for Voice
and Ensemble*, CRI 782, 1998. Bradstreet's Prologue to *The Tenth Muse* is included in *The Complete Works of Anne
Bradstreet*, ed. Joseph R. McElrath, Jr., and Allan P. Robb (Boston: Twayne, 1981 [1650]), 6.

[18] Ardito, "Miriam Gideon," 213.   [19] Rosenberg and Rosenberg, "Miriam Gideon," 68.

[20] LePage, "Miriam Gideon," 125.

[21] The annual Bloch Award was instituted by the United Temple Chorus to stimulate Jewish composition for
female and mixed chorus. See Abraham W. Binder, *The Jewish Music Movement in America* (New York: Jewish
Music Council of the National Jewish Welfare Board, 1975 [1963]), 9.

[22] Valdes, "Miriam Gideon Among Most Honored," D9.

I never understood that. Some of us were offensive to the people who ran the Guggenheims . . . They ran it, they never pretended not to. They ran everything in those days. They ran the Guggenheims, they ran the American Academy . . . The person I couldn't understand [not receiving a fellowship] was Miriam. Here is a sweet woman, her music obviously couldn't have offended anybody, and obviously it was very well written and very serious music – she was constantly turned down. Now if somebody wanted to say it was feminism, I mean, I have no doubt, it might have been at one time . . . I never understood why Miriam didn't get it. I never figured out what they had against her. There was something there somewhere.[23]

In response to a query about whether her career was hindered because of her sex, Babbitt said, "There's no question that in some ways she and other women have been hurt by this. Certainly her career was complicated by being a woman."[24]

In a 1970 interview, Gideon made the striking claim that gender difference may be imprinted on the music of women composers: "I strongly believe a woman composer can have something special to say, in that there is a very particular woman's way of responding to the world – and this is in some basic way quite different and yet no less important than a man's."[25]

As well as demonstrating that her feelings about being a woman composer were far from settled, Gideon's journals provided a site in which she could sort out her thoughts about a number of difficult family issues, including frank assessments of the struggles that her mother, the former Henrietta Shoninger, faced. Gideon's mother worked as an elementary school teacher at the turn of the century, a profession that was "considered unfeminine in that era" according to Gideon;[26] she stopped teaching shortly before marrying Abram Gideon, who supported the family, first as a professor of philosophy at State Teachers College in Greeley, Colorado, and then at the University of Wyoming and the University of California.[27] Their daughter observed:

Parents' relationship – marriage – seemed factually correct: children, devotion, etc. – yet may have covered up a great deal . . . She cooked & sewed, and taught us both [Miriam and her sister Judith], but I never felt prettily dressed – all this a chore. Mother itemized her life (children, household duties, etc.) yet did not have surge of feeling to carry it all along . . . Facade of ideal marriage with actual factors that were not is very confusing climate to be brought up in.[28]

In writing critically of her mother's domestic duties, duties that as a woman she was routinely expected to shoulder in the early twentieth century, Gideon recognized

---

[23] Interview with Milton Babbitt, 4 October 1997.

[24] Valdes, "Miriam Gideon Among Most Honored," D1. One award that Gideon did receive, from the National Federation of Music Clubs for *The Seasons of Time*, was earmarked for women composers and she received it late in her career, when she was 63. See Marion Morrey Richter, "1970 NFMC [National Federation of Music Clubs] 'Parade' Concert in New York, *National Federation of Music Clubs Magazine* (Spring 1970), 13.

[25] Weisser, "An Interview with Miriam Gideon," 39. Gideon also included this sentence in her *Perspectives of New Music* statement (Gideon, "Response," 301).   [26] MGj-NYPL.

[27] LePage, "Miriam Gideon," 118; Miriam Gideon, "Miriam Gideon" (Biographical statement for press release), n.d., in MGf-BMI.   [28] MGj-NYPL.

the ways that traditional gender roles constricted her mother's life and left her profoundly unfulfilled.

Dream of mother – leaving her house of horror – also of her pale, sick face . . . Dream shows sequence in their relationship: romantic, German, flowery – then sickness & horror – then flattened into food, housekeeping trivia.[29]

Witnessing her mother's unhappiness in performing duties traditionally designated as "women's work" might have been a factor that influenced Gideon to seek a career that she considered masculine. In a journal entry, she reflects that her mother was "probably anti-feminine" and speculates that her mother "wished to obliterate my femininity," but a few lines later, she writes that "my mother wished me to be feminine as she was not."[30] Although Gideon initially intended to pursue certification from New York University that would enable her to secure a teaching position in the public school system, she did not like her courses in education, and turned instead to composition.[31] Perhaps in order to reconcile her competing desires to have both "a career and life," as Ruth Crawford articulated the choice,[32] Gideon became a composer, professor, and wife, but not a mother – instead, according to Lucille Field Goodman, she "considered Fred's children [from a previous marriage] her children."[33]

In a number of journal entries, Gideon struggles with the question of whether or not to have children. One important factor in her deliberations seems to have been a concern with how her sister, Judith, would react to a pregnancy: "I have feared being greedy, having something J. doesn't have – like children" and "[p]erhaps my unwillingness to have children may have come from this sense of further outrage for J. – something else to make amends for."[34] In some entries she expresses apprehen-

---

[29] *Ibid.* By "German," Gideon is probably referring to her parents' Germanic lineage and their connections to Germany: all four of Gideon's grandparents were German, and her father earned a degree in philosophy at the University of Marburg. Gideon's parents also spoke German at home (Rosenberg and Rosenberg, "Miriam Gideon," 65). In 1991, recalling her parents' home in New York, Gideon called it "a dismal household – my father truly wasn't very well" (Ardito, "Miriam Gideon," 206).   [30] MGj-NYPL.

[31] Valdes, "Miriam Gideon Among Most Honored," D9. Gideon has credited Martin Bernstein, a faculty member in the New York University Music Department from 1926 to 1972, with encouraging her to compose ("I'll always be grateful to Martin Bernstein . . . He said 'Why, you're a composer!' That meant a lot to me at the time because he could just as well have said, 'Oh, you need an awful lot of study,' or, 'What do you mean, you want to compose, you're a woman . . .').". Quoted in Rosenberg and Rosenberg, "Miriam Gideon," 62.

[32] "I must discover for myself whether it is a 'career' or life that I want. I can have a career and life too, but even though the former will be enriched by the latter, there must be sacrifices. I am beginning to think life is what I want. That it is richer." RCd-LC, 1 August 1929; quoted in JT-RCS, 99.

[33] Telephone interview with Lucille Field Goodman. The pianist Şahan Arzruni recalls many dinner parties at Gideon and Ewen's tiny studio apartment in New York, occasions that suggest a few ways in which Gideon negotiated the demanding cooking and hostessing duties often assumed by a wife. For these parties, both she and Ewen cooked; they saved time in planning the menu by serving exactly the same meal at each dinner: a shrimp dish doused with sherry that had not been cooked off; a salad of watermelon, cantaloupe, and melon; Minute Rice; and pie with whipped cream – that the rice was of the instant variety demonstrates that Gideon had no qualms about taking culinary shortcuts (telephone interview with Şahan Arzruni, 8 July 1997). Goodman also recalls observing that Gideon spent "very little time cooking, very little time cleaning."

[34] MGj-NYPL.

sion about having children, interpreting a dream of "taking new apt. filled with terrors – whereas old seems desirable but lost forever" to signify "my fears regarding becoming pregnant." In another entry, she fears *not* having children, describing "my own fears re anxiety at menopause – tied up with not having children – feeling of thus it is ordered – doom. Tho other immediate and practical fears are there, this is at the center." And in still another entry, she acknowledges that she does not know whether she wants to have children or not: "I test out his [Frederic Ewen's] reaction to having children – not sure of my own feelings – confusing in regard to his answer."[35]

The tangle of contradictions that Gideon experienced – between her self-image as both masculine and feminine, between wanting and not wanting children, between her mother's wish that she be both feminine and unfeminine – is made clear in these writings. Her feminist voice, often muted in interviews and articles, can be heard distinctly in her journals, professional correspondence, other published writings, and, as I shall argue, in her music.

Gideon's "Night is my Sister," the second of her 1952 *Sonnets from Fatal Interview*, illustrates her pivotal statement about the perspective a woman can bring to her music.[36] The text is based on Sonnet VII from Edna St. Vincent Millay's 1931 *Fatal Interview*, a sequence of fifty-two Petrarchan sonnets that chronicle an affair from a woman's perspective. The title of the sequence refers to a line from John Donne's *Elegy XVI: On his Mistris*, "By our first strange and fatall interview, / By all desires which thereof did ensue," which Millay includes as an epigraph.[37]

In contrast to Donne's poem, Millay's *Fatal Interview* employs a female first-person speaker, tracing her turbulent affair with an unnamed man from the first throes of passion to the emotional devastation she experiences when confronted by his indifference. By addressing the theme of a woman's suffering from a painful love affair, Millay explores what Jane Stanbrough identifies as "woman's psychological disintegration."[38]

Each of the three sonnets by Millay that Gideon set for voice and string trio – Sonnets VII ("Night is my Sister"), XXI ("Gone in Good Sooth You Are"), and XXVII ("Moon, that against the Lintel of the West") – depicts the protagonist's despair about the destructive relationship rather than the pleasure she sometimes takes in it. Millay's reputation as a daring, independent, politically radical woman

[35] MGj-NYPL.

[36] Two further explorations of how Gideon's music can be understood to express a "woman's way of responding to the world" are Marianne Kielian-Gilbert's discussion of Gideon's 1966 piano suite *Of Shadows Numberless* in "Of Poetics and Poeisis," 44–67, and Jennifer Shaw, "Moon Tides and Male Poets: (En)gendering Identity in Miriam Gideon's *Nocturnes*," paper presented at the Feminist Theory and Music III conference, University of California at Riverside, 1995.

[37] John Donne, "Elegie XVI: On his Mistris," in *The Complete Poetry and Selected Prose of John Donne*, ed. Charles M. Coffin (New York: The Modern Library, 1952), 77.

[38] Jane Stanbrough, "Edna St. Vincent Millay and the Language of Vulnerability," in *Shakespeare's Sisters: Feminist Essays on Women Poets*, ed. Sandra M. Gilbert and Susan Gubar (Bloomington: Indiana University Press, 1979), 198.

Night is my sister, and how deep in love,
How drowned in love and weedily washed ashore,
There to be fretted by the drag and shove
At the tide's edge, I lie – these things and more:
Whose voice alone between me and the sand,
Whose arm alone, whose pitiful breath brought near,
Could thaw these nostrils or unlock this hand,
She could advise you, should you care to hear.
Small chance, however, in a storm so black,
A man will leave his friendly fire and snug
For a drowned woman's sake, and bring her back
To drip and scatter shells upon the rug.
No one but Night, with tears on her dark face,
Watches beside me in this windy place.

Figure 7.1 Edna St. Vincent Millay, "Night is my Sister"

may also have attracted Gideon, who shared Frederic Ewen's "very liberal political views."[39]

Figure 7.1 gives the text of Sonnet VII.[40] "Night is my Sister" offers a tale of a drowned woman "weedily washed ashore," one for whom there is "Small chance, however, in a storm so black / A man will leave his friendly fire and snug / For a drowned woman's sake." It thus provides an opportunity to examine Gideon's song in relation to an overtly gendered narrative. Her turbulent setting of Millay's sonnet effectively underscores a feminist reading of the text by presenting a compassionate portrait of the unfortunate female protagonist while it criticizes the male character's refusal to help her.[41] Not only do the violin, viola, and cello establish the song's haunting mood, but they also comment on the woman's grim situation and attempt to influence her deliberations.

Example 7.1 gives the score (note that accidentals carry through each measure). Marked "tumultuous," the song opens with the violin, viola, and cello alone. Gideon establishes a trichordal harmonic texture in the trio accompaniment, which employs all three instruments continuously throughout the song, save for two bars (mm. 33–34) that separate the sonnet's octet from its sestet.

Milton Babbitt has remarked that the concept of motivic saturation, or the immersion of a musical motive in a composition, was "very familiar to Miriam . . .

[39] Ardito, "Miriam Gideon," 208. Millay supported Nicola Sacco and Bartolomeo Vanzetti, the Italian immigrant anarchists who were executed by the Commonwealth of Massachusetts for their alleged role in a robbery and murder. She also helped to raise funds to support the writing of Emma Goldman's autobiography. See Suzanne Clark, "*Jouissance* and the Sentimental Daughter: Edna St. Vincent Millay," in *Gendered Modernisms: American Women Poets and Their Readers*, ed. Margaret Dickie and Thomas Travisano (Philadelphia: University of Pennsylvania Press, 1996), 143.

[40] Edna St. Vincent Millay, *Collected Sonnets*, rev. and exp. edn (New York: Harper & Row, 1988 [1931]), 76.

[41] Gideon also arranged *Sonnets from Fatal Interview* for voice and piano (New York: American Composers Alliance, 1961).

Example 7.1 Gideon, "Night is my Sister" for voice, violin, viola, and cello

Example 7.1 (*cont.*)

Circle Blue Print Co., Inc.
225 West 57th Street
New York 19, N. Y.

Example 7.1 (*cont.*)

Example 7.1 (*cont.*)

Example 7.1 (*cont.*)

that's what obviously influenced her very much . . . she considered herself a motivic composer."[42] Motivic saturation organizes the structure of the vocal line and of the instrumental trio, and is a means through which Gideon unifies the song.

Measure 1 presents the two types of trichords that take the greatest structural significance in the piece. The first type, which appears as a harmony on the second eighth note, is the set class 3–3 [014]: the cello plays B3, the viola plays B♭3, and the violin plays D4. The trichord on beat 3, first eighth note (A2–F3–A♭4) is also a member of [014]. The second type, which appears as the final simultaneity in m. 1, beat 3, third eighth note, is the set class 3–2 [013]: the cello plays G♯3, the viola plays G4, and the violin plays B♭4.

These two primary set classes, 3–2 [013] and 3–3 [014], can also be understood in terms elaborated by Adolph Weiss, Schoenberg's first American student, in his 1932 article "The Lyceum of Schönberg."[43] This significant record of Schoenberg's teachings and ideas sets forth a few fundamental principles of his middle-period compositional technique. According to Babbitt, the article had a "tremendous effect on people like Miriam, because it had to do with the things you can do with the motive."[44]

"Night is my Sister" beautifully illustrates Weiss's comments on the motive's role in creating compositional coherence. The two main trichords of the song – "germ-cells" to use Schoenberg's metaphor – undergo "musical mitosis," which Weiss defines as the "continued subdivision of the original germ-cell."[45] The first two pitches played by the viola in m. 1, B♭3 and A3, form a dyadic motive of two notes a semitone apart, an interval common to both motivic set classes 3–2 [013] and 3–3 [014] and a mitotic subdivision of these trichords, as well as to the interval that can transform [013] into [014] and vice versa.

In m. 1, beat 3, the viola presents F4–E4 on the first and second eighth notes and G4 on the third eighth note, three pitches that form a melodic [013] trichord. In m. 2, beat 1, Gideon transposes the viola's motive up a tritone, from F4–E4 on the first and second eighth notes to B4–A♯4 on the second and third eighth notes. Combined with the violin's D5, the resulting trichord is another member of 3–3 [014]. The minor third between the viola's B4 and the violin's D5 in m. 2, beat 1, second eighth note, is transposed down a major third on beat 2, second eighth note,

---

[42] Babbitt, interview with the author. He added, "I don't think anyone uses [motivic saturation] anymore," but then noted that the tradition is being carried on by Donald Erb and other composers at the Cleveland Institute of Music. Babbitt classifies Gideon's 1958 "Fantasy on a Javanese Motif" for cello and piano as an example of her motivic writing. He observes that the total composition is generated by a three-note motive, and identifies the "motival identification of linear and harmonic components" in the Fantasy as a compositional feature "characteristic of the composer's more extended and personal work." See Milton Babbitt, liner notes to Seymour Barab and William Masselos, *A Recital of New Music for Cello and Piano* (Paradox 10001, n.d.).

[43] Adolph Weiss, "The Lyceum of Schönberg," *Modern Music* 9/3 (March–April 1932), 99–107. Schoenberg's *Fundamentals of Musical Composition*, ed. Gerald Strang and Leonard Stein (New York: St. Martin's Press, 1967) develops some of the ideas summarized by Weiss in "The Lyceum of Schönberg." See particularly Chapters 3 and 4 ("The Motive" and "Connecting Motive-Forms"), 8–19.   [44] Babbitt, interview with the author.

[45] Weiss, "The Lyceum of Schönberg," 101.

$$Bb4 \longrightarrow Bb4$$
$$0$$

$$G4 \longrightarrow F\#4$$
$$-1$$

$$A4 \longrightarrow A4$$
$$0$$
[013]   [014]

Figure 7.2 Parsimonious voice leading between set classes 3-2 [013] and 3-3 [014]

to G4 in the viola and Bb4 in the violin, while the viola continues its dyadic gesture, playing G4–F#4. When the viola's dyad is combined with the violin's Bb4, another member of 3-3 [014] (F#4–G4–Bb4) results.

Inspecting the voice leading more closely, we observe that the simplest or most "parsimonious" way to move from a [013] simultaneity to a [014] simultaneity is to retain as common tones the two pitches that lie interval class (ic) 1 apart, and to move the remaining pitch one semitone closer to the other two.[46] Figure 7.2 shows an example of parsimonious voice leading from A4–G4–Bb4, a member of [013], to A4–F#4–Bb4, a member of [014]. A4 and Bb4 are held as common tones, and G4 moves down a semitone to F#4.

Figure 7.3 shows how Gideon avoids parsimonious voice leading in mm. 5–6. The pitches played by the cello, viola, and violin in m. 5, beat 3, third eighth note, are given in the left column, in low, middle, and high registers, respectively. That is, the cello's A4 is listed at the bottom of the left column, the viola's G4 is listed above it, and the violin's Bb4 is listed at the top. The right column gives the pitch of each instrument in m. 1, beat 1: the cello's A4 is listed at the bottom of the right column, the viola's A#4 is listed above it, and the violin's C#5 is at the top. The arrows from the left column to the right column indicate motion within an instrumental voice, and the integer beneath each arrow indicates the distance, measured in semitones, that each voice moves; + indicates ascent and – indicates descent. The violin's motion from Bb4 to C#5 is thus indicated by "+3," which means that its second pitch lies three semitones higher than its first pitch. The prime form of each trichord is given in brackets underneath each column.

To move from [013] to [014] using parsimonious voice leading, or what

46 Richard Cohn discusses parsimonious voice leading as a feature of triadic music in "Neo-Riemannian Operations, Parsimonious Trichords, and Their *Tonnetz* Representations," *Journal of Music Theory* 41/1 (Spring 1997), 1–66. By inspecting voice leading between different members of a trichord class, Cohn demonstrates that of the mod-12 trichord classes (except for the trivial case of 3–12 [048]), 3–11 [037] is capable of the greatest degree of voice-leading parsimony as defined by the operations that maximize pitch-class intersection between pairs of different triads. In contrast to Cohn, I inspect voice leading between members of two different trichord classes.

m. 5   m. 6

B♭4 ⟶ C♯5
+3

G4 ⟶ A♯4
+3

A4 ⟶ A4
0
[013]   [014]

Figure 7.3 Circuitous voice leading between set classes 3-2 [013] and 3-3 [014], mm. 5-6

Schoenberg dubbed "the law of the shortest way," Gideon could have simply lowered the viola's G4 to F♯4, retaining A4 and B♭4, as shown in Figure 7.2.[47] By leading two of the pitches in [013] to new pitches in [014], she instead uses anti-parsimonious voice leading, or what I call "circuitous voice leading," which may be defined as voice leading between trichords that avoids double common-tone retention, thus requiring at least two instrumental voices to move to different pitches.[48] In contrast, parsimonious voice leading between [013] and [014] would retain as common tones the two pitches that lie a semitone (mod 12) apart. For [013] → [014], parsimonious voice leading would move the remaining pitch one semitone farther from the other two pitches; for [014] → [013], it would move the remaining pitch one semitone closer to the other two pitches.

Figure 7.4 summarizes the voice leading in the song between the most significant harmonic presentations of set classes 3-2 [013] and 3-3 [014] that occur in close proximity. Each trichord is numbered by its measure number; when two or more occur in a measure, the measure number is followed by a letter (e.g. 1a, 1b). The occurrence of each trichord listed in Figure 7.4 is noted by its measure number in Example 7.1 below each system.[49]

This survey of voice leading between the song's two central trichords shows that as a general principle Gideon favors circuitous voice leading over parsimonious voice leading between structurally prominent members of set classes 3-2 [013] and 3-3 [014]. Figure 7.4 shows that throughout the song circuitous voice leading fre-

---

[47] "[E]ach voice will move only when it must; each voice will take the smallest possible step or leap, and then, moreover, just that smallest step which will allow the other voices also to take small steps" – Arnold Schoenberg, *Theory of Harmony*, trans. Roy E. Carter (Berkeley: University of California Press, 1983 [1911]), 39.

[48] Different pitches within the same pitch class (e.g., E4 and E5) do not count as common tones in my formulation, which operates within pitch space rather than in pitch-class space. In a theory of circuitous voice leading in pitch-class space, different pitches within the same pitch class *would* count as common-tone retention.

[49] I hear the cello's final pitch in m. 13, D3, as combining with the dyad in m. 14 – B♭3 played by the viola and D♭4 played by the violin – to form a trichord, even though the D3 is not actually sounding in m. 14. Because this trichord begins in m. 13, the first attack in m. 14 is labeled "13b."

quently connects [013] and [014]. The instruments tend to speak through a communal effort in the trio or as a pair of voices bound together through voice leading, rather than as a single effort by one instrument. United in this way, the three instruments may be understood to have the role of a chorus commenting on the events as described by the singer.

Some of the trichords shown in Figure 7.4 are connected by an intervening pitch a semitone away from one of its neighbors – for example, in m. 1, the viola plays F4 in trichord 1a, E4, and G4 in trichord 1b. The resulting melodic trichord is a member of [013]. In m. 6, the viola plays A♯4 in trichord 6a, F♯4 and G4 in trichord 6b. These three pitches form a [014] melodic tetrachord. Similarly, in m. 14, the viola plays B♭3 in trichord 14a, A4, and C4 in trichord 14b, forming a [013] melodic tetrachord.[50] By providing a +1/−1 voice-leading connection through the inclusion of intervening pitches in these and other measures, Gideon saturates the musical space with the primary trichord motives.

In mm. 1–3, the cello plays a melody with a jagged contour consisting of upward leaps off the beat and downward leaps on the beat. In m. 5, it pauses on a quietly pulsating A4 before sustaining the pitch in m. 6 for five eighth notes. The dyad motive also propels m. 5 to m. 6 via an eighth-note pulse felt within the 9/8 meter. In m. 1, the motive takes the form in the viola of −1 between B♭3 and A3, and F4 and E4; in m. 2, between B4 and A♯4, and G4 and F♯4; in mm. 3–4, of +1 in the violin between D4 and D♯4; and in m. 5 in the viola, the motive undulates between −1 and +1 between G4 and F♯4. Measure 5, the final measure of instrumental introduction, restates the two basic trichords of the opening, set classes 3–2 [013] and 3–3 [014]: the upper two voices play another [014], made up of the violin's repeated B♭4 and the viola's G4–F♯4–G4 triplet figure, while the sonority formed from the viola's two pitches and the cello's repeated A4 belongs to [013].

In m. 6, beat 1, the trio again states a [014] trichord: the cello sustains the A4 which it played in the previous bar; the viola moves a semitone above the cello, to A♯4; and the violin plays C♯5. After a fleeting 3–11 [037] on the second eighth note of beat 2 when the viola plays F♯4 under the cello's A4 and the violin's C♯4, forming a melodic [014] with its pitches A♯4–F♯4–G4, [013] reappears in the last half of the measure, when the viola plays G4 and the violin plays B♭4 over the cello's A4.

As soon as the vocalist sings her first pitch, C♯5, the steady eighth-note pulse established in the instrumental introduction immediately freezes on the word "Night." The violin solidifies the voice's C♯5 in m. 6 by doubling it. The viola breaks up this moment by returning to the eighth-note pulse on beat 2, second eighth note, with its descent from A♯4 to F♯4. The voice's switch to a duple meter

---

[50] In m. 31, the cello's intervening A3 is flanked by G♯2 and G♯4, creating two +11 connections that suggest the +1/−1 dyad motive rather than the full trichords from which the motive is derived.

m. 1   m. 1   m. 5   m. 6   m. 6

A♭4 $\longrightarrow$ B♭4   B♭4 $\longrightarrow$ C♯5 $\longrightarrow$ B♭4
   +2   +3   −3

F4 $\longrightarrow$ G4   G4 $\longrightarrow$ A♯4 $\longrightarrow$ G4
   +2   +3   −3

A2 $\longrightarrow$ G♯3   A4 $\longrightarrow$ A4 $\longrightarrow$ A4
  +11   0   0
[014]   [013]   [013]   [014]   [013]

1a   1b   5   6a   6b

m. 13   mm. 13–14   m. 14   m. 20   m. 22   m. 24   m. 25

D4 $\longrightarrow$ D♭4 $\longrightarrow$ E♭3   B♭5 $\longrightarrow$ A3   C5 $\longrightarrow$ A4
  −1   +2   −25   −3

B3 $\longrightarrow$ B♭3 $\longrightarrow$ C4   A4 $\longrightarrow$ G3   B♭4 $\longrightarrow$ F4
  −1   +2   −10   −5

C♯4 $\longrightarrow$ D3/D4 $\longrightarrow$ D4 F♯4 $\longrightarrow$ F♯3   A2 $\longrightarrow$ G♭2
  +1   0   −12   −3
[013]   [014]   [013]   [014]   [013]   [013]   [014]

13a   13b/14a   14b   20   22   24   25

m. 27   m. 27   m. 27   m. 28   m. 31   m. 31

A♭5 $\longrightarrow$ A♭4   B♭4 $\longrightarrow$ A5   C5 $\longrightarrow$ B♭4
   0   +11   −2

F5 $\longrightarrow$ E5   F♯4 $\longrightarrow$ F♯5   A4 $\longrightarrow$ G4
  −1   +12   −2

G4 $\longrightarrow$ G4   G4 $\longrightarrow$ G♯2   G♯2 $\longrightarrow$ G♯4
   0   −23   +24
[013]   [014]   [014]   [013]   [014]   [013]

27a   27b   27c   28   31a   31b

Figure 7.4 Voice leading between selected members of set classes 3-2 [013] and 3-3 [014]

Figure content:

m. 46   m. 46   m. 48   m. 48   m. 48   m. 49   m. 49   m. 49

C♯5 ⟶ E5   D4 ⟶ D4 ⟶ D4 ⟶ F4 ⟶ E4 ⟶ B♭4
     +3   0   0   +3   −1   +6

A♯4 ⟶ C♯5   B3 ⟶ A♯3 ⟶ B3 ⟶ D4 ⟶ D4 ⟶ A4
     +3   −1   +1   +3   0   +7

A4 ⟶ D♯3   C♯4 ⟶ C♯4 ⟶ C♯4 ⟶ C♯4 ⟶ C♯4 ⟶ C♯4
    −18   0   0   0   0   0
[014]   [013]   [013]   [014]   [013]   [014]   [013]   [014]

46a   46b   48a   48b   48c   49a   49b   49c

m. 53   m. 53   m. 55   m. 56

D5 ⟶ D♭5   A♯3 ⟶ G3
    −1   −3

B4 ⟶ B♭4   G3 ⟶ E3
    −1   −3

C♯2 ⟶ D2   F♯2 ⟶ F♯2
    +1   0
[013]   [014]   [014]   [013]

53a   53b   55   56

Figure 7.4 (*cont.*)

in m. 7 further checks the pace of the melodic line in m. 9, and suggests the woman's dreamy lack of awareness of her surroundings. Gideon's arresting of the rhythmic pulse contributes further to the sense of the woman's emotional numbness brought on by her metaphorical drowning ("how deep in love, / How drowned in love") and her literal drowning ("and weedily washed ashore").

In his article "The Music of Miriam Gideon," Perle remarks upon the method of doubling in her 1945 work *The Hound of Heaven* for voice, oboe, viola, and cello. In this composition, he points out specific passages in which the voice is "doubled by a line whose register in relation to the voice constantly changes and whose components are distributed among the different instruments."[51] In "Night is my Sister," Gideon employs the method of doubling that Perle describes. For example, the

[51] George Perle, "The Music of Miriam Gideon," *American Composers Alliance Bulletin* 7/4 (1958), 4.

voice's first four pitches in mm. 6–7, C♯5–F♯4–A♯4–A♮4, are doubled by violin, cello, viola, and viola, respectively.[52]

In addition to the traditional task of supporting the singer, Gideon's method of doubling in the song draws out specific melodic segments of two to six pitches. In m. 7, for example, the viola's doubling of the voice's successive pitches A♯4 and A♮4 extracts a motive from the longer vocal phrase which is also the dyad motive with which the viola opened the piece, transposed up an octave.

Gideon's technique of doubling is significant not only for the smaller motives or segments that it elicits, but also because it strengthens particular pitches. In m. 21, for example, the voice's F♯4 is doubled by all three instruments – the violin plays F♯4, and the viola and cello F♯3. Sung to the word "these," which marks the moment just before the "more" of the woman's situation is explained, the F♯ doubling gives greater emphasis to the word which is sung.

The phrase begun in m. 6 with the word "Night" is completed by the words "is my sister" in m. 7, sung to F♯4–A♯4–A♮4–F♯4. A member of set class 3-11 [037] opens the voice's melodic line (C♯5–F♯4–A♯4) in mm. 6–7, and set class 3-3 [014] is formed by F♯4–A♯4–A♮4. The poem sets forth the night's sympathetic relationship with the woman, and in mm. 8–9, the trio plays A4–B♭3–C♯4 which extend [014] harmonically while the singer discloses in mm. 9–10 what is most important to her – that she is "deep in love," three words sung to D5, B4, and A♯4, pitches that form another melodic [014].

In m. 8, the viola reasserts the dyad motive, the gently insistent B♭3–A3 from m. 1. It continues playing the dyad motive in m. 10 as D4–C♯4, but with a third pitch, E4, added on the third triplet eighth note, which results in a melodic [013] trichord akin to that in m. 1, beat 3. The viola continues to present the dyad motive through m. 18.

In mm. 9–11, the cello doubles all five of the pitches that are sung to the words "and how deep in love," suggesting the importance of the relationship. In mm. 10–14, the vocal melody is permeated by [014]: D5–B4–A♯4 with the phrase "deep in love"; B4–D♯4–D♮4 with "how drowned"; F♯4–A♯4–A♮4 with "and weed-"; and G♯4–A4–C5 with "-ily washed." The vocalist's pitches on the words "how drowned," B4–D♯5–D5, are doubled by the viola. The viola's prominence on these words stresses the woman's lamentable state of being "drowned" in love rather than "deep" in love. As well as the central conveyor of the dyad motive, the viola briefly steps out of the trio texture to present a solo comment on the events in this passage.

The woman grows more agitated in this passage, singing *poco crescendo* as she describes her situation of being "fretted by the drag and shove." The first instance of all three instruments doubling the voice occurs here – in m. 17, beat 2, the violin, viola, and cello double the singer's B4 to the syllable "-ted" of "fretted," stressing

---

[52] This method of scattering the doubled pitches among the accompanying instruments is a technique that Gideon uses in several other works for voice and chamber ensemble – for example, the first and third songs of *Sonnets from Fatal Interview*, and *The Seasons of Time*. For a further discussion of Gideon's method of doubling, see Petersen, "The Vocal Chamber Music of Miriam Gideon," 244.

the hardness of the word "fretted" and the physicality of the woman's suffering. To punctuate the word, Gideon includes another [014] harmony on beat 2, second eighth note (B3 in viola, B4 in cello, C5 and E♭5 in violin), sung to "-ted," and the voice repeats the [014] with C♯5–B♯4–E5 in m. 18, sung to "drag and shove." The woman's vexation dissipates by the end of m. 18, where she drops to *pianissimo* as she serenely describes her situation ("at the tide's edge I lie") in a six-note phrase that neatly breaks down into three two-note clusters of C5–D♭5 ("at the"); F5–G♭5 ("tide's edge"); and E♭5–D5 ("I lie") reverting to the motivic dyad.

Gideon underscores the woman's solitude by *not* doubling E♭5, the pitch sung to "I," which is the only significant word in the poem thus far that does not have an instrumental double. By de-emphasizing the word "I" through its rhythmic placement on the last eighth note of a 6/8 bar, Gideon's setting further emphasizes Millay's withholding of the subject ("I") until the end of the sentence, indicating that the woman is thinking less of herself than of her lover. As if to rouse her out of her reverie, each instrument repeats and accents its pitches from the second beat of m. 19, and again on the first two beats of m. 20. On the third beat, all decisively play *piu forte* while converging on an accented F♯ in m. 21, as if to urge her onward. She takes their advice and proceeds, singing "These things and more."

This significant moment in the poem, in which the woman begins to question her lover's commitment to her, is marked by the repeated and prominent use of [014] and [013] in the trio and in the vocal melody. In mm. 19–20, the cello's F♯4, the viola's A4, and the violin's B♭4 provide [014] harmonic support for the voice's [013] trichord in m. 19 – F5–G♭5–E♭5 ("tide's edge I") – and for its [014] trichord G♭5–E♭5–D5 in mm. 19–20 ("edge I lie"). In m. 20, beat 3, the violin and viola leap up an octave while the cello leaps up two octaves. In m. 21, beat 1, all voices temporarily converge on pitch class F♯. The voice then presents another melodic [014] with its subsequent A4–B♭4 in m. 21 ("things and more"); in m. 22, the trio switches to [013] harmonic support with the cello's F♯3, the viola's semitone ascent from F♯4 to G3, and the violin's drop from F♯4 to A3. (Figure 7.4 summarizes this voice leading from mm. 20–22 without the intervening F♯s of m. 21.)

As the woman reflects upon the ways in which her lover could help her ("Whose arm alone between me and the sand, / Whose voice alone, whose pitiful breath brought near, / Could thaw these nostrils or unlock this hand"), the vocal line, marked with a crescendo starting in m. 26, builds to a *forte* on the word "thaw" in m. 28. The ensemble joins the singer in producing the crescendo. The thickened texture and more deliberate duple rhythm emphasize the pathos of her situation, her nostrils and hands frozen while she awaits release from her suffering by her lover.[53]

A brief passage of trio alone in the last seven eighth notes of m. 30 connects the first seven lines of the poem's octet, which describe the woman's situation, to its last

---

[53] Debra Fried notes that a recurring theme in Millay's sonnets is the image of eros as prison; see her "Andromeda Unbound: Gender and Genre in Millay's Sonnets," in *Critical Essays on Edna St. Vincent Millay*, ed. William B. Thesing (New York: G. K. Hall, 1993), 236–37.

line, sung in mm. 31–32. The text is now narrated not by the woman but by a third person who speaks directly to her, proposing that "she [Night] could advise you, should you care to hear."

The completion of the octet presents the turning point of the scene – the woman comes to understand that it is not the unnamed man who will help her, but her companion, the night.[54] In mm. 34–36, with the first line of the sestet, she indicates that she has changed, from a person deep in love who dreamily lies at the edge of the tide waiting for her lover to rescue her, to a woman who ruefully pictures the more likely scenario ("Small chance, however, in a storm so black"). To emphasize the improbability that the man will actually help the woman, the violin and viola double the pitches to which each syllable of "Small chance, however" are sung.

Measure 33 marks a turn in the woman's perception of her situation with a change in rhythm, meter, and pitch. The trio becomes more impassioned and disturbed, *poco piu animato*, and the rhythm returns in m. 34 to a more propulsive composite sixteenth-note pulse; Gideon also uses a 2/4 meter for the first time in the song, and the entrances of the instruments are staggered in mm. 33–34. The cello's G♯2–A2–A3–C4 – another [014] – in m. 33 introduces the ascending octave leap that characterizes the first eight bars of this section (mm. 33–40) in both the cello and violin.

Gideon's use of doubling in this section emphasizes the woman's growing awareness that she has been abandoned. After the violin and viola double the voice's pitches in mm. 34–36, key words in the next line ("black," "a man," "friend-" of "friendly," "fire") are all sung without instrumental doubling, suggesting that the woman now realizes, without the prodding of the trio, that her lover probably will not help her.

Measure 41 contains the culminating moment of the song. The word "drowned," sung *forte*, takes up an entire measure and is set melismatically, to six pitches, D♯5–D♮5–C♯5–C♮5–A4–G♯4, a string of three pairs of dyads connected by a semitone. The setting of this crucial word recalls the dyad motive first played by the viola in m. 1. The viola doubles all six pitches of the voice, while the violin shadows them three semitones higher (F♯5–F♮5–E5–D♯5–C5–B4) and the cello intones a perfect fourth, E2–A2. The emphatic setting of this word can be heard as a harsh criticism by the trio of the man, who is so indifferent that he will not even bother to help a *drowned* woman.[55] The interval of a semitone that was largely avoided as a single-voice connection between [013] and [014] thus emerges at the

---

[54] Holly Peppe finds the traditional gendering of night as female in Millay's sonnet significant: "During moments of great sadness, the speaker recognizes that only another female presence (a "sister") can empathize with her anguish"; Holly Peppe, "Rewriting the Myth of the Woman in Love: Millay's *Fatal Interview*," in *Millay at 100: A Critical Reappraisal*, ed. Diane P. Freedman (Carbondale: Southern Illinois University Press, 1995), 60.

[55] In *Feminism and Poetry: Language, Experience, Identity in Women's Writing* (London: Pandora, 1987), Jan Montefiore suggests that the male lover in this sonnet adopts a stereotypically feminized role: reluctant to leave his warm and cozy home to help someone who will "drip and scatter shells upon the rug," he is "a domesticated creature who doesn't want his room messed up" (119).

song's climax. Its melodic presentation is underscored by the dynamic marking, change of meter, and doubling.

In the viola's and voice's six-note string of m. 41, a downward leap of a minor third connects the fourth pitch to the fifth, C5 to A4. This makes possible another [014], C5–A4–G♯4, which gives way to [013] in m. 43, A♯4–C♯5–C5, sung to the words "bring her back." The C5 is used in turn with an elided [013], C5–B♭4–A4 sung to the words "back to drip." A third [013] ends the measure, G♯4–B4–A♯4 ("and scat-ter"). The doubling of the vocal line by the viola on the words "drowned woman's sake" extends the doubling in m. 12 of the voice's D♯5–D♮5 on the single word "drowned," which in the poem then stood for her metaphoric rather than literal drowning.[56] The viola's tiny dyad motive established in m. 1 and the +1/−1 voice leading connection thus comes to full flower by the song's conclusion.

Starting in m. 45, the woman falls silent for five bars to contemplate her bleak situation, and the trio steps in to provide further musical commentary. Entering *subito forte*, the strings indignantly join forces, marcato, with jagged leaps in the violin and viola's two initial pitches (+11 and +8, respectively). In m. 44, the elided [013] that ended the last vocal phrase (F×4–G♯4–A♯4 and G♯4–A♯4–B4) reappears in m. 45 as D♯–D♯–F in all three instruments, and is quickly transformed into [014] in the violin's line in m. 46 (A♭5–F5–E5; F♯5–E5–C♯5; C♯5–C5–E5) to cite three examples, as well as in the first three notes of the viola in m. 46. The viola's shadowing of the violin's line in m. 46 three semitones higher evokes the second setting of "drowned," as well as the earlier pairing of these two instruments in m. 1.[57] Measures 47–49 are similarly rich with [014] and [013] harmonies.

After the trio's vigorous commentary on the woman's wretched situation, her final two lines show that she has indeed come to realize that her lover's comfort is more important to him than her anguish: "No one but Night, with tears on her dark face, / Watches beside me in this windy place." The harmony in m. 54 supporting the last word of the poem ("place") is [014]: the cello plays F♯4, the viola D5, and the violin F5. These three pitch classes, played in m. 12 as harmonic support for the first setting of "drowned," provide a further connection to that word; the dyad motive is played again in mm. 53–54 by the violin as G♭5–F5, and by the viola and voice as E♭5–D5. These latter two pitches evoke the voice's enharmonic equivalent D♯5–D♮5 on the word "drowned" from mm. 12 and 41 one last time. As Figure 7.4 shows, the harmony and voice leading in m. 53 (of C♯2–B4–D5 to D2–B♭4–D♭5) are identical to that in m. 13 (C♯4–B3–D4 to D4–B♭3–D♭4). Not only does the conclusion invoke the phrase "drowned in love" one last time through this wordless musical connection, but the use of voice leading by semitone in each of the three instrumental voices between the two central trichord types also emphasizes the unfolding of the initial motivic semitone and the abandoned woman's acknowledgment of the man's apathy.

---

[56] In "The Music of Miriam Gideon," Perle connects these two settings of the word "drowned" (5).

[57] In m. 46, the viola's C5 on its fifth sixteenth note appears to be a miscopied pitch. A4 rather than C5 would continue the violin's and viola's parallel motion in thirds that has been established.

Susan McClary has suggested that many twentieth-century women composers have disregarded the issue of gender because of lingering pernicious essentialist assumptions about music composed by women.[58] Although Gideon has often been understood to be a composer who rejected the label "woman composer," her personal papers and professional correspondence suggest that she was much more aware of the potentially beneficial and deleterious consequences of being identified as a woman composer than has been previously represented. The persona she tended to project in interviews, of being unconcerned with the category of the "woman composer," contrasts with that presented in her journals, in which she identified herself as a woman composer and grappled with the category's negative associations. Perhaps in order to avoid having to discuss publicly professional struggles attributable to her sex, Gideon preferred to downplay the difficulties of being a woman composer, allowing her innermost thoughts about being a woman in the profession to surface in the privacy of her journals rather than in published articles and interviews. In composing a setting of Millay's "Night is my Sister" which critically observes the female protagonist's transformation from a passive recipient of a man's occasional affection to a perceptive reader of his indifference, Gideon poignantly unveils a feminist sensibility sympathetic to the woman's plight.

[58] Susan McClary, *Feminine Endings*, 19.

8

FEMINIST AGENCY IN GIDEON'S "ESTHER"

> One picture of myself is [of] a passive person – led like a child by the hand
> – actually it appears I have shown much initiative and action of my own.
>
> -Miriam Gideon

To celebrate its centenary in 1945, the Reform synagogue Temple Emanu-El in New York commissioned a composition from Miriam Gideon. For such an occasion, her decision to set a portion of Francis Thompson's 1889 poem *The Hound of Heaven*, a Catholic text about conversion to faith, was unanticipated.[1] After Thompson was rejected for the priesthood and became addicted to opium, he wrote *The Hound of Heaven* as a metaphorical account of his acceptance of faith; the title refers to the poem's description of the process in which the speaker allows God, the heavenly hound, to capture his soul.

Discussing her choice of text for this particular occasion, Gideon noted that she interpreted the underlying message of Thompson's poem *The Hound of Heaven* to be that difficult life experiences "mar, in order to make, the human being."[2] She eloquently argued for the poem's relevance to Jewish suffering, understanding its central question addressed to God – "Designer infinite! Must Thou Char the wood / Ere Thou canst limn with it?" – as one that "might well be posed by the Jewish people in terms of its tragic history"[3] and that suggested to her that "we must suffer . . . in order to live deeply."[4]

The Hound of Heaven is a pivotal work in Gideon's career and marks a significant shift toward her stylistic maturity. In her words, it was "probably the first piece in what I would call my own style."[5] Its free atonality marks a clean break from the more traditional diatonicism of her earlier compositions. As an occasional work, it demonstrates her ability to alter a pre-existing text to fit specific circumstances – in setting the poem, Gideon omitted the poem's overtly Catholic allusions, including references to "our Lady-Mother" and to "him enwound / With glooming robes purpureal, cypress-covered."

---

[1] Francis Thompson, *The Hound of Heaven* (New York: McCracken Press, 1993 [1890]).
[2] Miriam Gideon, Liner notes to *The Hound of Heaven*, CRI SC 286, 1971; repr. in liner notes to *Miriam Gideon: Music for Voice and Ensemble*, CRI 782, 1998. [3] Albert Weisser, "An Interview with Miriam Gideon," 40.
[4] *Ibid.* [5] Rosenberg and Rosenberg, "Miriam Gideon," 65.

It also demonstrates a way in which a composer makes her music correspond to her particular subjectivity – that is, her setting of *The Hound of Heaven* corresponds to her identity as a Jew. It stands as a turning point in the forging of her identity, one constituted by a complex of traits including gender, ethnicity, temperament, religion, and nationality. Her compositions reveal aspects of her identity and provide a musical counterpoint to a biography that can be written through letters, diaries, journals, papers, her own recollections, and those of her contemporaries.

As I argued in Chapter 7, Gideon's journals complicate her image as a woman whose professional success was unaffected by the obstacles often faced by female composers. They suggest that Gideon was aware of the traditionally gendered nature of her profession and of her place within it. As I have argued in the cases of Crawford and Bauer, music offered Gideon a psychic space to substitute for the physical space creative women need, famously described by Virginia Woolf.

One recurrent topic in Gideon's journals is her anxiety about forming and voicing her opinions: "Sense of panic is tied up with unclear vision – I must learn to see and think for myself."[6] She mentions in particular her insecurity in relation to men and male authority:

Dream of party at Bianca and Peter's: I do not speak up – but recognize in music what I should have done. (Not assertive, but think of assertive passage in Beethoven.) Father & uncle [Henry Gideon, with whom she lived in Boston and who cultivated her early musical talents], like P. [Peter Rosoff, Gideon's first husband] . . . often wrote script for me, so that I was confused as to who I really was – who was author of my feelings.[7]

In a later entry, she reflected that "I have no autonomy in many spheres; act only when permission is given" and then she added in parentheses "*in music I have—.*" Gideon's identification of music as a domain that enabled her to have the autonomy she sought provides a way to link music, gender, and identity: music can be understood as a site in which Gideon is the agent, a space necessitated by cultural and societal constraints on women's artistic creativity.

Gideon mentions a gendered dimension of the musical space in a subsequent journal entry: "Music is a means of secret communication with men, not for the sake of the music but for the secret language."[8] Considered in the context of her comments about male authority figures in her life (her father, her uncle, and her ex-husband Rosoff), this remark can be understood as one answer to the question she posed in the entry about the "author of my feelings" – with music she found a way to communicate as an equal with the men in whose presence she felt insecure.

Gideon's embracing of an atonal musical idiom enabled her to break away from the influence of her uncle Henry:

The more I found my own style, verging toward the avant-garde in those days, the less my uncle seemed to approve, though he never said so outright.[9]

---

[6] MGj-NYPL.   [7] *Ibid.*   [8] *Ibid.*

[9] Hannah Hanani, "Portrait of a Composer," *Music Journal* 34/4 (April 1976), 24.

Music could also be a "secret language" for Gideon because it was not her husband's. (Frederic Ewen's field was literature, and he published on Brecht and Heine.) Gideon's friend and colleague Leo Kraft recalls that while she and Ewen generally did not work together in any formal way, they were close intellectual and creative companions.[10]

[Fred] listened to her music very intently and always had something to say about it . . . They were very close. Very very close. She read all of his prose works as he was writing them, and he listened to her music, and they collaborated in that kind of spiritual sense.[11]

Lucille Field Goodman, a former student of Gideon at Brooklyn College who knew her for over fifty years, also found Ewen very supportive of Gideon's career and observed that he was "so proud of her."[12]

In Chapter 7, I offered a feminist reading of Gideon's song "Night is my Sister," a composition with text. An instrumental work that also suggests a feminist compositional sensibility is her *Three Biblical Masks* for violin and piano (1960).[13] The work portrays the three main Biblical figures in the Purim story after which each movement is named: Haman, the prime minister who secured a decree from King Ahasuerus of Persia for the destruction of the Jews; Queen Esther, who prevented Haman from carrying out his plan; and Mordecai, who aided his cousin Esther.

After King Ahasuerus's wife Vashti refuses to attend a banquet in which she is commanded to appear before the guests so that they may admire her beauty, the king dismisses her and decides to select a new wife from a group of virgins.[14] Esther, a young woman raised by her cousin Mordecai after the death of her parents, wins the competition to please Ahasuerus and becomes queen. At Mordecai's bidding, she does not reveal her Jewish identity to King Ahasuerus.

After Mordecai refuses to bow down to Haman, Haman vows that he will revenge himself upon Mordecai by massacring Jews throughout the kingdom. Mordecai appeals to Esther to rescue the Jews, and she invites the king and Haman to a banquet, at which Haman has set up a gallows to hang Mordecai. At the banquet, the king recalls a previous incident in which Mordecai saved his life, and wants to reward him. Esther entreats the king to spare her and her people, and identifies Haman as the wicked person who would have her killed. Haman is hanged upon the gallows intended for Mordecai, and Mordecai becomes prime minister. The day originally scheduled for the massacre of the Jews is now celebrated as Purim.

The Book of Esther, or the *Megillah* (scroll) is a problematic text for many feminists. Although a woman is featured as the central heroic character who rescues the

---

[10] Ewen wrote the text for the first song of Gideon's 1979 song cycle *The Resounding Lyre*, "Mutterbildnis."

[11] Leo Kraft, interview with the author, 10 July 1997.

[12] Lucille Field Goodman, Telephone interview with the author, 21 December 1999.

[13] Gideon composed a version of *Three Biblical Masks* for organ in 1958.

[14] *The Revised English Bible* (N.p.: Oxford University Press and Cambridge University Press, 1989), 424–30. All Biblical references will be to this edition unless otherwise noted.

Jews, Esther's status as a female Jewish role model is complicated by the fact that she attains her position of power through her relationship to prominent men, her beauty, and her ability to please the king. As Alice Laffey notes, the defiant behavior of King Ahasuerus's first wife, Vashti, stands in sharp relief to Esther's obedient demeanor: the insubordinate woman who resists patriarchal expectations is banished while the virtuous woman who conforms to them ultimately triumphs.[15] Esther Fuchs's critique notes that like other women characters in the Bible, Esther achieves her success through deception and manipulation; she fulfills her expected role as a dutiful wife but does not have a forceful presence on her own.[16] Celina Spiegel observes that it is Mordecai who is responsible for much of Esther's success: he advises Esther on how to conduct herself, saves King Ahasuerus's life, discovers Haman's plot to destroy the Jews, and supplants Haman as prime minister.[17]

Yet the story of Esther also supports a positive feminist reading, one that recognizes her transformation from a compliant and passive maiden into an assertive and independent woman who rescues the Jews. Michael V. Fox proposes that change is the distinctive feature in Esther's portrayal.[18] He argues that her character develops from passive at the opening of the story, to active once she tells Mordecai to assemble the Jews and orders them to fast, and finally to authoritative when she asks the king to lift the decree to massacre the Jews, and he suggests that the author of the Book of Esther is "something of a protofeminist."[19]

Rivkah Lubitch also interprets Esther to be a woman with two strikingly different personalities: Esther in the beginning of the Book plays a stereotypically feminine role in contrast to the later, feminist Esther, who stops acquiescing to Mordecai and tells him what to do ("Mordecai then went away and did exactly as Esther had bidden him", 4:17).[20] It is this feminist reading of the story – of Esther's transformation from a passive female whose actions are dictated by her older male cousin into a decisive and independent agent who successfully rescues the Jews from being slaughtered – that undergirds Gideon's composition "Esther," the second movement of her *Three Biblical Masks* for violin and piano.

In her journals, Gideon remarked on her difficulty in forming definitive opinions about politics: "I look to others (Fred espec) for political opinions – helpless, like a little girl."[21]

Inability to know where I stand on politics etc. – "shadow boxing" – retreating from literal people with meaningless statistics to equally meaningless "hunches" – perhaps recreates situation of mother attempting to face facts with unrealistic father spinning arabesques. I show same inability to take a stand or have my own values in personal relationships as well. I do

---

[15] Alice L. Laffey, *An Introduction to the Old Testament: A Feminist Perspective* (Philadelphia: Fortress Press, 1988), 216.

[16] Esther Fuchs, "Status and Role of Female Heroines in the Biblical Narrative," *The Mankind Quarterly* 23/2 (Winter 1982), 149–60.

[17] Celina Spiegel, "The World Remade: The Book of Esther," in *Out of the Garden: Women Writers on the Bible*, ed. Christina Buchmann and Celina Spiegel (New York: Fawcett Columbine, 1994), 192.

[18] Michael V. Fox, *Character and Ideology in the Book of Esther* (Columbia: University of South Carolina Press, 1991), 196.   [19] *Ibid.*, 209.   [20] Rivkah Lubitch, "A Feminist's Look at Esther," *Judaism* 42 (Fall 1993), 438, 442.

[21] MGj-NYPL.

not inquire or think things thru and use my own resources in so doing – but retreat into little girl questions and protestations of confusion.[22]

Because of Ewen's political views, Gideon lost her job at Brooklyn College during a period in which McCarthyism forced out faculty in the City University of New York system and in other colleges and universities across the country.[23] In 1940, Ewen refused to testify before the Rapp-Coudert Committee, a panel that was investigating allegations of "subversive" activities in New York City's public schools and colleges.[24] Rather than have to go before a committee to discuss his and others' political views, Ewen gave up a tenured position at Brooklyn College in 1952. In a 1991 interview, Gideon said that because of her association with Ewen and his liberal political views, which she shared, she was told at the end of the fall academic term in 1954 that her services were no longer required at Brooklyn College, where she had taught as an instructor since 1944.[25] After learning that Bella Dodd, a former member of the Teachers Union and of the Communist party, would testify before the McCarran Committee, Ewen opted for early retirement.[26] In order to avoid having to go before a committee to identify leftist colleagues at the City College of New York (CCNY) in 1955, Gideon announced that she would no longer be available to teach there.[27] She was appointed later that year at the Cantors Institute of the Jewish Theological Seminary, which had opened in 1952.[28] Arranged by Hugo Weisgall, a friend of Gideon and Director of the Cantors Institute, this position helped Gideon and Ewen to support themselves.[29]

Gideon noted her dissatisfaction with her deferential manner:

I'm inclined to give too much credit to others – for things I've done myself – whether out of a desire to be grateful or some other reason.[30]

In light of her journal entries that critically assess her passivity and difficulty in forming and expressing her opinions, Gideon's view of Esther and her musical

---

[22] *Ibid.*

[23] Interview with Frederic Ewen by Ellen Schrecker, 7 November 1980; cited in Ellen Schrecker, *No Ivory Tower: McCarthyism and the Universities* (New York: Oxford University Press, 1986), 287–88.

[24] *New York Times*, "Frederic Ewen, 89, Ex-Professor of English," 19 October 1988, B5.

[25] Linda Ardito, "Miriam Gideon," 208.

[26] Schrecker, *No Ivory Tower*, 169. In *Many Are the Crimes: McCarthyism in America* (Boston: Little, Brown, and Company, 1998), Ellen Schrecker notes that rather than being fired outright, many victims of McCarthyism were eased out of their jobs (ix), as in Ewen's case.

[27] Ardito, "Miriam Gideon," 208. David R. Holmes documents the efforts to purge Communism at Brooklyn College in *Stalking the Academic Communist: Intellectual Freedom and the Firing of Alex Novikoff* (Hanover, NH: University Press of New England, 1989), 25–54. A more general discussion of the Cold War's effects on university English departments appears in Richard Ohmann, "English and the Cold War," in *The Cold War and the University: Toward an Intellectual History of the Postwar Years* (New York: The New Press, 1997), 73–105.

[28] Ardito, "Miriam Gideon," 208–9; Binder, *The Jewish Music Movement in America*, 20.

[29] Weisgall had assisted Gideon's career on several previous occasions: while stationed in England as an army sergeant, he attempted to get some of her pieces performed in Europe (letter from Hugo Weisgall to Mr. and Mrs. Peter Rosoff [Gideon was married to Rosoff at the time], 5 June 1943; MGP-NYPL), and he conducted her *Lyric Piece* for String Orchestra with the London Symphony in April 1944; see David Ewen, "Miriam Gideon," in *Composers Since 1900* (New York: H. W. Wilson Co., 1969), 222.   [30] MGj-NYPL.

representation of the character can be understood to reflect traits that she sought to acquire. Her portrait of Esther emphasizes the title character's transformation from a passive to a decisive figure who freely speaks out and takes command of the situation.

Several of Gideon's friends and colleagues have noted that in her later years she made her opinions known, musical and otherwise. Leo Kraft, who met Gideon when she was 54, remarks that "I don't think she took criticism from anybody" and that "[there was] nobody more independent . . . she stuck to her principles."[31] Barbara Petersen recalls an occasion in which she and Gideon endured a "*dreadfully long piece at a new music concert we were obligated to attend*" and Gideon's "clever but cutting comments, ever louder" during its performance.[32] A 1963 letter by Gideon to Broadcast Music, Inc. disapprovingly noted that her name had never appeared in their publication *News About BMI Music and Writers*, and directed the news department to "get acquainted with the names of BMI composers," closing the letter with "Mine is / Miriam Gideon."[33] Milton Babbitt also remembers Gideon as "very forthright."[34]

Example 8.1 presents the score of "Esther" (note that accidentals carry through each measure). On the title page to *Three Biblical Masks*, Gideon characterizes Esther as "gracious and humane," and her sonic portrayal of Esther begins gently and unobtrusively, *piano* and *con sordino*.

In mm. 1–2, the violin's melody tentatively explores the major second from F5 to G5 over static harmonic support. The melody later abandons its initial inclination to explore a fixed melodic space and becomes increasingly independent and propulsive. It takes on a bold and assertive character through larger melodic leaps, increased rhythmic activity, and a crescendo to *forte* in m. 26. The violin's eventual separation from the piano further depicts Esther's increasing independence, affirmed in the final section of the piece, in which the violin assumes the role of leader to the piano's role as follower. In musically portraying Esther, Gideon avoids lingering on those aspects that prove problematic for a female role model – namely, that she is passive and dutiful, and acquires power only through her beauty and familial relationships. Instead, Gideon emphasizes Esther's transformation into an authoritative woman who persuades King Ahasuerus to spare the Jews by altering the relationship of the violin and piano in the piece.[35]

---

[31] Kraft, interview with the author.

[32] Barbara A. Petersen, "Remembering Miriam Gideon," remarks read at a concert of Gideon's music at the Jewish Theological Seminary, New York City, 5 June 1997.

[33] Letter from Gideon to news department, BMI, 6 January 1963; MGp-BMI.

[34] Milton Babbitt, interview with the author, 4 October 1997.

[35] Gideon's presentation of a feminist reading of this Biblical story in her musical setting suggests one way in which she reconciled her beliefs about female agency with a religious tradition that did not permit the full and equal participation of women. In 1959, when the music historian Irene Heskes was interviewed by Hugo Weisgall in order to enroll in courses at the Jewish Theological Seminary's Cantors Institute, she felt she had to assure him that she was "not going to be a troublemaker" (Irene Heskes, interview with the author, 8 July 1997). Hugo Weisgall's daughter, Deborah Weisgall, gives a first-hand account of the exclusion of women from the Orthodox Jewish musical tradition in the 1950s in her memoir *A Joyful Noise: Claiming the Songs of My Fathers* (New York: Atlantic Monthly Press, 1999).

Example 8.1 Gideon, "Esther," from *Three Biblical Masks* for violin and piano

Example 8.1 (cont.)

Example 8.1 (*cont.*)

Example 8.1 (*cont.*)

Example 8.1 (*cont.*)

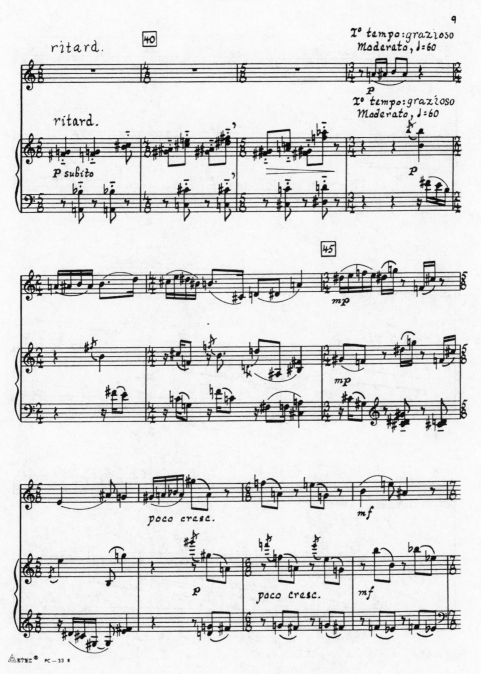

Example 8.1 (*cont.*)

Example 8.1 (*cont.*)

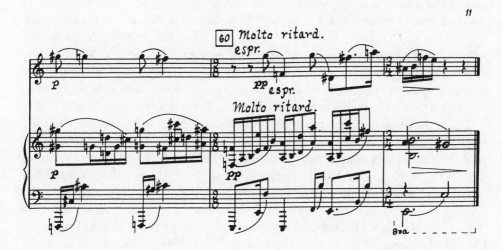

"Esther" is divided into four sections, distinguished by tempo, texture, and artic-ulation. Section I (mm. 1–13) is marked *grazioso* with a tempo marking of quarter note equals 60, and introduces the violin's principal motive of set class 3–1 [012]. Section II (mm. 14–26) contrasts with Section I by proceeding in a faster tempo marking, first of quarter note equals 144 in mm. 14–20 and then of eighth note equals 160 in mm. 21–26. Further contrast is established by the violin's *ponticello* for seven measures, a profusion of seconds, staccato articulation, and harmonic dyads in both the violin and piano's right hand. Section III (mm. 27–41) begins by restoring the initial tempo of Section II and continues the dyads in the piano. The violin is mostly silent in this section, playing only four dyads in all, in mm. 36 and 38. Section IV (mm. 42–61) returns to the original tempo in Section I and to the violin's initial [012] motive, but with the violin's new role of leader firmly estab-lished.

The violin opens the work by presenting its primary melodic motive, set class 3–1 [012], stated as ordered pitch intervals (ips) <+1 +1>. It plays F5–F♯5 on the pickup beat to m. 1 and reaches G5 in m. 1, beat 1. On beat 2, the violin lands on F♯5 for a half note and immediately retraces its limited melodic terrain from F5 to G5 in m. 1, beat 4, through the half note in m. 2. The [012] motive reappears in m. 6, beat 3, and again in m. 12, beat 1, over a four sixteenth–note figure. In Section I, the violin's melody tends to move by nothing larger than a perfect fifth; in only a few instances does it stray from this relatively limited motion. The shy, hesitant character of the violin's music, established by the dynamic marking, tempo, and small compass of the melody, suggests Esther's meek and malleable disposition in the beginning of the story; it is in the violin's music that Gideon's musical portrait of Esther can be located.

The constraining environment within which Esther exists is symbolized by the piano's statically harmonic music, which begins in m. 1, beat 3. The left hand strikes a perfect fourth, G4/C5, while the right hand plays D6 as a grace note, which leads to F♯5. In Section I, pitches are often doubled between the piano and violin or lie an interval class (ic) 1 apart – for example, the violin's F♯5 in m. 5 is doubled in the piano's right hand and also lies ic 1 from G4 in the left hand. This doubling by octave demonstrates Esther's initial restrictions – she is not yet an independent actor and is unable to move more than a limited span.

The violin's next statement further establishes its lack of independence from the piano. In m. 2, its G5 on beats 1–2 is doubled by the piano's G4, and with the C5 it plays on beat 3 pitch interval (ip) 5 is formed. These pitch classes were introduced in m. 1 in the piano's left hand. After creeping up by a semitone from C5 to C♯5, the violin plays an ascending perfect fourth in m. 3, from C♯5 to F♯5, and returns to C♯5 on beat 2.[36] The three notes in m. 3 that form the ascending and descending perfect fourth, C♯5–F♯5–C♯5, lie ic 6 away from the piano's inverted figure of C4–G3–C4; the middle note of the violin's figure, F♯5, is also doubled by the piano's F♯4 in the right hand.

In mm. 3–4, the violin repeats the [012] motive with which it opened the piece, playing F♯4–G4 in m. 3, beat 3, and completing the three-note cluster with G♯4 in m. 4, first eighth note. The violin's pitch class is again doubled by the piano – this time by a G♯5 grace note preceding beat 1 – and is followed by another harmonic ip 5, A3/D5, on beats 1–2.

In Section II, the relationship between violin and piano changes dramatically. The two instruments begin to work in tandem rather than as two voices that are somewhat reluctantly bound together through octave doubling, ic 1, and the perfect fourth. In mm. 14–20, the upper pitches of the violin's harmonic dyads are doubled by the piano's right hand, which plays octaves or occasionally single pitches throughout the section, while the left hand contributes eighth notes that are most frequently inserted between the right hand's attacks, though they sometimes coincide with the right hand at cadences.

The violin first asserts its independence from the piano in m. 17, beat 3, breaking loose from the dyad texture by using [012], played as a trichord of three sixteenth notes, G♯4–A4–G4, <+1 −2>. In m. 18, the violin repeats its music from m. 14 transposed down a perfect fourth, and in m. 19 begins a more varied presentation: instead of transposing the second dyad up five semitones as in m. 15, m. 19 transposes the second dyad up seven semitones; the resulting dyad, E♭5/F5, is then transposed up a semitone rather than transposed down three semitones, as in m. 15. The

---

[36] Gideon has remarked that each of her characterizations – of Haman, Esther, and Mordecai – is based on transformed cantillation motives from the Book of Esther (Weisser, "An Interview with Miriam Gideon," 39). The relationship between the cantillation motives and this movement is, however, remote – only the perfect fourth in the violin's and piano's music is a principal interval in the cantillation motives for the reading of the Scroll of Esther. The cantillation motives are listed in A. W. Binder, *Biblical Chant* (New York: Philosophical Library, 1959), 93–94.

corresponding third measure of the passage, m. 16, is omitted and in m. 20, beats 1–2, proceeds directly to the cadential dyads of four and five semitones that were first heard in m. 17. On beat 3, the violin again plays [012] as three sixteenth notes, <+1 –2>.

This second entrance of [012] in Section II leads into an extended passage in which the violin begins to take command. Crescendoing into m. 21 while slowing the tempo from quarter note equals 144 to eighth note equals 160 in a 6/8 meter, the violin abandons its *ponticello* playing and begins to lead. In m. 21, the violin's first eighth note, D♭6, is doubled at pitch and one octave higher by the piano with its D♭6/D♭7 octave on the second eighth note. The upper pitch of the violin's dyad on the second eighth note, F5, is similarly doubled one octave higher by the piano on the third eighth note, and its B♭5 on the fourth eighth note is likewise doubled at pitch and an octave higher one eighth note later, on the piano's fifth eighth note. Both pitches of the violin's last dyad in m. 21, F5/E♭6, are doubled by the piano an octave higher, but this time the four pitches are played simultaneously.

The next four measures, mm. 22–25, proceed with the general pattern established thus far: the violin introduces a single pitch or dyad, which is echoed by the piano, and towards the end of each measure, the two voices are drawn together on the same eighth note by a doubling. In m. 22, the violin's D6 is answered by the octave D6/D7 on the second eighth note; its B♭5 on the second eighth note is followed by the piano's B♭6 on the third eighth note, and its E6 on the fourth eighth note is answered by the piano's octaves E6/E7 as a simultaneity on the fifth eighth note. In m. 23, the violin's G6 on beat 1 is followed by the octave G6/G7 an eighth note later, and its B5 on the fifth eighth note is doubled by the upper pitch of the piano, as is D♭6 on the seventh eighth note. In m. 24, the violin's C6 is echoed by the octave Cs on the second eighth note, its G5 on the fourth eighth note is repeated by the octave Gs in the piano an eighth note later, and the E4 is restated by the octave Es on the subsequent eighth note. Measure 25 continues this pattern of the piano responding to the violin's pitch an eighth note later until the seventh and ninth eighth notes, at which point the two instruments together play the pitch classes B♭ and D. This doubling continues into m. 26, where the second and fourth beats receive similar treatment: on the second eighth note, the violin's A5–B5 dyad is doubled by the piano an octave above, and on the fourth eighth note, the upper note of its G5–F6 dyad is similarly doubled by the piano.

The simultaneities in Section II are dominated by the two interval classes present in the initial [012] that opened the piece: each trichord is a member of set class 3-1 [012], 3-5 [016] or 3-8 [026], drawing upon ics 1 and 2 of the motivic [012] from the opening. The three tetrachords in mm. 21–26 – set class 4-7 [0145] in m. 22, last eighth note; 4-18 [0147] in m. 25, ninth eighth note; and 4-10 [0235] in m. 26, fourth eighth note – also contain either ic 1 or 2 and ic 5.

In the latter half of Section II (mm. 21–26), the violin expands ips 1 and 2 by playing their inversions, ips 11 and 10. While mm. 15–20 presented pitch intervals in the violin's double stops no larger than a tritone (2, 3, 4, 5, and 6), the double stops in mm. 21–26 expand into larger intervals. In m. 21, last eighth note, the violin plays ip 10 with an F5/Eb6 double stop; in m. 23, the D5–Db6 is ip 11; and in m. 26, the final violin dyad is G5–F6, or ip 10. Measure 26 concludes the section, *forte*, with a *poco ritard*, emphasizing the violin's increasingly assured character.

Section III returns to the scherzando that began Section II, and continues the previous section's use of harmonic dyads. A significant change in Section III is the virtual absence of the violin, which plays for only four dyads, in mm. 36 and 38.

Rather than a retreat to its formerly passive state, the violin's temporary silence may be understood to parallel the moment in the Biblical story when Esther waits to approach King Ahasuerus with her request that he spare the Jews. Although the King tells Esther on the third day of the Jews' fast that "Whatever you ask will be given to you" (5:6), Esther merely requests that he and Haman attend a second banquet on the next day. It is not until this second banquet that she asks that the lives of the Jews be spared (7:1–3). Esther's postponement of her request is ultimately successful because, as Fox notes, it piques the King's curiosity and defers identifying Haman as the agent behind the plot until after the King's anger has been kindled.[37]

In Section III, the piano does not maintain the octave texture in the right hand, but instead copies the violin's music in Section II – it plays relatively small dyads, ranging from ip 2 to 5 in mm. 27–32. The opening of Section III presents a nearly identical pattern of dyads as in the opening of Section II: m. 27 presents ips 2–3–5–3–5 in 5/4 while m. 14 presents 2–4–6–3–5 also in a 5/4 meter. Similarly, the composite rhythm in the piano alone in Section III imitates the composite rhythm of violin and piano in Section II: m. 27 corresponds to m. 14, and m. 28 corresponds to m. 15. The bars with the groupings of three sixteenth notes (mm. 17, 20, 29, and 32) slightly disrupt this pattern. The piano's rhythmic imitation of Section II, a section in which piano and violin played together, culminates at m. 33, where the piano's right hand imitates the violin's rhythm from m. 21. The piano's mimicking of the violin serves to reinforce the violin's new role as leader.

As in Section II, the trichordal harmonies in Section III belong to only a handful of set types. Set classes 3-3 [014], 3-4 [015], and 3-5 [016] are most frequently represented in the passage from m. 27 to m. 34. These trichords continue to present pitch intervals 1, 2, and 5, which can be linked to the initial 3-1 [012] motive and the perfect fourths that predominated in the opening. In restating [012] as a group of three sixteenth notes in mm. 29 and 32, F4–F#4–E4 and G#5–A5–G5, as <+1 –2>, the piano returns to the motive with which the violin opened the piece, and so the tables are turned.

In mm. 36 and 38, the only two measures in Section III in which the violin plays, the piano briefly leads: in m. 36, the piano plays the dyads C#6/E6 and C5/Eb5, which the violin imitates at the octave below, on the third and fourth eighth notes of each bar; similarly, in m. 38, the piano plays E5/F#5 and C4/Eb4; the violin plays E4/F#4 and C4/Eb4 two eighth notes later. That the violin temporarily follows the

[37] Fox, *Character and Ideology*, 201.

piano parallels Esther's plan to play a deferential role ("If I have found favor with your majesty, and if it please you, my lord, what I ask is that my own life and the lives of my people be spared," 7:3) in order to win the King's sympathy by emphasizing her role as defenseless victim of Haman's plot.

Section IV, the final section, begins in m. 42. The tempo returns to *tempo primo* – quarter note equals 60 – and to the *grazioso* indication of the opening. The violin also renders the [012] pitch-class grouping of m. 1, this time as <+1 +1 −1> rather than as <+1 −2> as it did in the middle two sections. Yet Section IV does not merely present a transposed or slightly modified variant of Section I, but fundamentally alters the relationship between violin and piano. The violin's previous tentativeness in Section I is discarded in favor of a freely moving, assertive melody that suggests the authoritative character that Esther now assumes.

Whereas the two instruments in Section I were linked by doublings of ic 1, the violin emerges in Section IV as the instrument with the more commanding presence. In m. 42, the violin enters with the piano close on its heels. The peak of the violin's [012] figure, B4, falls on beat 2, and this pitch class is echoed in the piano's B5 grace note tied to beat 3 and in the B4 that is struck immediately after the B5 sounds.

Subsequent phrases continue this order of instrumental presentation. In m. 44, the violin's B4 on beat 2 is followed by B4 in the piano's right hand a sixteenth note later; in m. 45, D♯5–G5 and F4–C♯5 on beats 2 and 3 are followed an eighth note later in the same octave, again in the piano's right hand. Additional instances of this rhythmic staggering occur in m. 47, beat 2 (G♯5–A4 is echoed an eighth note later) and m. 48, beats 1 and 2 (F5–A4 and E5–G4 are likewise echoed an eighth note later).

A second way in which the violin demonstrates Esther's transformation from tentative in the beginning of the story to newly forceful and outspoken in Section IV is through the use of [012]. Although its ordered pitch intervals return in the initial <+1 +1 −1> guise in mm. 42, 43, 45, and 47, the motive never recurs in its rhythmically hesitant form of the eighth-, eighth-, quarter-, half-note pattern of m. 1. Instead, it appears in several modified forms. In m. 50, for example, the three pitch classes starting on the fifth eighth note, A♯–B–C, establish [012] but with a new order of pitch intervals, <+2 −1>, A♯5–C6–B5, and with a rhythm of dotted eighth-sixteenth-sixteenth.

Measure 52 contains another example of [012] in expanded form. Here, the violin plays E♭6–D6–D♭6 over the first four eighth notes, but with an intervening pair of sixteenth notes B♭5–A5 between E♭ and D. This method of motivic variation illustrates one of the nine methods for motivic variation that Adolph Weiss presents in "The Lyceum of Schönberg," that of interpolation. Here the original motive is stretched over a longer span and uses register to gather the pitches into a musical unit.[38]

---

[38] Weiss, "The Lyceum of Schönberg," 99–107. As noted in Chapter 7, Milton Babbitt recalls that Gideon was familiar with Weiss's article.

Measures 54–55 take up this idea of motivic expansion through the use of intervening pitches, and present A♯5–B5–A6 with G6–B♭6 in m. 55, beat 1, inserted
between B5 and A6. After a more straightforward <+1 +1> presentation in m. 56
(C5–C♯5–D5) of another [012], the sixteenth-note pulse slows in m. 57 to eighth,
quarter, eighth, quarter, which restates the [012] now as a grand <−1 −1> gesture.
Measure 58 offers two additional instances of <−1 −1> embedded in each of its two
sixteenth note groupings: D6–C♯6–C6 on the second, third, and fourth sixteenth
notes of the first grouping, and B5–B♭5–A5 on the second, third, and sixth sixteenth notes of the second grouping – again, [012] is established through register.

Ordered pitch intervals <−1 −1> continue to structure the violin's melody in m.
59. G♯5 moves to G5, which in turn descends another semitone to F♯5 over an
eighth-quarter-eighth-quarter rhythm. Measure 60 elaborates <−2 +1> by dropping fourteen semitones from G5 to F4, and after returning to G5, descends one
semitone to F♯5 after an interpolated D♯4 <−14 +14 −1>. This F♯5, furthermore,
precedes F♯5 in the piano one sixteenth note later, in m. 60, last eighth note. The
violin's A5 on the last sixteenth note of m. 60 is similarly followed by A4 in m. 61,
beat 1.

The final indication that the violin has indeed forged a path independent from
the piano's is contained in m. 61. The violin plays A♯4–B4–F5–E5 over four sixteenth notes, or <+1 +6 −1>, a gesture that emphasizes ic 1 one last time, and then
exits, leaving the piano to complete the piece with a E2–G♯4 dyad held for a half
note over beats 2–3.

As I have argued, Gideon's private insecurities and views about personal traits that
she wished to change, including her lack of assertiveness in the presence of older
men, may well have influenced her musical interpretation of the Book of Esther.
By means of pitch doubling, rhythmic staggering, and motivic variation, Gideon's
portrait draws out a feminist reading of the Biblical story, one that presents the
transformation of an initially pliant youth into a strong, independent, and assertive
woman. In "Esther," Gideon thus creates a work that successfully merges compositional identity, motivic transformation, and optimism.

COMMON THREADS

Over the past two decades, feminist music scholarship has made a significant impact upon the discipline of musicology. Music theory has been slower than musicology to incorporate feminist methodologies, perhaps because of the extreme gender imbalance in the profession at large and the challenges inherent in bringing a political discourse like feminism to a traditionally formalist discipline like music theory.[1] Through the imaginative efforts of theorists such as Lori Burns, Marion Guck, Marianne Kielian-Gilbert, David Lewin, Judy Lochhead, Fred Maus, and Joseph Straus, and of musicologists such as Susan McClary and Suzanne Cusick who have published music-theoretical writings, the discipline of music theory has been recently invigorated by feminist approaches and by the growing interest in the rich repertoire of compositions by women, one that still remains largely unanalyzed at the end of the twentieth century.

This study offers readings of a portion of that repertoire – seven compositions by three American women – by interweaving history, biography, feminist theory, formalist theory, and analysis. Attention to contour, narrative, musical drama, and aspects of performance undergirds the analyses as a whole. Because of the singular structure of these compositions, each required different analytical treatment and I accordingly devised new analytical tools. For example, I invented a "twist" tool that reveals a hidden dimension of the third movement of Crawford's String Quartet; this method of measuring the relationship of the four instrumental voices strengthens my interpretation of the movement as a double-voiced, gendered discourse. The unusual shifting relationship between the hands of a pianist while she performs Bauer's Toccata led to my formal exploration of hand dominance throughout the piece and to the musical narrative that emerges when the piece is contemplated within this dimension. The use of what I call "circuitous voice leading" in Gideon's "Night is my Sister" binds the instrumental trio together, reinforcing its role as a critical commentator on the female protagonist's wretched situation and fortifying the idea that Gideon's musical setting of Millay's sonnet is feminist.

What ties these diverse explorations together is my conviction that musical analysis and social critique can be fundamentally entwined. Formalism and feminism

---

[1] A 1999 study by the Society for Music Theory showed that women constitute only eighteen percent of the Society's membership. See "Report from the Committee on the Status of Women," *SMT Newsletter: A Publication of the Society for Music Theory* 22/2 (1999), 6–7.

have frequently been understood as irreconcilably and fundamentally opposed, especially in the discipline of music theory, which has traditionally not combined a study of historical and social contexts with close readings of "the music itself." By describing how these compositions were in fact produced by women whose lives were inescapably gendered, raced, sexualized, and classed, and by placing my analyses within these historical and social frameworks, I demonstrate that the lives of Crawford, Bauer, and Gideon may be related to the very fabric of their music.

This study does not attempt to offer a global theory about "difference" in the structure of music by female composers. Such a theory would have to consider music by men as well as music by women and would have to inspect a much larger sampling than I have done here. The conclusions of such a project would, moreover, be dubious. If composers are made, not born, then there is no reason that music composed by those of the same sex would necessarily share certain fundamental properties.

Yet if certain women composers shared a common experience of being excluded, silenced, and steered away from particular professional and personal choices, then their craft, of creating works in a sonic medium, might well have offered them a site in which they could record and encode their circumstances while resisting debilitating societal norms. My readings of these compositions celebrate their creators' freedom to construct new, inventive, and liberating musical discourses.

BIBLIOGRAPHY

Ammer, Christine. *Unsung: A History of Women in American Music*. Westport, CT: Greenwood Press, 1980; rev. edn, Portland, OR: Amadeus Press, forthcoming

Ardener, Edwin. "Belief and the Problem of Women." In *Perceiving Women*, ed. Shirley Ardener. New York: John Wiley & Sons, 1975, 1–18

"The 'Problem' Revisited." In *Perceiving Women*, ed. Ardener, 19–28

Ardito, Linda. "Miriam Gideon: A Memorial Tribute." *Perspectives of New Music* 34/2 (Summer 1996), 202–14

Babbitt, Milton. Liner notes to Seymour Barab and William Masselos, *A Recital of New Music for Cello and Piano*. Paradox 10001, n.d.

"Twelve-Tone Invariants as Compositional Determinants." *Musical Quarterly* 46 (1960), 246–59

Words about Music, ed. Stephen Dembski and Joseph N. Straus. Madison: University of Wisconsin Press, 1987

Bach, Wilhelm Friedrich Ernst. "Das Dreyblatt." In *Music of the Bach Family: An Anthology*, ed. Karl Geiringer. Cambridge, MA: Harvard University Press, 1955, 231–36

Bauer, Marion. Papers 1936–51. Bobst Library Archives, New York University

"A Furious and Outraged Audience, a Debasing Program." *The Musical Leader* 56 (3 January 1929), 8. Quoted in David Metzer, "Reclaiming Walt: Marc Blitzstein's Whitman Settings." *Journal of the American Musicological Society* 48/2 (1995), 251

Twentieth Century Music: How It Developed, How to Listen to It. New York: G. P. Putnam's Sons, 1933; rev. edn 1947; repr. New York: Da Capo Press, 1978

Binder, A[lexander]. W. *Biblical Chant*. New York: Philosophical Library, 1959

Binder, Alexander W. *The Jewish Music Movement in America*. New York: Jewish Music Council of the National Jewish Welfare Board, 1975 (1963)

Block, Adrienne Fried. *Amy Beach, Passionate Victorian: The Life and Work of an American Composer, 1867–1944*. New York: Oxford University Press, 1998

Bradstreet, Anne. Prologue to *The Tenth Muse*. In *The Complete Works of Anne Bradstreet*, ed. Joseph R. McElrath, Jr. and Allan P. Robb. Boston: Twayne, 1981 (1650), 6

Burns, Lori. "Analytic Methodologies for Rock Music: Harmonic and Voice-Leading Strategies in Tori Amos's 'Crucify'." In *Expression in Pop-Rock Music: A Collection of Critical and Analytical Essays*, ed. Walter Everett. New York: Garland, 2000, 213–46

Citron, Marcia J. *Gender and the Musical Canon*. Cambridge: Cambridge University Press, 1993

Clark, Suzanne. "*Jouissance* and the Sentimental Daughter: Edna St. Vincent Millay." In

Gendered Modernisms: American Women Poets and Their Readers, ed. Margaret Dickie and Thomas Travisano. Philadelphia: University of Pennsylvania Press, 1996, 143–69

Clinkscale, Edward H., and Claire Brook, eds. *A Musical Offering: Essays in Honor of Martin Bernstein*. New York: Pendragon Press, 1977

Cohn, Richard. "Neo-Riemannian Operations, Parsimonious Trichords, and Their *Tonnetz* Representations." *Journal of Music Theory* 41/1 (Spring 1997), 1–66

Crawford, Ruth. Seeger Collection. Library of Congress, Washington, D.C.

Cusick, Suzanne G. "Feminist Theory, Music Theory, and the Mind/Body Problem." *Perspectives of New Music* 32/1 (1994), 8–27

  "Gender, Musicology, and Feminism." In *Rethinking Music*, ed. Nicholas Cook and Mark Everist. Oxford: Oxford University Press, 1999, 471–98

  "On a Lesbian Relation with Music: A Serious Effort Not to Think Straight." In *Queering the Pitch: The New Gay and Lesbian Musicology*, ed. Philip Brett, Gary C. Thomas, and Elizabeth Wood. New York: Routledge, 1994, 67–83

Daly, Mary. *Beyond God the Father: Toward a Philosophy of Women's Liberation*. Boston: Beacon Press, 1973

DeKoven, Marianne. "Modernism and Gender." In *The Cambridge Companion to Modernism*, ed. Michael Levenson. Cambridge: Cambridge University Press, 1999, 174–93

de Lauretis, Teresa. *Alice Doesn't: Feminism, Semiotics, Cinema*. Bloomington: Indiana University Press, 1984

Denning, Michael. *The Cultural Front: The Laboring of American Culture in the Twentieth Century*. London: Verso, 1996

Donne, John. "Elegie XVI: On his Mistris." In *The Complete Poetry and Selected Prose of John Donne*, ed. Charles M. Coffin. New York: The Modern Library, 1952, 77

Dorian, Frederick. *The Musical Workshop*. New York: Harper & Bros., 1947

Duckworth, William. *Talking Music: Conversations with John Cage, Philip Glass, Laurie Anderson, and Five Generations of American Experimental Composers*. New York: Schirmer Books, 1995

Dunaway, David K. "Charles Seeger and Carl Sands: The Composers' Collective Years." *Ethnomusicology* 24/2 (May 1980), 159–68

  "Unsung Songs of Protest: The Composers' Collective of New York." *New York Folklore Quarterly*, 5/1–2 (Summer 1979), 1–19

Elson, Louis C. *The History of American Music*. New York: MacMillan, 1925 (1904); repr. New York: B. Franklin, 1971

Ewen, David. *American Composers Today: A Biographical and Critical Guide*. New York: H. W. Wilson, 1949

  "Miriam Gideon," in *Composers Since 1900*. New York: H. W. Wilson, 1969, 222

Fertig, Judith. "An Analysis of Selected Works of the American Composer Miriam Gideon (1906–) in Light of Contemporary Jewish Musical Trends." M.A. thesis, University of Cincinnati, 1978

Forte, Allen. *The Structure of Atonal Music*. New Haven: Yale University Press, 1973

Fox, Michael V. *Character and Ideology in the Book of Esther*. Columbia: University of South Carolina Press, 1991

Freud, Sigmund. *Leonardo da Vinci and a Memory of his Childhood*, ed. James Strachey, trans. Alan Tyson. New York: W. W. Norton, 1964 (1910)

Fried, Debra. "Andromeda Unbound: Gender and Genre in Millay's Sonnets." In *Critical

Essays on Edna St. Vincent Millay, ed. William B. Thesing. New York: G. K. Hall, 1993, 229–47

Friedmann, Michael. "A Methodology for the Discussion of Contour: Its Application to Schoenberg's Music." *Journal of Music Theory* 29/2 (1985), 223–48

"My Contour, Their Contour." *Journal of Music Theory* 31/2 (1987), 268–74

Fuchs, Esther. "Status and Role of Female Heroines in the Biblical Narrative." *The Mankind Quarterly* 23/2 (Winter 1982), 149–60

Gaume, Matilda. *Ruth Crawford Seeger: Memoirs, Memories, Music.* Metuchen, NJ: Scarecrow Press, 1986

"Ruth Crawford Seeger." In *Women Making Music: The Western Art Tradition, 1150–1950*, ed. Jane Bowers and Judith Tick. Urbana: University of Illinois Press, 1986, 370–88

Gideon, Miriam. Miriam Gideon files. Broadcast Music, Inc., New York City

Miriam Gideon papers. Music Research Division, New York Public Library.

"Hommage à Roger." *Perspectives of New Music* 16/1 (Spring–Summer 1978), 118–19

Liner notes to *The Hound of Heaven*. CRI SD 286, 1971; repr. in liner notes to *Miriam Gideon: Music for voice & ensemble*. CRI CD 782, 1998

Response to questionnaire from Elaine Barkin sent to women composers. *Perspectives of New Music* 20/1–2 (1981–82), 301

"The Secular Chamber Music of Mozart with Particular Reference to the Quintets." M.A. thesis, Columbia University, 1946

Gilbert, Sandra M., and Susan Gubar. *The Madwoman in the Attic: The Woman Writer and the Nineteenth-Century Literary Imagination*. New Haven: Yale University Press, 1979; 2nd edn, 1984

No Man's Land: The Place of the Woman Writer in the Twentieth Century, vol. 1: *The War of the Words*. New Haven: Yale University Press, 1988

Gilbert, Sandra M., and Susan Gubar, eds. *The Female Imagination and the Modernist Aesthetic*. New York: Gordon and Breach, 1986

Goss, Madeline. *Modern Music-Makers: Contemporary American Composers*. New York: Dutton, 1952; repr. Westport, CT: Greenwood Press, 1970

Greer, Taylor A. "Critical Remarks," Preface to "Tradition and Experiment in (the New) Music," by Charles Seeger. In *Studies in Musicology II: 1929–1979*, ed. Ann M. Pescatello. Berkeley: University of California Press, 1994, 27–38

"The Dynamics of Dissonance in Seeger's Treatise and Crawford's Quartet." In *Understanding Charles Seeger, Pioneer in American Musicology*, ed. Bell Yung and Helen Rees. Urbana: University of Illinois Press, 1999, 13–28

A Question of Balance: Charles Seeger's Philosophy of Music. Berkeley: University of California Press, 1998

Guck, Marion A. "A Woman's (Theoretical) Work." *Perspectives of New Music* 32/1 (1994), 28–43

Gyory, Andrew. *Closing the Gate: Race, Politics, and the Chinese Exclusion Act*. Chapel Hill: University of North Carolina Press, 1998

Hanani, Hannah. "Portrait of a Composer." *Music Journal* 34/4 (April 1976), 24–25

Harrison, Daniel. "Some Group Properties of Triple Counterpoint and Their Influence on Compositions by J. S. Bach." *Journal of Music Theory* 32/1 (1988), 23–49

Holmes, David R. *Stalking the Academic Communist: Intellectual Freedom and the Firing of Alex Novikoff.* Hanover, NH: University Press of New England, 1989

hooks, bell. *Yearning: Race, Gender, and Cultural Politics.* Boston: South End Press, 1990

Howard, John Tasker. *Our Contemporary Composers: American Music in the Twentieth Century.* New York: Thomas Y. Crowell, 1941

Hull, Gloria T., Patricia Bell Scott, and Barbara Smith, eds. *All the Women Are White, All the Blacks are Men, But Some of Us Are Brave: Black Women's Studies.* Old Westbury, NY: The Feminist Press, 1982

Hutcheon, Linda. *A Theory of Parody: The Teaching of Twentieth-Century Art Forms.* New York: Methuen, 1985

"In response" (responses to questionnaire from Elaine Barkin sent to women composers). *Perspectives of New Music* 20 1/2 (1981–82), 288–330

Isaacson, Eric J. "Similarity of Interval-Class Content between Pitch-Class Sets: The IcVSIM Relation." *Journal of Music Theory* 34/1 (Spring 1990), 1–28

Kielian-Gilbert, Marianne. "Of Poetics and Poiesis, Pleasure and Politics – Music Theory and Modes of the Feminine." *Perspectives of New Music* 32/1 (1994), 44–67

   "On Rebecca Clarke's Sonata for Viola and Piano: Feminine Spaces and Metaphors of Reading." In *Audible Traces: Gender, Identity, and Music,* ed. Elaine Barkin and Lydia Hamessley. Zurich: Carciofoli Press, 1999, 71–114

Kim, Hyung-chan, ed. *Dictionary of Asian American History.* New York: Greenwood Press, 1986

   A Legal History of Asian Americans, 1790–1990. Westport, CT: Greenwood Press, 1994

Klumpenhouwer, Henry. "A Generalized Model of Voice-Leading for Atonal Music." Ph.D. diss., Harvard University, 1991

Kozinn, Allan. "Miriam Gideon, 89, a Composer of Vocal and Orchestral Music." *New York Times,* 20 June 1996, D21

Laffey, Alice L. *An Introduction to the Old Testament: A Feminist Perspective.* Philadelphia: Fortress Press, 1988

Lambert, J. Philip. "Interval Cycles as Compositional Resources in the Music of Charles Ives." *Music Theory Spectrum* 12/1 (1990), 43–82

LePage, Jane Weiner. "Miriam Gideon." In *Women Composers, Conductors, and Musicians of the Twentieth Century,* vol. 2. Metuchen, NJ: Scarecrow Press, 1983, 118–41

Lewin, David. *Generalized Musical Intervals and Transformations.* New Haven: Yale University Press, 1989

   Musical Form and Transformation: 4 Analytic Essays. New Haven: Yale University Press, 1993

   "Women's Voices and the Fundamental Bass." *Journal of Musicology* 10/4 (Fall 1992), 464–82

Lieberman, Robbie. *"My Song is My Weapon": People's Songs, American Communism, and the Politics of Culture, 1930–1950.* Urbana: University of Illinois Press, 1989

Lim, Shirley Geok-lin, and Mayumi Tsutakawa, eds. *The Forbidden Stitch: An Asian American Women's Anthology.* Corvallis, OR: Calyx Books, 1989

Lindsay, Vachel. "The Chinese Nightingale: A Song in Chinese Tapestries." In *The Chinese Nightingale and Other Poems.* New York: Macmillan, 1918, 3–13

Litzmann, Berthold. *Clara Schumann: An Artist's Life, Based on Material Found in Diaries and Letters,* vol. 1, trans. Grace E. Hadow. New York: Da Capo Press, 1979. Originally published as *Clara Schumann: ein Künstlerleben, nach Tagebüchern und Briefen,* vol. 2. Leipzig: Breitkopf & Härtel, 1910–12

Lochhead, Judy. "Joan Tower's 'Wings' and 'Breakfast Rhythms I and II': Some Thoughts on Form and Repetition." *Perspectives of New Music* 30/1 (1992), 132–57

Lomax, John A., and Alan A. Lomax, eds. *Our Singing Country*. New York: Macmillan, 1941

Lubitch, Rivkah. "A Feminist's Look at Esther." *Judaism* 42 (Fall 1993), 438–46

Lupton, Ellen. "Love, Leisure, and Laundry." In *Mechanical Brides: Women and Machines From Home to Office*. New York: Cooper-Hewitt National Museum of Design/Princeton Architectural Press, 1993, 15–27

Marvin, Elizabeth West, and Paul A. Laprade. "Relating Musical Contours: Extensions of a Theory for Contour." *Journal of Music Theory* 31/2 (1987), 225–67

Maus, Fred Everett. "Masculine Discourse in Music Theory." *Perspectives of New Music* 31/2 (Summer 1993), 264–93

"Music as Narrative." *Indiana Theory Review* 12/1–2 (1991), 1–24

McClary, Susan. *Feminine Endings: Music, Gender, and Sexuality*. Minneapolis: University of Minnesota Press, 1991

"Getting Down Off the Beanstalk: The Presence of a Woman's Voice in Janika Vandervelde's Genesis II." In *Feminine Endings: Music, Gender, and Sexuality*. Minneapolis: University of Minnesota Press, 1991, 112–31

"Narrative Agendas in 'Absolute' Music: Identity and Difference in Brahms' Third Symphony." In *Musicology and Difference: Gender and Sexuality in Music Scholarship*. Berkeley: University of California Press, 1993, 326–44

"Paradigm Dissonances: Music Theory, Cultural Studies, and Feminist Criticism." *Perspectives of New Music* 32/1 (1994), 68–85

Metzer, David. "Reclaiming Walt: Marc Blitzstein's Whitman Settings." *Journal of the American Musicological Society* 48/2 (Summer 1995), 240–71

Millay, Edna St. Vincent. *Collected Sonnets*. Rev. and exp. edn, New York: Harper & Row, 1988 (1931)

Miner, Valerie, and Helen E. Longino, eds. *Competition: A Feminist Taboo?* New York: The Feminist Press, 1987

Montefiore, Jan. "Case-histories versus the 'Undeliberate Dream': Men and Women Writing the Self in the 1930s." In *Difference in View: Women and Modernism*, ed. Gabriele Griffin. London: Taylor & Frances, 1994, 56–74

Feminism and Poetry: Language, Experience, Identity in Women's Writing. London: Pandora, 1987

Moraga, Cherríe, and Gloria Anzaldúa, eds. *This Bridge Called My Back: Writings by Radical Women of Color*. Watertown, MA: Persephone Press, 1981; 2nd edn, Latham NY: Kitchen Table, Women of Color Press, 1983

Morgan, Robert P. Liner notes to Ruth Crawford Seeger, String Quartet, The Composers Quartet. Nonesuch H-71280, 1973

Morris, Robert D. *Composition with Pitch-Classes: A Theory of Compositional Design*. New Haven: Yale University Press, 1987

"New Directions in the Theory and Analysis of Musical Contour." *Music Theory Spectrum* 15/2 (1993), 205–28

Mura, David. "Strangers in the Village." In *Multi-Cultural Literacy: Opening the American Mind*, ed. Rick Simonson and Scott Walker. St. Paul, MN: Graywolf Press, 1988, 135–53

Nattiez, Jean-Jacques. "Can One Speak of Narrativity in Music?" *Journal of the Royal Musical Association* (1989–90), 240–57

New York Times. "Frederic Ewen, 89, Ex-Professor of English." 19 October 1988, B5

Newcomb, Anthony. "Schumann and Late 18th-Century Narrative Strategies." *19th-Century Music* 11/2 (Fall 1987), 164–74

Nicholls, David. *American Experimental Music, 1890–1940*. Cambridge: Cambridge University Press, 1990

Ohmann, Richard. "English and the Cold War." In *The Cold War and the University: Toward an Intellectual History of the Postwar Years*. New York: The New Press, 1997, 73–105

Oja, Carol J. *Making Music Modern: New York in the 1920s*. New York: Oxford University Press (in press)

"Marc Blitzstein's *The Cradle Will Rock* and Mass-Song Style of the 1930s." *Musical Quarterly* 73/4 (1989), 445–75

"'New Music' and the 'New Negro': The Background of William Grant Still's *Afro-American Symphony*." *Black Music Research Journal* 12/2 (Fall 1992), 145–69

"Women Patrons and Crusaders for Modernist Music: New York in the 1920s." In *Cultivating Music in America: Women Patrons and Activists since 1860*, ed. Ralph P. Locke and Cyrilla Barr. Berkeley: University of California Press, 1997, 237–61

Osumi, Megumi Dick. "Asians and California's Anti-Miscegenation Laws." In *Asian and Pacific American Experiences: Women's Perspectives*, ed. Nobuya Tsuchida. Minneapolis: Asian/Pacific American Learning Resource Center and General College, University of Minnesota, 1982, 1–37

Page, Tim. "Gideon and Talma at 80 – Composers and Neighbors." *New York Times*, 19 October 1986, H23

"Two Lives in Harmony: The Parallel Paths of Trailblazers Miriam Gideon and Louise Talma." *Washington Post*, 25 August 1996, G02

Pasler, Jann. "Narrative and Narrativity in Music." In *Time and Mind: Interdisciplinary Issues*, ed. J. T. Fraser. Madison, CT: International Universities Press, 1989, 233–57

Peppe, Holly. "Rewriting the Myth of the Woman in Love: Millay's *Fatal Interview*." In *Millay at 100: A Critical Reappraisal*, ed. Diane P. Freedman. Carbondale: Southern Illinois University Press, 1995, 52–65

Perle, George. "The Music of Miriam Gideon." *American Composers Alliance Bulletin* 7/4 (1958), 2–9

"A Tribute to Miriam Gideon." Memorial statement read at American Academy and Institute of Arts and Letters meeting, New York City, 1996

Pescatello, Ann M. *Charles Seeger: A Life in American Music*. Pittsburgh: University of Pittsburgh Press, 1992

ed., Introduction to *Studies in Musicology II: 1929–1979*, by Charles Seeger. Berkeley: University of California Press, 1994, 1–16

Petersen, Barbara A. "Remembering Miriam Gideon." Remarks read at a concert of Miriam Gideon's music held at the Jewish Theological Seminary, New York City, 5 June 1997

"The Vocal Chamber Music of Miriam Gideon." In *The Musical Woman*, vol. 2, ed. Judith Laing Zaimont, Catherine Overhauser, and Jane Gottlieb. New York: Greenwood Press, 1987, 223–55

Pettis, Ashley. "Second Worker's [*sic*] Music Olympiad." *New Masses* 11/8 (22 May 1934), 28–29

Pickett, Susan. "Why Can't We Listen to Marion Bauer's Music?" *Providence Journal-Bulletin* (Rhode Island), 23 August 1994

Rahn, John. *Basic Atonal Theory*. New York: Longman, 1980

Reis, Claire R. *Composers in America: Biographical Sketches of Contemporary Composers With a Record of Their Works*. New York: Macmillan, 1938; rev. and enl., 1947

Reuss, Richard A. "The Roots of American Left-Wing Interest in Folksong." *Labor History* 12/2 (Spring 1971), 259–79

Richter, Marion Morrey. "1970 NFMC [National Federation of Music Clubs] 'Parade' Concert in New York." *National Federation of Music Clubs Magazine* (Spring 1970), 13

Ringer, Benjamin B. *We the People and Others: America's Treatment of its Racial Minorities*. New York: Tavistock Publications, 1983

Rosenberg, Deena, and Bernard Rosenberg. "Miriam Gideon." In *The Music Makers*. New York: Columbia University Press, 1979, 62–69

Rosenfeld, Paul. *An Hour with American Music*. Philadelphia: J. B. Lippincott, 1929; repr. New York: The New Press, 1979

   Musical Portraits: Interpretations of Twenty Modern Composers. New York: Harcourt, Brace and Howe, 1920

Schoenberg, Arnold. *Fundamentals of Musical Composition*, ed. Gerald Strang and Leonard Stein. New York: St. Martin's Press, 1967

   Theory of Harmony, trans. Roy E. Carter. Berkeley: University of California Press, 1983 (1911)

Schrecker, Ellen. *Many Are the Crimes: McCarthyism in America*. Boston: Little, Brown, and Co., 1998

   No Ivory Tower: McCarthyism and the Universities. New York: Oxford University Press, 1986

Scott, Joan Wallach. *Gender and the Politics of History*. New York: Columbia University Press, 1988

Seeger, Charles. "On Dissonant Counterpoint." *Modern Music* 7/4 (1930), 25–31

   "On Proletarian Music." *Modern Music* 11/3 (March–April 1934), 121–27

   "Reminiscences of an American Musicologist." Interview by Adelaide Tusler and Ann Briegleb, Oral History Program, University of California at Los Angeles, 1972

   "Ruth Crawford." In *American Composers on American Music: A Symposium*, ed. Henry Cowell. Stanford: Stanford University Press, 1933, 110–18; repr. New York: Frederick Ungar, 1962, 3–13

   "Tradition and Experiment in (the New) Music." In Charles Seeger, *Studies in Musicology II, 1929–1979*, ed. Ann M. Pescatello. Berkeley: University of California Press, 1994, 39–273

Seeger, Ruth Crawford. Seeger Collection. Library of Congress, Washington, D.C.

   American Folk Songs for Children. Garden City, NY: Doubleday, 1950; repr. Hamden, CT: Shoe String Press, 1993

Shaw, Jennifer. "Moon Tides and Male Poets: (En)gendering Identity in Miriam Gideon's *Nocturnes*." Paper presented at the conference Feminist Theory and Music III, University of California at Riverside, 1995

Showalter, Elaine. "Feminist Criticism in the Wilderness." In *The New Feminist Criticism: Essays on Women, Literature, and Theory*, ed. Elaine Showalter. New York: Pantheon Books, 1985, 243–70

Siu, Paul C. P. *The Chinese Laundryman: A Study of Social Isolation*, ed. John Kuo Wei Tchen. New York: New York University Press, 1987

Smith, Barbara. "Toward a Black Feminist Criticism." In *All the Women Are White, All the*

Blacks are Men, But Some of Us Are Brave: Black Women's Studies, ed. Gloria T. Hull, Patricia Bell Scott, and Barbara Smith. Old Westbury, NY: The Feminist Press, 1982, 157–75

Smith, Catherine Parsons. "'A Distinguishing Virility': Feminism and Modernism in American Art Music." In *Cecilia Reclaimed: Feminist Perspectives on Gender and Music*, ed. Susan C. Cook and Judy S. Tsou. Urbana: University of Illinois Press, 1994, 90–106

Spiegel, Celina. "The World Remade: The Book of Esther." In *Out of the Garden: Women Writers on the Bible*, ed. Christina Buchmann and Celina Spiegel. New York: Fawcett Columbine, 1994, 191–203

Stanbrough, Jane. "Edna St. Vincent Millay and the Language of Vulnerability." In *Shakespeare's Sisters: Feminist Essays on Women Poets*, ed. Sandra M. Gilbert and Susan Gubar. Bloomington: Indiana University Press, 1979, 183–99

Stewart, Nancy Louise. "The Solo Piano Music of Marion Bauer." Ph.D. diss., University of Cincinnati, 1990

Straus, Joseph N. *Introduction to Post-Tonal Theory*, 2nd edn. Upper Saddle River, NJ: Prentice Hall, 2000

  The Music of Ruth Crawford Seeger. Cambridge: Cambridge University Press, 1995

Subotnik, Rose Rosengard. *Developing Variations: Style and Ideology in Western Music*. Minneapolis: University of Minnesota Press, 1991

Takaki, Ronald. *Strangers from a Different Shore: A History of Asian Americans*. Boston: Little, Brown and Company, 1989

Tarasti, Eero. "Pour une narratologie de Chopin." *International Review of the Aesthetics and Sociology of Music* 15/1 (1984), 53–75

Tchen, John Kuo Wei. "Believing is Seeing: Transforming Orientalism and the Occidental Gaze." In *Asia/America: Identities in Contemporary Asian American Art*. New York: The Asia Society Galleries/New Press, 1994, 12–25

Temperley, Nicholas. Introduction to *A Selection of Four-Hand Duets Published between 1777 and 1857*, vol. 19 of *The London Pianoforte School, 1766–1860*. New York: Garland, 1986

Tenney, James, with Larry Polansky. "Temporal Gestalt Perceptions in Music." *Journal of Music Theory* 24/2 (1980), 205–41

Thomas, Margaret E. "The String Quartet of Ruth Crawford: Analysis With a View Toward Charles Seeger's Theory of Dissonant Counterpoint." M.A. thesis, University of Washington, 1991

Thompson, Francis. *The Hound of Heaven*. New York: McCracken Press, 1993 [1890]

Tick, Judith. "Dissonant Counterpoint Revisited: The First Movement of Ruth Crawford's String Quartet 1931." In *A Celebration of American Music: Words and Music in Honor of H. Wiley Hitchcock*, ed. Richard Crawford, R. Allen Lott, and Carol J. Oja. Ann Arbor: University of Michigan Press, 1990, 405–22

  "Ruth Crawford's *Proletarian Ricercari*." *Sonus: A Journal of Investigations into Global Music Possibilities* 15/2 (Spring 1995), 54–79

  Ruth Crawford Seeger: A Composer's Search for American Music. New York: Oxford University Press, 1997

Trinh T. Minh-ha. *Woman, Native, Other: Writing Postcoloniality and Feminism*. Bloomington: Indiana University Press, 1989

Tsiang, H. T. *Poems of the Chinese Revolution*, English edn. New York: Liberal Press, 1929

Tsou, Judy S. "Gendering Race: Images of Chinese in American Popular Music." *repercussions* 6/2 (in press)

Valdes, Lesley. "Miriam Gideon among Most Honored." *Baltimore Sun*, 27 September 1981, D1, D9

Wallace, Michele. *Invisibility Blues: From Pop to Theory*. London: Verso, 1990

Weisgall, Deborah. *A Joyful Noise: Claiming the Songs of My Fathers*. New York: Atlantic Monthly Press, 1999

Weiss, Adolph. "The Lyceum of Schönberg." *Modern Music* 9/3 (March–April 1932), 99–107

Weisser, Albert. "An Interview with Miriam Gideon." *Dimensions in American Judaism* 4/3 (Spring 1970), 38–40

Weissweiler, Eva. *Fanny Mendelssohn: Ein Portrait in Briefen*. Frankfurt am Main: Ullstein Taschenbuch, 1985

Wilding-White, Ray. "Remembering Ruth Crawford Seeger: An Interview with Charles and Peggy Seeger." *American Music* 6/4 (1988), 442–54

Williams, Patricia J. *The Alchemy of Race and Rights*. Cambridge, MA: Harvard University Press, 1991

Woolf, Virginia. *A Room of One's Own*. San Diego: Harcourt Brace Jovanovich, 1989 (1929)

Wu, William. *The Yellow Peril: Chinese Americans in American Fiction, 1850–1940*. Hamden, CT: Archon Books, 1982

Yamada, Mitsuye. "Invisibility is an Unnatural Disaster: Reflections of an Asian American Woman." In *This Bridge Called My Back: Writings by Radical Women of Color*, ed. Cherríe Moraga and Gloria Anzaldúa. Watertown, MA: Persephone Press, 1981; 2nd edn, Latham, NY: Kitchen Table, Women of Color Press, 1983, 35–40

Yasser, Joseph. *A Theory of Evolving Tonality*. New York: American Library of Musicology, 1932; repr. New York: Da Capo Press, 1975

Zuck, Barbara A. *A History of Musical Americanism*. Ann Arbor: UMI Research Press, 1980

INDEX